W9-BJI-662

First-Time
Around the World

written and researched by
Doug Lansky

ROUGH
GUIDES

www.roughguides.com

First-Time **Around the World** |**INTRODUCTION**

Introduction to

First-Time
Around
the World

The world is flat. Or so the thinking went, until someone actually went off to circumnavigate it. You may not make such a colossal discovery during your own global journey, but what awaits you "out there" is something only you can find: your very own adventure. Beyond your part of the planet lie mountain ranges with echo-bending canyons, tangled jungles, deserts that stretch into sanguine sunsets and yellow savannah veiling lions, wildebeest and springbok. There are retina-burning white beaches tapering off into vodka waters that serve as a playground for dolphins, turtles and manta rays. Not to mention over

6000 languages, countless botanical wonders, architectural masterpieces and geological anomalies. All that is already out there. The decision to find it is yours.

World fact file

- **World population** over 6 billion
- **Circumference** of the earth 40,000km
- **Height** of Mount Everest 8850m/29,035ft
- **Depth** of the Mariana Trench, Western Pacific Ocean 10,924m/35,840ft
- **Highest temperature** El Azizia, Libya 136°F/58°C
- **Lowest temperature** Vostok, Antarctica -126°F/-88°C
- **Tourism** The World Tourism Organization estimated there were 698 million international tourist arrivals in 2000, which generated $3.5 trillion and accounted for 11.7 percent of the world's GDP. Almost 200 million jobs (8 percent of all jobs worldwide) are supported by the travel and tourism industry. By 2020, they expect 1.6 billion arrivals.
- **Worldwide refugees** and asylum seekers 3,800,000

My own plan was to walk out the front door, head to Florida and try to hitchhike on yachts to South America – all on a budget stretched tighter than Liz Taylor's forehead. Without getting into details, my yacht-hitching scheme only got me as far as the Virgin Islands. And the only reason I made it that far was because I flew there. (Turned out I was trying to hitch south during hurricane season, when all the boats were headed north or into safe harbours.) This start, however rocky, did launch me on a two-and-a-half-year trip that forever changed my life. And not just because it ended with a car accident in Bangkok, which left me in the unfortunate position of having a broken ankle and amoebic dysentery – a tragic combination of constantly having to go to the loo, and never being able to get there quickly enough.

Before I get ahead of myself, though, I just want to assure you this book is not going to try to persuade you to travel, nor make grandiose assertions that stomping around the planet with a coated-nylon pack will somehow fulfil whatever may be missing from your life. Travel is an urge best cultivated from within. In fact, one of the biggest favours you can do for yourself is to travel if and when you're ready, not when someone else thinks you should. The more eager you are to open yourself up to life on the road, the more willing you are to embrace the unknown rather than sign up for a pre-packaged air-conditioned experience, the more likely you are to reap real rewards.

Believe it or not, nearly anyone can get around the world in one piece (or in my case, two), and I'd be lying if I

Meeting locals

It's hard to pick up a travel magazine, brochure or guidebook without seeing an exotic cast of faces. The unspoken message seems to be that this is who you'll meet in these countries. The people you're far more likely to encounter, however, are other travellers. And the local people you'll mostly come in contact with are vendors, taxi drivers, guides and hotel clerks – people serving you. To make more genuine contacts takes some effort. Volunteering or working in a place is one of the best ways (see p.66). But even if you're just looking to take a picture of someone, a thoughtful approach might lead to a more meaningful connection; see p.208 for more.

Time and space

Two things that travellers often forget to mentally prepare for are altered concepts of time and space. With buses that don't leave until they're full, boats that wait at the harbour for the captain to return from his family holiday, and mechanical problems that require spare parts sent by cargo ship from Australia, the hardcore traveller's mantra of "no watches, no calendars, no worries" begins to seem like a healthy response. Your personal space, on the other hand, is likely to shrink, whether you're speaking with someone who insists on standing almost nose-to-nose during the conversation or you're packed into a six-person mini-van with seventeen other passengers.

Plan for twice as much transport time as you think you need, try to grab a seat near a window so you can control the fresh-air supply – and make sure you've got something to read. See p.135 for more tips.

told you that you needed this book to come back alive. However, the down side to blindly winging it is that you'll make mistakes, some potentially dangerous, many costly and some just plain embarrassing. By the time you get through the first section of this book, you should be savvy enough to chart an itinerary for your trip and avoid nearly all the snares that await you. With a glimpse of life on the road, a feel for the essentials, and by addressing a number of travel's most testing issues ahead of time, you'll be well on your way.

The regional profiles in the second part of the book tell you what it costs to get around, how long it'll take to cross the various landmasses and if there are any rail, bus or air passes you may wish to buy ahead of time to make things cheaper and more convenient. You'll notice we took some liberties in dividing up the world into eight regions: North America, for instance, normally includes Mexico, but because of popular overland routes, a shared language and its latitude, it has been placed in the Central America and the Caribbean section. The regional maps are meant to provide ballpark estimates of the times and costs of overland travel on common routes. They are by no means instructing you to take such routes (it's always better to find your own way), nor are they completely accurate, since prices change, exchange rates fluctuate and delays do occur, particularly in less-developed regions.

Of course, you'll want more specific information eventually, either from websites or publications listed in the Basics section at the end of this book or from your guidebook once you arrive. But at this point, much more information than what you'll find provided here will bog down your planning process instead of helping it along. And remember that there's such a thing as too much planning. One of the greatest thrills of travel is trying to make your way between two points by the least travelled, most arduous route, chancing rides and roads and climates as you go.

> **One of the biggest favours you can do for yourself is to travel if and when you're ready, not when someone else thinks you should.**

25

things to enrich your journey

Adventure and cultural insights can be found almost anywhere.
How you decide to travel and what you decide to do is far more
important than where you decide to go and what you intend to see.
Thinking in terms of "doing" rather than "seeing" will enhance
that most vital, often elusive dimension to your travels: depth.

01 **Relax on a desolate beach** Costa Rica

02 Spend the night some-where unusual The Ice Hotel, Jukkasjärvi, Sweden

05 Try ancient transport Felucca, The Nile, Egypt

04 An elephant provides a perfect perch for wildlife viewing

06 **Test the street food** Beijing

07 **Make friends with other travellers** Rainbow Gathering, Queensland, Australia

08 **Take in the cultural scene** Roman theatre, Orange, France

09 **Head underwater** Saparura Island, Indonesia

10 **Go underground** New Mexico, USA

11 **Check out a sporting event** Mongolian wrestling

12 **Ride a bicycle** Bolivian salt flats

13 **Get close to some wildlife** King's Canyon, Australia

14 **Navigate without your guidebook**

15 **Bargain at the local market** Delhi

16 **Take a bath** Hammam, Istanbul, Turkey

17 **Experience the power of a river** Nepal

18 **Wake up early to see a sight in solitude** Red Square, Moscow, Russia

19 Make a trip to the hair-dressers China

20 **Sample the local firewater** Prague, Czech Republic

21 **Participate in a festival** Buñol, Spain

22 **Spend a few days in the jungle** Tikal, Guatemala

23 **Wander the backstreets of a city** Paris, France

24 **Try out a new sport** Sandsurfing

25 **Climb a mountain** Kilimanjaro, looking out over Tanzania

Contents

Colour section

The ultimate journey

Regional profiles

Basics

Index

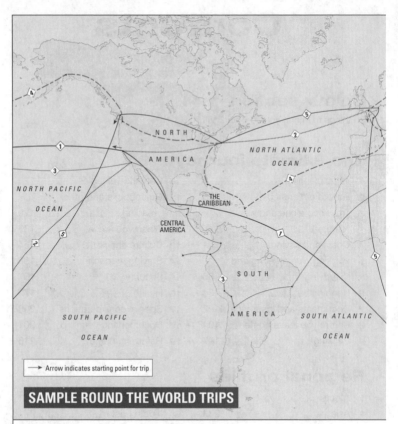

Arrow indicates starting point for trip

SAMPLE ROUND THE WORLD TRIPS

#1
Start in San Francisco; fly to Japan, work as an English teacher in karaoke bar; fly to Beijing; bus to Hong Kong, work as a private English tutor; fly to Hanoi; bus to Saigon; bus to Phnom Penh; fly to Bangkok, kickboxing school; bus to Kuala Lumpur; fly to Kathmandu; fly to Kenya, volunteer to build a school; overland truck to Cape Town; fly to Mexico City; bus to San Francisco.

#2
Start in Sydney; cheap one-way ticket to Christchurch, NZ; bus to Bay of Islands; catch lift on yacht to Fiji, work as a diving instructor in resort; one-way flight to Los Angeles; bus to San Francisco, work as a private gardener; car "drive-away" service to New York; one-way ticket to London, work in pub; Europe train pass, stop in Greece; one-way ticket to Bombay; train to Calcutta; one-way ticket to Bangkok; bus to Malaysia, work as a diving instructor in a resort; bus to Singapore; bus/ferry to Bali; one-way ticket to Darwin; bus to Alice Springs; hitch a lift to Sydney.

#3
Start in Israel; fly to Salvador for Carnival; bus to Bolivia, tour Salar de Uyuni salt flats; bus to La Paz, Passover; bus to Cuzco, walk the Inca Trail; bus to Ecuador; trip to Galapagos Islands; bus to Colombia; fly to Guatemala, visit Tikal ruins; bus to Mexico City; bus to Los Angeles, work moving furniture; fly to Japan, sell fake designer bags on the street; fly to Bangkok; fly to Nepal for trekking; bus to India, New Year's rave party in Goa; fly to Israel.

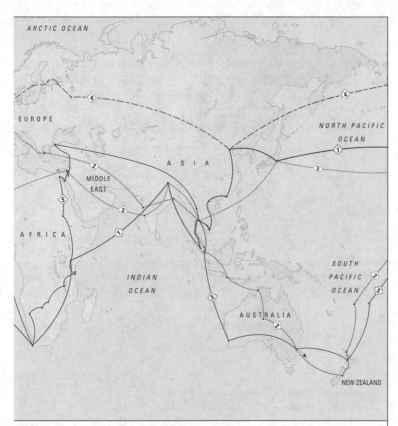

First-Time Around the World

The ultimate journey

1

Initial planning

Figuring out where to go, how to get there, what to do and how long to stay is a lot easier than it sounds. In this chapter, the planning process is dissected into smaller, easier-to-chew pieces that will get you under way, from choosing activities to avoiding troublesome weather to catching the festivals you don't want to miss.

Should you see the world on a tight budget?

Independent budget travel isn't for everyone. Especially if you're not thrilled about riding on buses that use the horn as a turn signal, greeting *and* emergency brake. Or using toilet paper better suited for removing barnacles from the underside of harboured yachts. Or spending the occasional night in a place that considers the urine stain on the mattress all the decoration the room needs. If this little sample didn't faze you (much), you're in luck. The cultural and social payoff of budget travel is enormous, the experience invaluable, and it's unlikely to bankrupt you, or your parents.

This book is primarily designed for the independent budget traveller because... well, they're the ones who need the most information. if you're not ready to travel on the cheap, you'll still get plenty of essential information and itinerary ideas from the ensuing pages, but you should be aware that a thick wallet has a tendency to insulate you from the very culture you're trying to experience. Also, you may have to limit your time on the road, or knock off a bank. A year of air-conditioned tours, meals served on real tablecloths, and comfortable hotel rooms could set you back $100,000/£64,000. Whereas it can be done for as little as $10,000/£6400. Or, with a few tips from Chapter 4, for even less than that.

How much time do you need?

With 191 countries stretched around the planet's 47,000-kilometre girth, it would take several lifetimes to see it all and do it all. Almost everywhere you go, you'll meet travellers who will tell you about amazing places you won't have time to visit. The truth is, you won't know how long you'll want to go for until you get out there. Your best defence, therefore, is to try to carve out as much time as you can beforehand, since it's easier to come back early than try to push back deadlines once you're on the move.

If you already know how long you've got, you should be thinking about the pace of your trip. How many countries, cities and activities should you try to tackle in that amount of time? A good guideline is this: don't plan more than four major activities per month in advance. (Sorry, visiting India does not count as a single activity. But things like a two-day cooking class, short stay with a relative, a few days exploring a major city and a hiking trip do.) If you plan to see, say, Paris and Rome in June, that doesn't mean you just see these two cities. It means you get to make up the rest of your plans on the move as you travel between them. This approach allows for ample flexibility, plus any transport delays you may encounter.

If the length of your trip is largely dictated by budget, check out Chapter 4 to help calculate your time on the road and maximize the funds you have (rough budget estimate: $12–55/£8–35 a day not including major transport costs). However, you don't necessarily need to let your initial funds shorten your trip. Chapter 5 covers jobs and volunteer projects, so you can leave home with minimal funds or stretch your trip for years.

A year off has a nice ring to it. Besides, most round-the-world tickets (see p.26) are designed with that as an upper limit. It almost seems like this is the length of time society and the travel industry have deemed appropriate. Much shorter and you may get accused by "hardcore" travellers of not getting a real taste of the road. Much longer and people back home may start to think you've completely lost it. Even if you have to be back in a year, better to tell people (and yourself) that you're returning when you're ready.

Where to go

Since no traveller can do it all, the tendency is to head for the "best" places. What are the best places? It feels like a natural question, but you're better off refraining from asking it as you gather information about your upcoming trip because it isn't going to reveal much useful information. Ninety percent of your travel experience will be made up of the people you meet, the weather, spontaneous adventures and little cultural discoveries you make along the way. It goes the other way as well: a bad experience is coloured with random mishaps ranging from bus breakdowns to bed bugs to boring travel companions. I'm not a big fan of Bangkok, for example, but my perspective includes the fact that I was run over by a car and spent time in the hospital there. I know others who love it. Besides, what may seem awful at the time may, in retrospect, prove to be the most life-changing event of your journey.

The only person to ask about where you should go is yourself. Grab a pencil, take a look at the four points below, and start jotting down places, sights and activities that sound appealing. You can figure out how to connect them later See p.ii–iii for a map depicting sample itineraries.

Go where you speak the language

No, not English. A second language. (Although an English-speaking country is a fine place to start your travels.) Even if you can just read a menu and a few street signs, you're off to a good start. You can begin to interact with a country in an independent, real way. And once you start using a language, once you start looking around and trying to decipher the words or communicate where you need to go, the learning curve becomes nearly vertical.

Go where you have family or friends

Don't be afraid to look up that childhood pen pal in Ghana or your third cousin once removed in Hungary. To cover your bets, bring along some kind of document or a snapshot to help bridge any gaps. With a little luck, you'll find you've got yourself a cultural guide. You'll almost certainly get a free place to stay and, if nothing else, an inside look at the way they live, from food and interior decor to bowling and strip clubs, or whatever your relatives happen to do for fun.

Go somewhere you've longed to see

A little wanderlust goes a long way. If you've read about a place, heard other people talk about it for ages, or had some sort of childhood fascination with it, that's not a bad reason to go. At the very worst, it's a decent starting point (many of the travellers who end up in Timbuktu are there because they like the sound of it).

Follow your interests

This is perhaps the best tool to use to start picking your destinations. The concept is simple enough: instead of thinking about what you'd like to see, think about what you'd like to do. Approach the trip as a chance to collect unique experiences, not postcards. If you're a golfer, you might pursue the sport to its roots with a round at the Old Course in St Andrews in Scotland. Or try a twist, and stop for a game of sand golf in the United Arab Emirates. There's even ice golf in Finland, where you can play with a bright orange ball, tee it up on an ice cube you hack out of the fairway, and putt on icy "whites". If you like to cook, you might take a pastry course at the world-famous Cordon Bleu school in Paris or try a day of curry preparation at the Oriental Hotel in Bangkok. The more original your approach, the more unique your experience is likely to be.

Wonders of the world

Nothing seems to attract visitors like a Wonder of the World. And, once you start travelling, these Wonders seem to be everywhere. You may start to wonder yourself which Wonders are actually Wonders (not to mention UN "World Heritage" status, which is currently conferred on 730 sites in 125 countries). Only one of the Seven Ancient Wonders remains intact today: the Great Pyramids. The list, first referenced in the *History of Herodotus* in the fifth century BC and then by chief librarian Callimachus of Cyrene (305 BC–240 BC), proved to be such a public relations success that historians, writers and architects have been trying to create updated versions ever since. Not surprisingly, they can't quite reach consensus. Some assert, for instance, that the ancient list was flawed because the Greeks were unaware of such marvels as the Great Wall of China. Today, several "official" lists of geological anomalies and man-made structures

Is it ethical to visit oppressed countries?

Should you go to Burma (Myanmar) and allow your tourist dollars to fuel the junta that's withholding basic human rights, practising forced labour, and manoeuvring Nobel Laureate and pro-democracy leader Aung San Suu Kyi in and out of house arrest. Are you lending legitimacy to a Chinese-occupied Tibet with even a quick visit to Lhasa?

A limited influx of tourist money might make those in power realize that they could make more by catering to tourists' desires with a free society. It might also deter them from taking action; they could argue that tourists are coming anyway. Aung San Suu Kyi appeals to foreigners to boycott travel to Myanmar. Nobel Laureate and spiritual leader, his holiness the Dalai Lama, is encouraging visitors to Tibet. In both cases, some money goes to the oppressed, some goes to the oppressors. Should you decide to visit one of these places, while you're there, you can help a little. Rather, you can minimize the damage. You can steer clear of government-run tour agencies, hotels and shops, so that more of your money buys bread instead of bullets.

To some extent, your real impact depends on what you do afterwards. Your visit in and of itself may not help the causes of the oppressed, but what you learn about them and pass on to others can. The Dalai Lama is counting on visitors' tales to fight the giant Chinese propaganda machine. You can give money to various good causes. You can give money or volunteer your time at Amnesty International. You can write to your local representative and insist on more political pressure to not do business with those in power. Even a "Free Tibet" bumper sticker on your car is a step in the right direction.

Can you do these things without visiting the country? Of course. But if you plan to raise your voice in protest, it can be helpful to get a first-hand look.

But where should you draw the line? You don't like the death penalty in America? Maybe you shouldn't spend your tourist dollars there either (or shouldn't go to the states where it's permitted). The Australians haven't been historically kind to Aboriginals. The Brazilians are wiping out the Amazonian rainforest. The Turks, Iraqis, Syrians, Armenians, Iranians and Azerbaijanis have it in for the Kurds. The Norwegians and Japanese are hunting whales. The more you think about travelling ethically, the trickier it gets. Just about every country on the planet has dozens of skeletons in the closet if you choose to look closely enough. And once you start down that path, it's hard to know where to stop. It becomes a very personal decision, with few whites and blacks, just a vast collection of greys. The best thing to do is arm yourself with as much information as possible, and pass on what you learn to others.

have emerged, each with its own merits. Because so many attractions are touting their particular wonder, this round-up may provide some perspective to the PR you're bound to encounter.

Seven wonders of the ancient world

- The Pyramids of Giza
- The Hanging Gardens of Babylon
- The Statue of Zeus at Olympia
- The Temple of Artemis at Ephesus
- The Mausoleum at Halicarnassus
- The Colossus of Rhodes
- The Lighthouse of Alexandria

Natural wonders

- Angel Falls in Venezuela
- The Bay of Fundy in Nova Scotia, Canada
- The Grand Canyon in Arizona, USA
- The Great Barrier Reef in Australia
- Iguaçu/Iguazú Falls in Brazil/Argentina
- Krakatoa Island in Indonesia
- Mount Everest in Nepal/Tibet
- Mount Fuji in Japan
- Mount Kilimanjaro in Tanzania
- Niagara Falls in Ontario (Canada) and New York State (USA)
- Paricutin Volcano in Mexico
- Victoria Falls in Zambia/Zimbabwe

"Forgotten" wonders

- Abu Simbel Temple in Egypt
- Angkor Wat, Cambodia
- The Aztec Temple in Tenochtitlan (Mexico City), Mexico
- The Banaue Rice Terraces, the Philippines
- Borobudur Temple in Java, Indonesia
- The Colosseum in Rome, Italy
- The Great Wall of China
- The Inca city of Machu Picchu, Peru
- The Leaning Tower of Pisa, Italy
- Mayan Temples of Tikal in Guatemala
- Moai Statues in Rapa Nui, Easter Island
- Mont-Saint-Michel in Normandy, France
- The Throne Hall of Persepolis in Iran
- The Parthenon in Athens, Greece

- Petra, the rock-carved city in Jordan
- The Shwedagon Pagoda in Burma (Myanmar)
- Stonehenge in England
- Taj Mahal in Agra, India
- The Temple of the Inscriptions in Palenque, Mexico

Modern wonders

- The Eiffel Tower in Paris, France
- The Empire State Building in New York, USA
- The Channel Tunnel, under the English Channel
- The Clock Tower (Big Ben) in London, England
- CN Tower in Toronto, Canada
- Gateway Arch in St Louis, USA
- Golden Gate Bridge in San Francisco, USA
- The High Dam in Aswan, Egypt
- The Hoover Dam in Arizona/Nevada, USA
- Itaipú Dam in Brazil/Paraguay
- Mount Rushmore National Memorial in South Dakota, USA
- The Panama Canal in Panama
- Petronas Towers in Kuala Lumpur
- Statue of Cristo Redentor in Rio de Janeiro, Brazil
- The Statue of Liberty in New York, USA
- The Suez Canal in Egypt
- Sydney Opera House, Australia

Want to try something new?

Here are thirty of today's most popular travel activities. Most are possible in thousands of locations, so you should be able to arrange a lesson or tour no matter where you go:

Alpine skiing • bike touring • bird-watching • canyoning • caving • deep sea fishing • fly fishing • golfing • horse-riding • kayaking • learning meditation • mountain climbing • painting • power-kiting • rock climbing • sampling haute cuisine • scuba diving • snowboarding • studying martial arts • studying photography • surfing • trekking • viewing wild animals • visiting castles/palaces • whale-watching • whitewater-rafting • windsurfing • wine tasting • cross-country skiing • yachting

These days, with seventy-year-olds waiting for hip replacements signing up for "adventure tours", it's hard to know exactly what the term means.

An adventure used to involve exploring uncharted waters and lands with hidden dangers. It meant not knowing where it would end up or how or if. Similarly, safari (borrowed from Swahili, originally meaning "a trip"), was once used to describe a hunting expedition in Africa and now encapsulates taking pictures of animals from a bouncing mini-van, then relaxing by the pool with a dry martini.

"Adventure travel" is typically applied to white-water rafting, bungee-jumping, trekking and getting spun about in jet boats, especially when these activities take place in foreign countries. The fact is, they're completely packaged activities with an outcome nearly as predictable as a fairground ride, rendering them closer to the X Games than what any explorer would dub an adventure. Does that mean you should avoid them? No. A little adrenaline is healthy and good fun. Does that mean there are no "real" adventures left? No. Just make sure you understand which kind you're signing up for. Come to think of it, if you need to sign up for the adventure, that's a pretty good indication of what kind it is.

Timing your trip

On a long trip you can't be everywhere at just the ideal time. And it's not worth trying. Usually, if it's too hot inland, you can head for the coast. And if it's too hot on the coast you can move to higher elevations, where temperatures are more mild. If there are monsoon rains in one place, an overnight train or bus can usually take you to the coast that's getting all the sun. This only requires one thing: flexibility. What you need to investigate, therefore, is not the ideal time to be in each location, but if there are any dates to absolutely avoid (see p.14). Much of this depends on what you plan to do. Southern Italy in January may be chilly but fine for city exploring, especially if you plan to be inside museums and churches, whereas in Nepal in January you may be unable to trek. If you plan to hitch sections of your journey on yachts, make sure you check out the seasonal schedule. Same for rough overland trips that could get snowed under or rained out. Likewise, you'll want to know if there are any dates not to miss. If you're applying for a seasonal job, there's usually a tight window. And it's a pity to unwittingly arrive in Venice a day after Carnevale has ended: you're stuck with the crowds but have missed the event.

Travel seasons

Tourist season is climatically favourable, but plagued with crowds and, as a result, more expensive. The advantages of travelling out of season are numerous: low-cost and less crowded flights, better chances of finding a room at the cheapest hostels, shorter queues at museums, less need for reservations, and – best of all – fewer visitors to distract you from the culture you came to observe. However, you may be looking at some hidden expenses. Some of the cheapest hotels shut down in the off-season, so you may be forced into nicer digs. If it's cold enough to rattle your teeth loose at night, expect to pay extra for a room with heat. If you've arrived in the hot and sweaty season, be prepared to pay more for air-conditioning. Sure, you can combat these with a good sleeping bag or a cold, wet sarong wrap, but you might not always be in the mood. As a general rule, the best times to visit are at the beginning and end of the tourist cycles, the so-called "shoulder seasons", when you get the good weather without the crowds.

Stuck in a typhoon

I can't even remember how many typhoons passed through while I was working in Hong Kong.

The most common local response to a typhoon warning is to shop. The stores might close while the storm passes, so people gather up food, flashlight batteries, that sort of stuff. The bread gets picked clean by the end of the day, but it's far from panic shopping. There's enough advance notice to keep things calm. You just pick up enough to get you by for a few days. Besides, you probably won't be going anywhere since the airport and the public transport to and from it are shut down during the worst of the storm.

When you're picking up some food, it's probably not a bad idea to get some Scotch tape as well. They say if you make a giant X across the window with it, it minimizes the danger of shattering. More commonly, though, the driving rain eventually seeps through the window – or bleeds through – so your things might get wet if you put them in the wrong spot.

The stronger typhoons are serious – flying trees and the like – but if you're inside you're fine. In fact, many places have typhoon parties with cheap beer and offers to "Come weather the storm here". If things officially close down due to weather, it becomes a designated typhoon shelter and everyone already inside is allowed to keep on partying.

Where I lived, when the eye of the storm passed over, everyone ran out to body surf. It was the only time we had big enough swells to do it.

Ron Gluckman, correspondent based in China for numerous magazines including *Time* (ⓦ www.gluckman.com)

Average temperatures and rainfall

	Jan	Feb	Mar	Apr	May	June	July	Aug	Sept	Oct	Nov	Dec
Alice Springs, Australia												
Av daily max (°C)	36	35	32	27	23	19	19	23	27	31	34	36
Rainfall	43	33	28	10	15	13	8	8	8	18	31	38
Anchorage, USA												
Av daily max (°C)	-7	-3	1	7	12	17	18	18	14	6	-1	-7
Rainfall	20	18	15	10	13	18	41	66	66	56	25	23
Auckland, New Zealand												
Av daily max (°C)	23	23	22	19	17	14	13	14	16	17	19	21
Rainfall	79	94	81	97	127	137	145	117	102	102	89	79
Bali, Indonesia												
Av daily max (°C)	28	28	28	28	27	27	26	26	27	27	28	28
Rainfall	394	311	208	115	79	67	57	31	43	95	176	268
Bangkok, Thailand												
Av daily max (°C)	32	33	34	35	34	33	32	32	32	31	31	31
Rainfall	8	20	36	58	198	160	160	175	305	206	66	5
Beijing, China												
Av daily max (°C)	1	4	11	21	27	31	31	30	26	20	9	3
Rainfall	4	5	8	17	35	78	243	141	58	16	11	3
Bombay, India												
Av daily max (°C)	28	28	30	32	33	32	29	29	29	32	32	31
Rainfall	2.5	2.5	2.5	0	18	485	617	340	264	64	13	2.5
Cairo, Egypt												
Av daily max (°C)	18	21	24	28	33	35	36	35	32	30	26	20
Rainfall	5	5	5	3	3	0	0	0	0	0	3	5
Cape Town, South Africa												
Av daily max (°C)	26	26	25	22	19	18	17	18	18	21	23	24
Rainfall	15	8	18	48	79	84	89	66	43	31	18	10
Caracas, Venezuela												
Av daily max (°C)	24	25	26	27	27	26	26	26	27	26	25	26
Rainfall	23	10	15	33	79	102	109	109	107	109	94	46
Copenhagen, Denmark												
Av daily max (°C)	2	2	5	10	16	19	22	21	18	12	7	4
Rainfall	49	39	32	38	43	47	71	66	62	59	48	49
Damascus, Syria												
Av daily max (°C)	12	14	18	24	29	33	36	37	33	27	19	13
Rainfall	43	43	8	13	3	0	0	0	18	10	41	41
Harare, Zimbabwe												
Av daily max (°C)	26	26	26	26	23	21	21	23	26	28	27	26
Rainfall	196	178	117	28	13	3	0	3	5	28	97	163

	Jan	Feb	Mar	Apr	May	June	July	Aug	Sept	Oct	Nov	Dec
Hong Kong, China												
Av daily max (°C)	18	17	19	24	28	29	31	31	29	27	23	20
Rainfall	33	46	74	137	292	394	381	367	257	114	43	31
Istanbul, Turkey												
Av daily max (°C)	8	9	11	16	21	25	28	28	24	20	15	11
Rainfall	109	92	72	46	38	34	34	30	58	81	103	119
Jamaica												
Av daily max (°C)	30	30	30	31	31	32	32	32	32	31	31	31
Rainfall	23	15	23	31	102	89	89	91	99	180	74	36
Kathmandu, Nepal												
Av daily max (°C)	18	19	25	28	30	29	29	28	28	27	23	19
Rainfall	15	41	23	58	122	246	373	345	155	38	8	3
London, England												
Av daily max (°C)	6	7	10	13	17	20	22	21	19	14	10	7
Rainfall	54	40	37	37	46	45	57	59	49	57	64	48
Manaus, Brazil												
Av daily max (°C)	31	31	31	31	31	31	32	33	33	33	33	32
Rainfall	249	231	262	221	170	84	58	38	46	107	142	203
Marrakesh, Morocco												
Av daily max (°C)	18	20	23	26	29	33	38	38	33	28	23	19
Rainfall	25	28	33	31	15	8	3	3	10	23	31	31
Mexico City, Mexico												
Av daily max (°C)	28	29	37	41	40	33	33	33	32	31	29	28
Rainfall	13	5	10	20	53	119	170	152	130	51	18	8
Moscow, Russia												
Av daily max (°C)	-9	-6	0	10	19	21	23	22	16	9	2	-5
Rainfall	39	38	36	37	53	58	88	71	58	45	47	54
Nairobi, Kenya												
Av daily max (°C)	25	26	25	24	22	21	21	21	24	24	23	23
Rainfall	38	64	125	211	158	46	15	23	31	53	109	86
New York, USA												
Av daily max (°C)	3	3	7	14	20	25	28	27	26	21	11	5
Rainfall	94	97	91	81	81	84	107	109	86	89	76	91
Quito, Ecuador												
Av daily max (°C)	22	22	22	21	21	22	22	23	23	22	22	22
Rainfall	99	112	142	175	137	43	20	31	69	112	97	79
Rio de Janeiro, Brazil												
Av daily max (°C)	29	29	28	27	25	24	24	24	24	25	26	28
Rainfall	125	122	130	107	79	53	41	43	66	79	104	137

continued	Jan	Feb	Mar	Apr	May	June	July	Aug	Sept	Oct	Nov	Dec
Rome, Italy												
Av daily max (°C)	11	13	15	19	23	28	30	30	26	22	16	13
Rainfall	71	62	57	51	46	37	15	21	63	99	129	93
San Francisco, USA												
Av daily max (°C)	13	15	16	17	17	19	18	18	21	20	17	14
Rainfall	119	97	79	38	18	3	0	0	8	25	64	112
San José, Costa Rica												
Av daily max (°C)	24	24	26	26	27	26	25	26	26	25	25	24
Rainfall	15	5	20	46	229	241	211	241	305	300	145	41
Santiago, Chile												
Av daily max (°C)	29	29	27	23	18	14	15	17	19	22	26	28
Rainfall	3	3	5	13	64	84	76	56	31	15	8	5
Sydney, Australia												
Av daily max (°C)	26	26	24	22	19	16	16	17	19	22	23	25
Rainfall	89	102	127	135	127	117	117	76	74	71	74	74
Suva, Fiji												
Av daily max (°C)	29	29	29	29	28	27	26	26	27	27	28	29
Rainfall	290	272	368	310	257	170	125	211	196	211	249	318
Tokyo, Japan												
Av daily max (°C)	2	2	6	13	18	21	24	26	22	17	11	5
Rainfall	25	43	61	84	102	160	188	155	160	147	56	38
Vancouver, Canada												
Av daily max (°C)	5	7	10	14	18	21	23	23	18	14	9	6
Rainfall	218	147	127	84	71	64	31	43	91	147	211	224

When not to go

The regions listed below don't necessarily share a common weather pattern, so it's difficult to broadly apply monsoon or dry-season dates. Consult the Regional Profiles at the end of this book for more information, plus country guidebooks or specific books on weather (such as the *Rough Guide to Weather*).

- **Africa** May–June & Oct: northern parts of Africa experience prolonged sandstorms. March–June: rains in eastern Africa can soak a safari and make roads muddy and impassable. May–Nov: rains in western Africa bog down roads and render Sahara transit difficult. Christmas season: southern African coastal resorts and safaris fill up with locals.

- **Asia** Mid-Dec to March: Himalayan trekking routes may get snow-bound. Nov–March: north central Asia can be wickedly cold. Oct–June: the Karakoram Highway and the road between Srinigar and Leh (Kashmir to Ladakh) officially close.
- **Australia/ New Zealand** Dec–March: heavy rains in northern Australia can flood roads. Dec–Feb: sweltering heat in the Outback. June–July: freezing nights in the Outback. Christmas summer holiday: resorts and transport busy.
- **Caribbean & Central America** June–Nov: hurricanes (can usually be avoided if you stay flexible and keep an eye on the news).
- **Europe & Russia** Nov–Feb: northern Europe is cold and rainy and snow can disrupt travel, especially in the Alps. Nov–March: Russia can be extremely cold.
- **Middle East** June–Aug: the heat can get downright uncivilized, especially if the Med isn't nearby for a cool swim. Keep an eye on the Jewish holiday calendar in Israel, as public transport and hotels can be swamped.
- **North America** Dec–Feb: mid- and north US, winter storms cause slow travel, and severe cold can limit time outdoors. June–Sept: hurricanes can hit the southeast coast, but are easily avoided. May–Aug: central US is prone to tornadoes.
- **South America** Jan–April: Inca Trail can get awfully wet. Mid-Dec to Feb: Christmas holiday rush in Brazil, Venezuela, Argentina and Chile – coastal resorts and transport fills up. Jan–April: Galapagos Islands are hot and rainy.
- **South Pacific** Jan: rains can get heavy in the southern islands.
- **Southeast Asia** Nov–April: northwest monsoon drenches the eastern coast of Thailand and the islands, and the east coast of Malaysia. March–Oct: on the west coast, southwest monsoon rains disrupt diving visibility and tanning.

Planning around local holidays and events

Your overnight train pulls into the station, you stagger over to the tourist information bureau, take a number and wait. When your number pops up, you head to the counter and say you're looking for some budget accommodation for a night or two. The person behind the counter is already nodding their head like a paint shaker before you finish the sentence. There's a Rotary Club convention in town and they've taken up all the rooms. The best the tourist office can do is a double room at the Ritz for $350/£225. Or, you can stay an hour's journey outside the city at a little hostel situated next to a maximum-security psychiatric ward.

Festival planning usually takes some advance legwork, as cities and towns can get booked up over a year in advance. Last-minute accommodation, if indeed there is any, usually gets snatched up several days before the event. But the extra effort it takes to attend a festival is almost always worthwhile. There are thousands to choose from. In some you can participate, in some the spectators become part of the spectacle whether they want to or not, but the exuberance is nearly always palpable (see ⓦ festivals.com and ⓦ www.world-party.com).

Africa

Great Migration Serengeti National Park, Tanzania. When a million wildebeest do anything together, it's pretty exciting to watch. Add 18,000 eland, about 200,000 zebras, and up to half a million Thompson's gazelles. Now throw in a few crocodile-infested rivers that must be crossed and hundreds of hungry lions and it gets really interesting. People pour in from around the globe to see this moving smorgasbord migrate, hot-air balloons providing great lookouts for highly inflated prices. May–Sept ⓦ www.tanzania-web.com

Americas

Burning Man Project Black Rock Desert, Nevada, USA. This pop-pagan, postapocalyptic gathering of 10,000-plus "burners" (gun-wielding prophets, nude chainsaw jugglers and so on) has only one stated mission: to burn a giant wooden thing that, even in poor lighting, only barely looks like a man. Aug–Sept ⓦ www.burningman.com

Carneval Rio de Janeiro and Salvador, Brazil. You get a choice: you can watch the world's most colourful parade in Rio (2 days, starting around 7pm and lasting until 5am), after which you'll never look at Liberace or Zsa Zsa Gabor the same way again. Or you can samba away three kilos a night dancing down the streets behind giant trucks loaded with speakers in Salvador. Feb–March (the week prior to Ash Wednesday) ⓦ ipanema.com/carnival

Day of the Dead Oaxaca, Mexico. There may not be life after death, but there's at least a party. The line between the breathing and the buried gets chucked aside for a day so the deceased can come out and play, complete with skeleton costumes and graveside bashes. Oct–Nov ⓦ www .turista.com.mx/puebla

Greenwich Village Halloween Parade, New York, USA. If you think New Yorkers are frightening in the daylight, check this out. The freak show gets even freakier during Halloween with over 20,000 kooks and spooks and 1.5 million spectators. Oct 31 ⓦ www.halloween-nyc.com

Mardi Gras New Orleans, USA. Good times have been rolling here since 1699. A bacchanalian party with parades that begins on January 6

(Epiphany) and builds to a feverish pitch that culminates on Shrove Tuesday. Feb–March (the week prior to Ash Wednesday) ⓦwww.mardigrasneworleans.com

Monarch Butterfly Migration Angangueo, Mexico. With 100–250 million monarchs attending, it's likely the most spectacular convention of insects in the world. There's butterfly carpet everywhere you look and orange and black clouds in the middle of the day. The deep shade of the oyamel fir trees in the forests outside of Mexico City lure these beasties from as far as 2000 miles away. Dec to mid-March ⓦwww.monarchwatch.org

Junkanoo Nassau, Bahamas. Even Santa takes a back seat at this Christmastime Caribbean-beat blowout. Bring a whistle, cow bell, or anything else that makes noise. Dec 26 & Jan 1 ⓦwww.bahamasnet.com/Junkanoo/w.junkhome.html

New Orleans Jazz Fest. Ten days of mind-bending jazz, funk, gospel, blues, zydeco, folk and bluegrass – 4000 musicians-worth of it – plus great food. April–May ⓦwww.nojazzfest.com

New Year's Eve Party, Times Square, New York. Wanna see a 500-pound ball slide down a pole? Sing "Auld Lang Syne" out of tune with half a million people? You may risk getting crushed to the size of this book but that's a small price to pay. More interesting than watching it on TV with 300 million others, anyway. Dec 31, arrive early ⓦwww.timessquarebid.org

Asia

Full Moon Party Koh Phangan, Thailand. Possibly the most popular travel party on the planet. With twelve raves per year, it's hard to miss. Howl at the moon, bark or just dance yourself into a trance. Thousands of lamps (and the odd fire-eater) illuminate the beach until sunrise. Full moon each month ⓦwww.kohphangan.com/travel/fullmoon.html

Holi Festival Northern and eastern India. Welcome to the festival of flying colours. Powder dyes are dumped off balconies or playfully thrown at you from ground level (ears, nose, mouth… no orifice is safe from the Technicolor assault). Feb–March during full moon ⓦwww.tourisminindia.com

International Dragon Boat Championships Hong Kong. Paddle power propels the participants (fuelled with traditional pyramid-shaped zongzi dumplings), as they pull through the waters just off Hong Kong in 11.6-metre boats. The boats have been battling for over 2000 years to commemorate the suicide drowning of the poet-politician, Qu Yuan. The festival is tied to the lunar calendar, so check for annual dates. June ⓦwww.hkta.org

Naadam Festival Ulaanbaatar, Mongolia. Sometimes called the Mongolian Olympics, Naadam focuses on three main events: wrestling, archery and

continured

horse racing. Throw in some folk dancing and fermented mare's milk, and you've got yourself a festival. July ⓦwww.visitmongolia.com/naadam _festival.htm

Pushkar Camel Fair Pushkar, India. If you ever need to get your hands on 30,000 camels, this is the place to go. In addition to the camel swap, there are races, camel polo matches, and other events, but people-watching plays a big role as the town's population increases by 2000 percent during the week. Nov ⓦwww.indolinks.com/websights/pushkar

Snow and Ice Festival Sapporo, Japan. Don your thermals along with two million others as the streets of Sapporo fill with hundreds of sculpted, glittering ice creations, some upwards of 20m tall. Feb ⓦjin.jcic.or.jp/kidsweb/ calendar/february/snow.html

Australia

Darwin Beer Can Regatta, Australia. Would-be yachtsmen can chug their way to the rank of captain in no time at this event: a coupling of aggressive drinking and aggressive sailing for the sake of charity. What more could you want from a pseudo-sporting event. Early Aug ⓦwww.tasgreetings.com /bcregatta.html

Sydney Gay and Lesbian Mardi Gras, Austrailia. Gays, bis, straights, and synthetic fibres are all warmly welcome as the gay and lesbian pride hits the streets, maximum exposure being the order of the day. Feb–March ⓦwww.mardigras.com.au

Europe

Ascot Races Berkshire, England. You can bet on the horses, but keep your eyes on the pomp on parade. Morning suits for men and formal dresses for women, not to mention hats of all sorts, from those with the shade coverage of a patio parasol to dainty little numbers not much bigger than a cinnamon roll. Third week in June, Tues–Fri ⓦwww.ascot.co.uk

Carnevale Venice, Italy. A decadent renaissance festival, pyjama party and three-day rager against the backdrop of the world's most picturesque sinking city. The costumes are as elaborate as they are expensive. And guess what? They're for sale. Feb–March (the week prior to Ash Wednesday) ⓦwww.venice-carnival.com

Cooper's Hill Cheese Roll Brockworth, England. People have been chasing a cheese down a sixty-degree slope here for over 200 years. Most tumble in a blur of legs, hands, and dislocated shoulders all the way to the bottom. Don't worry, there are plenty of ambulances standing by. Last Mon in May ⓦwww.visit-glos.org.uk

Kirkpinar Oil Wrestling Tournament Edirne, Turkey. Smear yourself with oil and wrestle for a camel and stack of cash? Believe it or not, it's been a winning formula for 600 years and it's still going. Over 1000 contestants sign up every year. July 5–11 ⓦwww.geocities.com/aydemiray

La Tomatina Buñol, Spain. Ingredients: one small town that produces cement, one town plaza, 30,000 mostly drunk lunatics and 40,000 kilos of tomatoes. Mix aggressively for one hour or until town is sufficiently red, then rinse at a local watering hole. Aug ⓦwww.lahoya.net/tomatina

Love Parade Berlin, Germany. At this uber-fest, you'll see mosaic tattoos, blinding hair colours, and more body piercings than you can shake a ... well, you'd better think twice before you shake anything at them. It's the world's largest rave. Millions of technophiles dance nonstop as they squirm through the crowds, exchanging sweat, drugs and exotic diseases. July ⓦwww.loveparade.de

Oktoberfest Munich, Germany. Just grab a seat and a frothy "mas" and start slidin' back the brew. The atmosphere (over 5000 buzzing, swaying, happy drinkers per tent) makes the beer taste even better. But don't be fooled by the name; most of the event takes place in September. Sept–Oct ⓦwww.muenchen-tourist.de

The Palio Siena, Italy. With bribes, religion and dirty tricks, this horse race is straight out of the Middle Ages. To be precise, 1147. Riders representing Siena's different neighbourhoods battle and race around the town square for three laps. Medical personnel are on alert for both riders and horses. The party starts for days before each of the two big races. Early July & mid-August ⓦwww.ilpaliodisiena.com

Paris Air Show France. You don't need to be on the market for your own private F-15 to attend. The public, 300,000 of them, turn out to see new models unveiled and flown every year on the spot Charles Lindbergh first landed. It's the biggest air show going. June (odd-numbered years only) ⓦwww.parisairshow.com

Running of the Bulls Pamplona, Spain. People have been testing out their insurance polices at this event for years. Eight days of drinking, revelling in the streets, and, oh yes, attempting to avoid stampeding bulls on a narrow, winding, cobblestoned street armed with nothing more than a pair of tennis shoes and a hangover. July ⓦwww.pamplona.net

Whirling Dervish Festival Konya, Turkey. The famed Whirling Dervishes spin their way closer to God only once a year, but the celebrations last a week. The dizzying ceremonial dance is accompanied with drums, flutes and camera shutters. Dec ⓦwww.turizm.gov.tr

Occasionally scheduling conflicts occur. A rock concert, business convention or sporting event unexpectedly disrupts your travel plans. So what do you do? First, just try to avoid the situation by keeping an eye on your guidebook for national holidays or other events that might cause a hotel-booking frenzy. Then, if you expect the city's accommodation to fill up, either email ahead for a reservation or stop at another, smaller town and delay your arrival until a more auspicious day. If you've already arrived, the easiest and most common route is to simply move on to the next town. For this, the tourist office can be quite helpful. It's an opportune time to head somewhere not mentioned in a guidebook. But before you do, ask for a list of accommodation the tourist bureau represents and a phone book. Cross-check their list with the one in the yellow pages. Often, there are several hotels, especially the cheaper digs, not on the list. Give those places a call first; they're the most likely to have room. Or look for less conventional places to stay, such as camping grounds that rent tents or university dormitories. Don't forget to ask about rooftop sleeping at hostels if the weather is favourable.

How much time do I spend in each place?

At least two days longer than you think. Maybe even two weeks. The faster you go and the more ground you cover, tempting though it may be, the less you'll see. The same way that slowing down improves your peripheral vision when driving, reducing your speed allows you to take more in while you travel. If you're not pressed to press on, you may take an extra day to forge a friendship with another traveller you met over breakfast or find out your favourite musician is giving a concert in an ancient amphitheatre nearby or that the local cultural centre is offering free palm-tree climbing lessons. With enough time and curiosity, something interesting is bound to happen.

Plan to take a break

Travel may sound romantic and adventurous, but finding your way around a city, coordinating train schedules, locating a place to stay, carting around three kilos of unex-changeable small coins, taking the stairs up every tall structure for a scenic overview, using perplexing toilets, sampling palate-numbing foods and happening upon nose-tweaking smells – the things that give independent travel its bite – combine to form an exhausting experience. Give yourself a chance to relax.

To some extent, taking a break is going to happen on its own. You might stumble upon a place you can't resist, get stuck waiting for a visa application to process or for a transport strike to end, find a fun person or group of travellers to hang out with or just hit the sensory-overload wall.

The last one will occur if the first four don't. This exhaustion – think of it as cultural burnout – may creep up on you, or just descend on you at once. It typically occurs after two to four months of continuous, fairly fast-paced travel, but you'll need to find your own threshold. Here's the main symptom: you spend more and more time in cafés and hostel lounges and less out exploring towns and museums. There's a simple remedy for recharging your wanderlust: stay put.

Give yourself a chance to absorb and process what you've seen. Write some long letters. Get to know a few locals. Take the oppor-tunity to earn some money. Who knows, stay in one place long enough and you might even fall in love.

On a long trip, allow yourself the flexibility to stop when you need it, or plan ahead so you end up at your dream white-sand hangout. If you hope to work or volunteer (see Chapter 5) or take a course or pay a relative an extended visit, you might try to plan some of that ahead of time as well. Whether or not you schedule a pit stop in advance, you should factor in some "down time": at least two weeks for every three months on the road.

Researching your trip

The Internet works a treat for trip planning. Let's say you speak Spanish and you like scuba diving: start at your favourite Web search engine. Type in "scuba" and "Spanish" and see what pops up, then narrow the search with words like "shark" or "tequila" or whatever diving aspects you deem essential. You can often find reviews and references online as well just by adding the words "reviews" or "references" to the search.

For specific activities, look in specialized magazines and newsletters. For a cooking course or fine dining, for example, you might look in *Gourmet Magazine*; for photography trips, *Outdoor Photographer*. If you're looking for general ideas, major-city newspaper travel sections are invaluable. A similar assortment with higher-budget adventures and more edgy writing can be found in magazines, with some of the best ideas located among the tour advertisements listed in the back. That doesn't necessarily mean you ought to sign up for their tours – many of those things you can do on your own for a fraction of the price. For a list of publications and websites, see p.300.

For information directly from other travellers, try ⊛roughguides .com's Travel Talk, where you can post and read messages on thousands of specific travel topics. Other sites, such as ⊛virtualtourist .com and ⊛lonelyplanet.com's Thorn Tree, offer similar discussion boards.

Your itinerary

You've got a few places in mind, some weather you want to miss and a few dates you want to hit for festivals or seasonal activities. Before you start stringing it together with your chosen methods of transport (see p.25), there are a few more things to consider.

If it's your first big trip, start out gently. If you're going to India, Chile and New Zealand, for example, India is the most challenging of the three and won't make the best starting point. Besides, after India, Chile and New Zealand won't seem nearly as interesting. If you start in New Zealand, it will still be exciting, but much easier. Once you get a feel of getting around on your own, move on to a more challenging country like Chile, where there's a decent infrastructure, but a language barrier. After that, navigating the train stations and markets of India will be significantly easier to handle.

Take a moment and consider the balance of your trip. You want a good mix of attractions, adventure, a few courses, a little wandering, ample breaks, an overland journey, maybe some sea passage, a measure of hiking, some kind of animal viewing and maybe even a dose of meditation. Chances are your trip may be thin in a few of these areas. Look back at the activity list on p.9 for some ideas on how you might round out your experiences. Just remember to space them out. You don't want to feel like you're trapped in a Jules Verne novel, racing the globe with Passepartout.

To find out how to connect the dots with the best-suited transportation, head on to Chapter 2. Just remember that by changing your departure date, you may be able to neatly sidestep any meteorological conflicts, or by stopping to work/volunteer/study/hang out you can achieve the same affect.

Checking political stability

Try to get into the habit of picking up an international newspaper and scanning the headlines for any turmoil in the area. America's State Department website tends to play up the dangers. This may help prevent lawsuits, but it can also scare people away from a reasonably safe destination. Instead, or at least as a comparison, try the UK's Foreign Office (@fco.gov.uk), Australia's advisories (@www.dfat.gov.au) or Canada's (@voyage.dfait-maeci.gc.ca), for a more sensible synopsis. Before heading anywhere you're not sure about, get a quick update from the Web. See p.168 for what to do if things turn sour while you're there.

Activity booking

Just because you find the ideal activity, that doesn't mean you have to book it. In fact, you can often save more than fifty percent of the cost by foregoing the middlemen and making arrangements once you arrive. However, there are some courses and tours that fill up well in advance. You can't always tell which these are, but it's possible to make a decent guess. If you reasoned, for example, that with constant treks heading out to Machu Picchu, there would be no trouble to finding a group, you'd be right. Whereas, there may be some size limit to a pastry course at the Cordon Bleu, so that would be worth booking in advance, or at least sending an email to find out about availability. Guidebooks often tell you which activities need to be booked in advance and which don't. When in doubt, check the Internet and follow up with a call or email.

Not planning at all

Here's another way to go about it: get a passport, rustle up some cash and hop on the next bus that passes. Connect to an airport, train station or harbour, and head in whichever direction cries out. If you need a visa to get there, no worries, just pick somewhere else. Or fill out a visa application, find a cheap hotel and wait for the visa to be processed. While you're waiting, you might look into a few vaccinations, study the language and meet a few locals. Or don't. Go with the wind and your whims.

The drawback to planning your trip, free spirits claim, is that, to a large extent, you decide in advance what you're looking for. So, while you'll probably find "it", you'll likely miss many of the unpredictable things that are subtly trying to find you.

2

How to get around the world

You can hop on a freighter across the ocean, then buy a motorcycle, or maybe a horse, and trade it in for a plane ticket when you're ready to move on. You can work your way from continent to continent on a yacht or circle most of the world on buses and trains. Price, length of journey, reliability of arrival and comfort vary drastically with each mode of transport, so you'll want to pick the ones that best fit your budget, itinerary (or lack thereof), and hardship threshold.

By air

The idea of flying around the world with a single ticket is not only possible these days, it's being done by an increasing number of travellers. However, it's not the only way to fly around the world or necessarily the best choice for your trip. In addition to the round-the-world (RTW) ticket option described below, you'll find two other flight alternatives, especially useful if you're planning to head to places that are off most airlines' radar, or if you want to leave open the possibility that you may be away for well more than a year. Determining your best option is generally a matter of matching your destination wish list (created using the tools in Chapter 1), travel comfort level and the deals available when you book a ticket.

RTW tickets

Because of their complexity, RTW tickets are best booked with a knowledgeable travel agent. The tickets come in two basic forms: a special RTW ticket provided by an airline alliance; and a series of cheap (often consolidated) one-way tickets sewn together by a booking agent.

With an alliance ticket, the standard arrangement is this:

- The ticket is valid up to one year
- You have to keeping going in the same direction around the planet (east to west or vice versa) although some tickets do allow back-tracking within a region
- You pay based on the distance you cover (which increases the more you deviate from a direct route around the globe and decreases with overland segments), or by the number of defined "zones" you stop in
- You have to pick your stops and dates when you book the ticket and pay a penalty fee (typically $75) for each ticket reissue
- High and low season only refers to the date that you make your first flight. If you leave during high season, you'll pay about $100/£125 more

With a "custom-made" ticket, it's possible to tweak it to get exactly where you want to go and even backtrack. However, sticking to major hubs is likely to decrease the cost of your trip (mention "South America" and "Africa" in the same sentence and watch dollar signs appear in the agent's eyes). And, if you start adding on extensive side trips, you're losing sight of the low prices that make RTW tickets worthwhile. The best deals are pieced-together consolidated tickets from a variety of different airlines, often the national airlines of the places you're flying into, which have been known to offer not only enticing stopovers, but government-subsidized flights to attract more foreign visitors. To get the best deals from this type of ticket, it helps if you're flexible with dates and destinations so a clever agent can make sure you get the latest bargains.

Numerous passes allow you to insert overland segments into your trip. Some even come packaged that way. The problem is, the more interesting and longer the overland route, the harder it will be to guarantee you can (or will want to) make your next connecting flight. Either your bus gets delayed at some washed-out bridge or you find so many mind-boggling things to do that you feel like you've grossly underestimated your time allotment. Which gets back to the flexibility of your ticket. How are you possibly going to know when you book the ticket that seventeen days is exactly the right amount of time to spend in Thailand? By paying extra or finding a ticket that allows flexibility, you may be thankful later. To design a trip and get a rough calculation on your own, try Airtrek's RTW online planner (@www.airtrek.com) or STA's UK-based online planner (@www.statravel.co.uk). To see some consortium deals, check out @www.star-alliance.com or @www.thegreatescapade.com. For a basic air-fare saving strategy, see the section on Costs on p.55. And to find out why air-couriering isn't ideal for RTW trips, see p.29.

Home base

You can also book a series of round-trip tickets with lengthy stopovers and open-jaw tickets (which allow you to fly into one country, out of another and travel overland in between) and simply return home for a quick break between journeys as you head around the world. For example, starting in Vancouver, you might book a round-trip ticket to Santiago, Chile, make some kind of loop around southern South America and then fly back home. From there, after a short breather, you might fly to Delhi with Thai airways, and take advantage of a free stopover in Bangkok (airlines generally stop at their hub city and allow you to stay for days, weeks or months), then make your way overland from Delhi to Kathmandu, and fly back home again (with another stay in Bangkok if you like). You won't necessarily circumnavigate the planet this way, but that's just a technicality. It can be nice to sort out some of the mail that may have piled up in your absence (even if it's coming to your parents' house), spend some time going over your travel pictures, meet up with some friends, grab a change of clothes and work up some thirst for your next destination. If you don't feel like returning home, or just want to save some money, pick a city with great international fares like London, Bangkok or New York and use it as a base.

Winging it

It's not only possible to book one-way flights as you go, it's usually pretty easy and inexpensive. Just pick up tickets from local travel agents and get visas and vaccinations at embassies and health clinics respectively. If the country you're entering next requires an onward ticket, no problem: simply buy a fully refundable onward ticket and cancel it once you arrive. Just remember to ask specifically where you can collect the refund as some airlines will only perform the service where you bought the ticket or at the corporate headquarters.

Steals and deals can be found at bucket shops – unbonded (aka uninsured) discount ticket consolidators that operate mainly in large gateways like Singapore, Bangkok, San Francisco, New York and London and, by acquiring large blocks of tickets (usually during less popular travel times), can offer savings of up to 30 percent. Many bucket shops are small-time operators that may go out of business overnight or try to pull a fast one. Insist on a receipt that lists complete restrictions and refunds and – just in case – purchase by credit card so you can stop payment if the ticket never materializes. How do you find them? Try the newspaper travel sections of the major cities mentioned above. Just look for the smallest ads with the lowest prices. The insured version is called a consolidator.

Most local travel agents can usually find you better deals to that country's popular destinations than you can find from home, because that's 99 percent of what they do. They make the deals and know the discounts. Depending on which points you're connecting, it's certainly possible to circle the globe this way for the price of a mid-range RTW ticket.

A "destination specialist" is a local travel agent, but the term generally refers to one that is a first- or second-generation immigrant and focuses on ultra cheap tickets to "the homeland" by buying large quantities of seats on certain flights (sometimes charters) and operating with lower margins. All agencies like to state that they're specialists, but a better giveaway for a destination specialist is if they have a country-specific name (such as Athens Travel for Greek flights, Taj Mahal Tours for Indian flights, and so forth). Small catch: they tend to specialize in round trips. If it's cheaper than a one-way fare, buy it and junk the return leg.

International flights are almost always more costly than domestic flights that cover the same distance. To get around costly international flights and taxes, it's often possible to string together domestic flights in neighbouring countries with short overland connections on buses or trains across the border.

Courier flights

Courier travel can make for some bargain getaway trips (see ⓦwww.aircouriertravel.com or ⓦwww.aircourier.org). But piecing together any sort of round-the-world journey this way is not a viable option. With a home base near a major international hub airport, single travellers can try to make use of the air courier option, a completely legal arrangement in which you give up your check-in luggage space (leaving you carry-on only, plus as many layers as you can wear) to transport goods for a courier service – you just carry an invoice, they handle all the actual carrying – and they give you a heavily discounted (typically 40–85 percent off) or free ticket in return. They get their freight delivered quickly and you get a good deal. In other words, you become a one-person FedEx. Now here's the fine print:

- You can put in requests for times and destinations, but for the most discounted tickets, you may be asked to leave on a day's or week's notice.
- You get a round-trip ticket that brings you back home within one or two weeks – this can be stretched up to several months, but don't count on it.
- This service operates most extensively out of major hub cities near the coast (eg San Francisco, London, Vancouver).
- You have to be over 18 or 21.
- There may be a lot of competition, especially to popular destinations and during popular times of year so, even if you get a flight, the discount may not be substantial.
- You often have to join a courier service (that is, pay a membership fee of about $50) before you can start getting transport assignments. If you're not deterred by the restrictions, the membership fee can be well worth it.

Travel clubs

Some people prefer travel clubs, another fee-based membership service that offers discounts in the range of twenty to sixty percent. Just check to make sure they offer discounts on the types of services you are likely to use. For example, great deals on four-star hotel suites may not be for you. Try the International Travel Club (🌐www.mytravelclub.com), Best Fares (🌐www.bestfares.com), Moment's Notice (🌐www.moments-notice.com) or Travelers Advantage (🌐www.travelersadvantage.com).

By sea

Rather than zipping over dimpled oceans at 30,000 feet, you could head for the high seas, especially if you've got a strong stomach. As the saying goes, "If a man has anything in him, travel will bring it out – especially ocean travel." On the plus side though, no other form of transport quite conjures up that special feeling you get arriving by sea: a grand entrance in the style of the great explorers and nineteenth-century travellers. You can circle the world on one ship, skip from boat to boat, or simply make it a segment of your journey. Catching a lift on a yacht is the cheapest option. After that it's a toss-up between cruise ships and cargo vessels. To find out which will work out best for your journey, read on.

By yacht

Private yachts of all types often need an extra pair of hands during a sea passage. Some are crewed by professional captains delivering a boat to a new owner and some by "old salt" couples who live aboard their vessels full time, follow general routes through regions and countries where anchorages are safe, the scenery is agreeable and (since many are retired) the prices are low – and simply want a little help or a little company on board.

It's possible to get a working passage or catch a free lift (though people may request $5–25/£3–16 per day to cover your food and drinks) while heading almost anywhere if you know the sailing seasons, yachting epicentres and routes and how to present yourself professionally. Most agreements to crew aboard a boat are made casually at the individual harbours, though you may have a written contract. Passages can be anything from a couple days to a couple of months, depending on the destination.

You don't need to be in peak condition to crew on a yacht, but if you're reasonably fit it certainly helps. Space is limited, so a compact kit will be appreciated. Show up pulling a Samsonite trolley and you've got a few strikes against you already. There's not much special gear involved, but in your collapsible bag you'll want some non-marking shoes, a good hat that won't land in the drink when the wind picks up, sun block, UV sunglasses with safety straps, motion sickness pills and some smart clothes that won't get you thrown out of the occasional yacht club. Naturally, it doesn't hurt your chances if you head to the yachting epicentres. The big three regions are the Mediterranean, Caribbean and the South Pacific.

You may be able to catch a ride right back to your departure point, but don't count on it. Even if you've pre-arranged a long round-trip berth, one thing or another may cause you to hop off earlier. Expect to cough up for a cheap one-way plane ticket, ferry ride or bus trip, depending on where you end up.

Where and when

Caribbean The sailing season begins in October following the summer hurricanes and lasts until May. If you want to head "down island" (south), show up in Miami or Fort Lauderdale from November to March. Antigua Race Week (end of April) is the big event, and the Antigua Yacht Club marina is an ideal place to pick up a berth to just about anywhere, especially South America, the US and Europe.

Mediterranean The season kicks off in June when yachts need crew for their summer charters to cruise the Med. Nearly all major marinas are active, but especially: Antibes, Las Palmas, Rhodes, Malta, Majorca, Alicante and Gibraltar. Then, at the end of November, there's a 2700-mile fun run of sorts from Las Palmas de Gran Canaria (Canary Islands) to Rodney Bay in St Lucia: the Atlantic Rally for Cruisers (ARC). Over 200 boats participate in the rally, and even more make the crossing unofficially. So from October to the end of November, there's a mass exodus to the West Indies. The standard point of departure for the two- to four-week Atlantic crossing is Gran Canaria. If you show up at the beginning of November or before and chip in some food money for the crossing

(about $250/£160), you've got a good chance of catching a lift. To
get a step ahead of the competition, start your search a few weeks
earlier in Mediterranean marinas around Spain or France to catch
the yachts before they pass through the Strait of Gibralter. It can be
a fairly rough passage from the Strait to Gran Canaria, which is why
so many prefer to skip it. By contrast, the leg from Gran Canaria
to the Caribbean is usually a smooth ride.

South Pacific The major springboard for the stunning islands of
the South Pacific are a few marinas in northern New Zealand:
Opua, Whangarei and Auckland, probably in that order. Most
boats leave in the autumn (end Feb to end April). If you're looking
for passage in the other direction (to New Zealand) or on to the
US, your best chances are July to October. Some prefer to start in
Australia. If so, try the marinas in the Whitsunday Islands, Arlie
Beach and Townsville. May to July is a promising time to head
north toward Indonesia.

How to look for passage

Head down to any major harbour and start by scanning the notice
boards. Then find the harbourmaster and ask if he knows any captains looking for crew. That way, you can slip in a personal reference

("the harbour master said I should speak to you about a crew position you're trying to fill"). If that doesn't yield any leads, ask if you can use his radio to announce on the local sailor's channel that you're looking for work. Before walking the docks in search of a captain, try a more informal place like the local sailing-supply shop or, better yet, the harbour bar. If you like to plan ahead, check the ads in yachting magazines and newsletters. There are also crewing placement agencies that specialize in this very service, but be prepared for a membership fee of around $50/£32. Or, if you prefer to see the boat and meet the skipper first (which is probably a good idea), you may be better off on your own.

If captains don't like how you look or conduct yourself, they may not reveal they have a position available. You need to dress smartly and demonstrate that you're easy-going and level-headed. Moreover, you'll need to learn some yachting manners. Always ask for "permission to board" before letting your foot cross the rail. If you're a good cook, mention it. If you've got technical experience, let the captain know. If you've got some solid job references, keep a few copies on hand. Tell the captain he's welcome to search your lug-

Finding crew work

First, you don't need to know how to sail to do a crossing: you need to be neat, clean and trustworthy. If you're doing day work for a boat in the harbour – which is a good way to get your foot in the door – show up on time and take it seriously. My first boat was pretty shitty. And the captain was mostly incompetent. But I had been working day jobs on various boats in the harbour in Antibes for three weeks and was getting desperate. He did, however, give me a free lift across the Atlantic. And after that, finding boats was easy. I went after the nice boats first. They usually had the best, most talented captains – and the most money. I even got paid over $1000 for the crossing back home after a few months in the Caribbean.

Jonas Persson

My friend and I flew right to Las Palmas, but there was so much competition, it took ten days of active looking before we got a free lift. We walked the docks, even borrowed a dinghy and rowed around to the boats that were anchored just off shore, but didn't get a lift until a captain saw me playing guitar at a party. He brought my friend and I along as onboard entertainment. It wasn't until we were well on our way across the Atlantic that I told him it was the only song I knew. Once we were in the Caribbean, it didn't take longer than five days to catch a lift. You just need to make sure that you don't get left someplace without a lot of yachts. Barbados, St Martin and Antigua are the places you want to be.

I saw a number of women hitching on boats alone, usually doing the cooking, but if it were me, I'd team up with another woman or man for safety.

Peter Laurin

gage (he may request this anyway) and that your travel documents are in order (make sure they are). The interview works both ways: you want to size up the captain and crew as well. Are these people you want to be stuck at sea with? Women travellers must especially be aware. Will you be the only woman on board? Can you speak to other women on board who have sailed with these men before? Find out. Once you set sail, it's too late.

By ship

Assuming the $130,395/£83,854 grand suite aboard the *Silver Cloud* for the 95-day round-the-world cruise is not the sort of independent budget travel you had in mind (or the $50,000/£32,000 standard cabin), there are some reasonably priced cruise ships – if your definition of reasonable is $120–250/£80 –160 a day – circling the world that will happily welcome you aboard for just a segment of the trip. Contact a cruise-booking specialist to see what's available. The bigger problem, as far as hardcore budget travellers are concerned, may be the image. The leg of your journey you made by cruise ship isn't going to be a big hit at the next youth hostel story-swap.

Cruise vs freighter

Now, here's the surprise: it's not much cheaper to take a freighter. The average per day may be lower ($70–120/£45–80) as human freight, but it'll take a bit longer (nearly double the time on some routes), and you may end up staying in a hostel for a few weeks waiting for the ship to leave for its "scheduled" departure, so the total price can easily end up about the same. Naturally, there'll be more to do on a cruise ship, especially if slot machines, shuffleboard and dancing the electric slide rev your engine, but travelling at the budget end of the scale will land you in a cruise-ship cabin so small you probably couldn't fall over in it. And the bathroom might be a walk down the hallway. By contrast, freighters tend to put you in fairly luxurious officer staterooms, many of which have been made available as the ships have become computerized. Groups are usually small (about twelve – more than that and the ship is required to carry a doctor), but some freighters have become quasi-cruisers and take 100-300 passengers.

Besides lengthy departure delays, one of the trickiest problems to overcome on many routes is the one-way issue. Ships give priority to round-trip travellers, so one-wayers generally end up on the waiting list. Also, single travellers may face a supplement of ten to twenty percent. If you're over 65, you'll want to bring a doctor's certificate of good health. And, finally, keep an eye out for pirates. No kidding. Indonesia's waters have the highest risk of armed attacks. Thailand comes in second, and Brazil third. Working aboard freighters for passage isn't likely to be a viable option, but they just might need some cleaning, an extra mechanic aboard or the services of a massage therapist. It never hurts to ask.

Container ship vs bulk freighter

The difference between a container ship and bulk freighter, as far as passengers are concerned, is the likelihood of delays and the number of days in each port. Container ships carry the giant metal box eyesores that can be dropped onto the back of a truck, which expedites the loading and unloading process. This means you may only get six to twelve hours in port to look around. It does help the ship keep on schedule, though. Bulk freighters may take two to three days in port, which gives you more time to explore, but increases the chances of falling behind schedule.

Overland

Overlanding is usually the cheapest, and by no coincidence most exhausting, way to travel. Anything can happen. . . and usually does. Buses break down in scorching heat, leaving you trapped next to a tin speaker blasting out Hindi remixes of Britney Spears songs at inhuman decibels; trains may for stop half a day for no discernible reason at all; and entire roads get washed away. There'll be times when you'll see a plane soar overhead and the thought of the cramped seats and rubber sandwiches of an economy-class cabin will send a wistful tear down your cheek. That said, kilometre for kilometre, overlanding is the most interesting way to get around, and no global trip would be complete without at least one land segment. Routes have sprung up over the years, some following ancient paths like China's Silk Road or Central America's Ruta Maya, or the 1960s contribution, The Hippie Trail (see p.84). Others have popped up to connect popular backpacker destinations, buttressed by glowing guidebook reviews. Some trails are better trod than others and sometimes the route branches then rejoins like stream flowing around a rock, and you'll pass hundreds, if not thousands, of other backpackers along the way.

Public transport

This is perhaps the best, most culturally enriching way to get around. Passenger status places you on equal footing with those around you and allows a precious peek into the daily travel experience of local people. It gives you a chance to strike up a conversation with them, or attempt one with a phrasebook and hand gestures.

Guidebooks contain the necessary travel details on major bus, train, and ferry lines. With the exception of the Trans-Siberian railway, a few popular ferry connections, and transport during local public holidays, tickets are rarely an issue and can be booked the same day (even a few minutes before departure).

Border crossings

Having the right visas, vaccination certificates and onward tickets can be vital when you're passing through certain countries. Often you can obtain everything you need for onward travel at the various border crossings for free or for a small charge, other times you need a stamp from an embassy, but count on the border guards turning you back if your papers aren't in order. Look ahead over your route and get updated visa information prior to departure, either from a guidebook or from national websites.

△ Cargo trucks make a mountain crossing, north India

The Trans-Siberian Express

Motherly Russian train attendants with enough facial hair to knit a pair of leg-warmers, food that most travellers would only eat on a dare and smoke in some cabins so thick you could conceivably cut off a piece of the seat and use it for a nicotine patch if you ran out of cigarettes... you might wonder how the Trans-Siberian Express has managed to maintain its exotic appeal. Still, it feels like the right way a traveller should head to Asia, or come home from Asia. Going both ways may be overkill. The actual Trans-Siberian line runs from Vladivostok (a Russian port city just north of China) to Moscow. Instead, most travellers take one of two trains from Beijing to Moscow, and – a point of much confusion – neither of them are called the Trans-Siberian, though people refer to them as such. There's the Trans-Mongolian, which takes six nights, passes through Mongolia (Russian and Mongolian visas required), and the seven-night Trans-Manchurian, which passes just south of Mongolia (Russian visa only).

Budget travellers usually opt for a four-bunk cabin with relatively comfortable bunk beds and luggage space above and below for an extra $100/£64. You can also ride in a more expensive first-class compartment with two beds, slightly softer seats and, on the Chinese trains, a shower. In both classes, attendants keep things clean and make your bed with rented sheets ($2/£1.20). The dining facilities on both trains may receive less than stellar reviews, but more interesting fare can be found off the train during the brief stops in Russia. Fresh smoked fish from Lake Baikal and other goodies are available for pocket change. There are samovars at the end of each car filled with hot water you can use to make your own soups and teas. Many travellers do in fact cross Asia on Cup-O-Soup and Earl Grey.

If you're not crossing in summer, bring warm clothes for the border checkpoint to stretch your legs or when the trains get a wheel change. (Russian and Chinese rails have different gauges, so they actually switch the train cars onto different wheel bases; this takes several hours, so a good novel will come in handy as well.)

Bring something to clean the outside windows. A cheap squeegee fastened to a long stick will make you tremendously popular, as many windows are coated in thick dust. Who knows, you might even be able to trade your window-washing services for a few drinks. In second class, ask for a top bunk so you can sleep when you want, not when your cabin-mates decide to relinquish your seat-bed. And pick up Bryn Thomas's *Trans-Siberian Handbook*, or *The Trans-Siberian Rail Guide* by Robert Strauss.

Both the Trans-Mongolian and Trans-Manchurian depart once per week.

Buying a Trans-Siberian ticket in China

Tickets can be booked through a travel agency or independently (and cheaper) through the Chinese rail office (CITS) in Beijing (@www.cits.net).

Taking the independent budget route (and taking your chances getting a seat), it's about $195/£125 for the Trans-Mongolian train and $220/£141 for the Trans-Manchurian. A local Chinese travel agency such as @www.monkeyshrine.com can help with visas, stopovers and accommodation in Moscow as well – and it should cost less than using travel agents closer to home. In fact, it's a decent starting point, no matter how you book your ticket. Stopovers are a bit tricky to arrange on your own since CITS insists that you buy separate tickets for each leg of your trip (eg one to Ulaanbaatar and one from Ulaanbaatar to Moscow), then refuses to sell you anything but the leg from Beijing to Ulaanbaatar. The leg from Ulaanbaatar to Moscow must be bought in Ulaanbaatar. That brings most people back to a booking agency.

Russian visas can be picked up at the Russian Embassy in Beijing. They cost $50/£32 (5 working days); $80/£51 (3 working days); or $100/£64 (same day). Try @www.hostels.ru or @www.visatorussia.com to get your "invitation" to Russia. For the Mongolian visa at the Mongolian embassy, it costs $30/£19 (3 working days) or $60/£39 (next-day service), but that just gets you 48 hours in the country. Remember to buy your train ticket before pursuing the visas. That's $160/£103 to get both visas in three days, or $80/£51 to get both visas in just under two weeks.

Buying a Trans-Siberian ticket in Russia or Finland

To do it yourself, head to Central Railway Agency in Moscow. The Trans-Mongolian costs around $165/£106 and requires Chinese and Mongolian visas. The Trans-Manchurian costs around $160/£103 and requires just a Chinese visa. For first-class fares, add about $100/£64. Booking with a local travel agent will add about $50/£32 to the fare. In Moscow, try Star Travel (wti_ket@startravel.ru) or Asia Hostel's @www.hostels.ru/rail for discount stopovers. In St Petersburg, the International Hostel can book tickets through its travel agency arm. In Finland, you can pick up a Trans-Siberian ticket at the train station in Helsinki, though it will cost more. If money is less of a concern, and you want some hand holding and a choice of diverse excursions, try the Russian Experience (@www.trans-siberian.co.uk), where a trip might cost around $2500/£1600.

A Mongolian visa can be picked up at the consular office in Moscow once you already have your Chinese visa. It can be processed the same day or next day for about $30/£19, but for anything more than a transit stay, you'll need an invitation. Moscow isn't the best place to pick up a Chinese visa, but it can be done. You'll need to show your train ticket and onward ticket from China. If you're leaving by an overland route you're making up as you go, try getting a letter of introduction from your country's embassy. If you're planning stops along the way, there are several trains you'll be able to catch throughout the week that don't go all the way to China.

Overland tours

If you find the idea of overlanding exhilarating but intimidating, you're not alone. There's an entire industry comprised of overland tour operators that load travellers into revamped army trucks (or some sort of steroid-enhanced transport), take care of all the paperwork, and drive them across Africa, Asia or South America. You typically sleep in tents or cheap hostels, share the cooking and cleaning chores and take the major attractions en route. It's not uncommon for travellers to use these tours as a sampler before heading off on their own or with a friend they've made in the group. However, there are some drawbacks: you're trapped with a group of travellers for weeks or months and chances are reasonably high that at least one person is going to tweak your nerves, and you may feel ready to jump off and go it alone long before your financial commitment is up. Companies are mostly London-based and charge around $325/£209–385/£248 per week depending on location and length of journey. Try: Dragoman ⊛www.dragoman.co.uk; Encounter Overland ⊛www.encounter.co.uk; Exodus Expeditions ⊛www.exodus.co.uk; or Guerba Expeditions ⊛www.guerba.co.uk.

Regional tours

This includes everything from four-star luxury tours to local packages that can be arranged in almost any mid-size city. There are thousands of tour companies to choose from at any number of levels, and it certainly helps to get a personal recommendation or find some favourable reviews. In many areas, hostels team up with local tour operators (or allow tour operators to leave posters around, for which the hostel may get a commission); the operators typically offer off-road budget trips to scenic spots in the area that are hard to access by local transport. Often these tours are good fun, but try to get a sense of what the guide is like, and trust your instincts.

Cars and motorcycles

It's possible to take a car or motorcycle across borders, and in Europe, North America, Australia and New Zealand, car travel can be a great way to save money and explore the backroads.

Guided excursions

Despite the general reluctance of independent travellers to sign up for just about anything, for small portions of a longer trip, jumping on a tour can be an excellent way to get some professional supervision while you do something you haven't done before. There are glacier treks, journeys by dugout canoe into the Amazon, kayak trips around the Fijian islands, hippo-dodging African canoe safaris – the list goes on. Some of these activities are difficult to arrange on your own and they can, in fact, be more expensive than a solo expedition. You can usually get good, impartial information from your guidebook and from other travellers while you're in the region.

A few good questions to ask when enquiring about an activity are:

1 How easy is it to book on the spot without a reservation?
2 Are there any possible (likely) weather-related conflicts with the intended activities or discounts if they're not available when you arrive?
3 Does the price include taxes and tips? If not, what's the total cost?
4 What are the living conditions like? Private room? Bathroom in room? Washing facilities?
5 What meals are included?
6 For walking and cycling tours, are baggage transfers or porters included?
7 What is the cancellation policy, and what kind of insurance is included?

In Asia, Africa and Latin America, prepare yourself well in advance for the mountain of paperwork and fees ahead. After you've specially prepped your vehicle for the trip, you'll need to get it a "Carnet de Passage" (automotive passport and guarantee; see box p.42) as well as credit for up to 600 percent of the vehicle's value. If your entry and exit stamps don't match up (that is, you came in with a car but didn't leave with one), that country has the right to collect on your carnet's down payment. You can get carnet insurance to help protect yourself, but expect to cough up a hearty deductible if a country calls in payment. If the vehicle dies on you and you decide to abandon it, you may be suspected of selling it and have to pay duties as well. For more details on documentation, preparation and international hassles you may encounter, take a look at *The Adventure Motorcycling Handbook* (Trailblazer) or *Russia and Central Asia by Road* (Bradt). And you'll see a few more suggestions in the Regional Profiles at the end of this book.

Tips for drivers

- Have multiple copies of everything. Even get some colour copies of your driving licence laminated so you can leave them with border guards who threaten to hold them for a bribe.
- Crosscheck maps in remote areas with local drivers. Some of the roads marked on your map may be planned projects while other roads simply don't exist.
- Crossing borders is more time-consuming for vehicle owners, so get there early or just after lunch to avoid the crowds, and try to steer clear of crossings during weekends or during local holidays.
- Keep things friendly at the border. Patience is paramount. If the border officers or police ask for money (a bribe), cheerfully asking for a receipt and their names might discourage them a little. If not, send a note to the country's tourist board.

Bringing your own vehicle

If you want to take your car or motorcycle around the world, you're going to need a Carnet de Passage en Douane (CPD). It's not necessary if you're bringing a car to Europe or North America, but for crossing continents the document works like a passport for your vehicle, allowing it to pass through customs with a set of stamps. The actual purpose of it, however, is to keep you from selling your vehicle in the countries you're travelling in (thus circumventing the local import taxes). So, while the Carnet itself only costs $70 – $200/£45 – £130 (depending on how many blank pages you want in it for stamps and if you're a member of the automobile association which issues it), to get it guaranteed you need to put down a refundable deposit of as much as six times the value of the vehicle. That means if you're taking a Land Rover worth $30,000/£19,290, you may have to leave as much as $180,000/£115,750 (and probably not less than $90,000/£57,870) to get a Carnet – though you can also pay an insurance company a fraction of that amount to guarantee the Carnet gets paid in the event you and your vehicle become separated. If you leave the country without the vehicle you came in with or overstayed your visiting time allotment, they'll presume you sold it (even if it died and you left it in a scrap yard), and the country is legally entitled to collect from the Carnet issuer an amount equalling whatever the import duties would have been, which can – you guessed it – be up to 600 percent of the vehicle's value in some countries.

However, if you're just shipping a vehicle to one country, such as Australia, you should look into the local import duties. It may very well be easier and cheaper to pay those than get a Carnet.

In the UK, pick up a Carnet from the AA (ⓦwww.theaa.com) or RAC (ⓦwww.rac.co.uk). In the US and Canada, this is handled by the CAA (ⓦwww.caa.ca). The AA also issues carnets in South Africa

- On a map, a town does not always equal a filling station, so tank up whenever you get the chance.

Bicycle

A bicycle involves much less paperwork than a car or motorbike, but few countries are set up for cyclists (not to mention people wearing spandex shorts with built-in crotch padding), which works both for and against you. In small towns off the main routes where few people with motors care to stop, you're an instant celebrity (or freak). But getting between them can be a dusty, muddy, traffic-dodging experience. Alternatively, some countries, such as the Netherlands or Denmark, are especially well suited for cycling. Find out what you're in for before packing the bike.

(🌐www.aasa.co.za), Australia (🌐www.aaa.asn.au) and New Zealand (🌐www.nzaa.co.nz). Outside of these areas, try the Swiss-based Alliance Internationale de Tourisme (🌐www.aitgva.ch) which administers the Carnet system. They have a public site with a listing of all affiliated members.

Below is a list of countries that currently require a Carnet. (Brazil only requires a Carnet for vehicles arriving by boat, not land. And in some African countries, it is not required, but because it facilitates the temporary importation of your vehicle, it may be worth picking up anyway.

Countries that require Carnets

Africa
Benin, Botswana, Burkina Faso, Cameroon, Central African Republic, Chad, Comoros, Congo, Egypt, Gabon, Ghana, Guinea-Bissau, Ivory Coast, Kenya, Lesotho, Libya, Madagascar, Malawi, Mali, Mauritania, Namibia, Niger, Senegal, Somalia, South Africa, Swaziland, Tanzania, Togo, Uganda

Asia
Bangladesh, India, Indonesia, Malaysia, Myanmar, Singapore, Sri Lanka

Australia, New Zealand, and the South Pacific
Australia, New Zealand, Vanuatu

Latin America
Argentina, Brazil, Chile, Colombia, Costa Rica, Dutch Antilles, Ecuador, Jamaica, Paraguay, Peru, Surinam, Trinidad & Tobago, Uruguay, Venezuela

Middle East
Bahrain, Iran, Iraq, Japan, Jordan, Kuwait, Lebanon, Oman, Pakistan, Qatar, Syria, United Arab Emirates, Yemen

If spare parts are a major concern or you want to get a firsthand look at local cycling conditions, wait until you arrive and buy a sturdy local model. And just because your bike holds four saddle bags, that doesn't mean you should bring all four. You will probably need four if you're camping. But if you're planning to stay at hostels or pensions, two saddle bags should be sufficient. The reduced weight is a godsend going up hills. But, more important, it makes daily security less of an issue. If you want to head into a market or restaurant or up a flight of stairs to check the availability of a hostel (something you'll be doing daily), it's easy to lock up the bike and carry two bags along. With four bags (or five including a front bag), that's not much of an option, so someone will get stuck guarding the gear – or you'll need one impressive security system.

Classic overland routes

London to Sydney
Distance: 19,900km
England–Belgium–Netherlands–Germany–Czech Republic–Slovakia–Hungary
–Romania–Bulgaria–Turkey–Iran–Pakistan–India–Nepal–Tibet–China–Laos–
Thailand–Singapore–Indonesia–Australia

Istanbul to Kathmandu
Distance: 16,997km
Turkey–Iran–Pakistan–India–Nepal

Beijing to Berlin
Distance: 7379km
China–Mongolia–Russia–Finland–Sweden–Denmark–Germany

Cairo to Cape Town
Distance: 8000km
Egypt–Sudan–Ethiopia–Eritrea–Kenya–Tanzania–Malawi–Zambia–Zimbabwe
–Botswana–Namibia–South Africa (Sudan/Ethiopia/Eritrea borders can be
problematic)

Anchorage to Tierra Del Fuego
Distance: 14,500km
Alaska–Canada–America–Mexico–Guatemala–Honduras–Nicaragua–Costa
Rica–Panama–Colombia–Ecuador–Peru–Chile–Argentina (Darién Gap,
between Panama and Colombia, can be problematic)

Istanbul to Cairo
Distance: 3500km
Turkey–Syria–Jordan–Israel–Egypt

Travelling alone
and with others

One of the biggest decisions facing any traveller is whether or not to go it alone. There are several factors to consider before making this choice and sizeable pros and cons for each, but, all things being equal, you'll probably want to travel solo, at least for some portion of your trip. Even if all things aren't equal and there's someone you'd really like to travel with, read through the section on travelling with a partner and make sure you're willing to take the risks.

Travelling alone

There's no question this is the most intimidating path to take, but it's also the most potentially rewarding. First, travelling alone does not necessarily mean you'll be travelling alone for the bulk of your trip. Quite the opposite, in fact. Most solo travellers just end up travelling with different people for different legs of their journey. Everywhere you go, from museums to hostels to cafés, you'll run into other solo travellers who'd be delighted to travel with someone and, because there are often significant price breaks on rooms for pairs, share the costs. Even shy travellers find the dialogue easy to start. You already have your travel destination and independent spirit in common; you might suggest swapping some travel notes or comparing shared frustrating experiences. At times, it can almost be more difficult to find periods to be on your own. For those who are still uncertain about their ability to meet travel partners on the trail, you can, virtually everywhere, sign up for a group tour along the way and surround yourself with an entire platoon of companions.

The benefits of travelling solo

You learn about yourself. You'll find out what your likes and dislikes are, and be able to act on them. Often travellers spur each other on to check off a "to do" list (with no one looking, maybe you'll give that famous museum a miss and rent a bike and head for the countryside instead.) You'll spend more time writing your journal, taking photos, reading, studying the culture – absorbing more of the country you're travelling in. You'll be less distracted by a friend and more likely to notice the small things happening around you. As a single traveller it can be easier to blend in, and you're less likely to be attracting attention by speaking English with your partner. Single travellers attract single travellers. You're much more likely to return home with an address book filled with great contacts from around the world. Plus, you'll be approached by more locals. They're often anxious to meet foreigners but can be intimidated by couples, feeling reluctant to interrupt a conversation or intrude.

My first trip alone was to Europe. I was 22. It was probably the three most eye-opening weeks of my life. I realized, for starters, that I could go to another continent and be entirely self-sufficient. I could travel from country to country, from one foreign language to another, order a meal, get a night in a room, and make friends with people all over the world. Learning I could do all that on my own was a revelation. If I had gone with a friend, I wouldn't have returned home with the same sense of accomplishment and satisfaction.

Jim Benning
Editor, ⓦ worldhum.com

Women alone

Women can and do travel solo throughout the world. Some countries make this quite easy, and thus provide a better starting point: Northern Europe, Australia, New Zealand, the US and Canada. In Southern Europe and parts of Latin America, catcalls are common, but you'll rarely feel threatened (for dressing and safety tips see p.173). In much of the world, however, you'll be seen as an oddity. All backpackers are a bit of an oddity (forsaking our creature comforts and spending more money than many locals will ever possess to wander about the globe with our worldly possessions in a nylon sack), but people may assume you have left your husband and children behind to undertake this journey. So long as your wardrobe is conservative, you'll often be afforded the same status as male travellers in most developing countries you visit, but expect numerous enquiries. It's helpful to have a story for the men (such as you're meeting up with your husband in the next town), but many questions will come from women, which is a great conversation starter and can offer interesting insights.

The possibility of rape and robbery should be taken seriously, but these are risks that can be minimized (see chapter 15). Most likely the harassment you get will be a mild irritant: an admirer on a long train ride who thinks he can charm you with a six-hour story. The trick is being able to distinguish between a tactless man and a dangerous one. Always trust your instinct. If any man makes you feel at risk, simply move to a train compartment where there are more safe-looking people (preferably women or other travellers), head to a more crowded street, pop into a crowded store or stop a police officer.

Covering up in India

When I started travelling on my own I was making all the typical mistakes. Perhaps the one I paid the highest price for was wearing tight-fitting clothes in India. I was often harassed on public transport and in crowded streets. It was at times so frustrating, some evenings I'd just go back to my room and cry.

After two years, I've learned to deal with it. I wear much baggier clothing now and keep my legs and shoulders well covered. I stopped initiating conversations with men and have become more abrupt with the ones who've approached me, as that too often seemed to signal some sort of green light. And I pay a little extra for the perks of air-conditioned second-class trains: doors that remain shut and passengers who are less likely to harass.

One of my favourite tricks is carrying my small daypack on my front in crowded areas. At least that protects my front from the anonymous hands searching for a quick feel. I'm also no longer afraid to lash out when I do get grabbed – and a little yelling helps get it out of my system.

If foreign women would cover up and respect local customs – as I wish I'd done from the start – it would make life easier for the rest of us.

Beth Wooldridge
Author, *Rough Guide to India*

If you're heading overland into a country or region that you're a little unsure of, you can almost always find a trustworthy travel companion (even a male companion, if limiting the sexual harassment is important) to accompany you for at least a few days, if not longer, provided you're going in the same direction. It may take a day or three to find the right person, but in places where the hassle factor is high, such as crossing from Spain into Morocco, a male companion can make things much easier (especially if you tell people you're married).

Travel with others

Travelling with a companion does minimize culture shock, gives you some medical security (they can help get you to a doctor if you get sick or carry you back to the hostel after you've passed out in a bar), and saves you money when double rooms, taxis and hiring guides are involved. For many, though, a travel partner's most important role is offering moral support for the never-ending onslaught of new situations you face. And helping avoid the fairly frequent party-of-one meals or having your ear bent by some garrulous locals.

The risks of bringing a friend

Twenty-four hours a day of reassurance and sharing for months on end can put a serious strain on any friendship. Having to make nearly constant decisions in often uncomfortable conditions can strain the tightest bonds. Just because you're the best of friends, there is no guarantee you'll travel well together. Something else to keep in mind: if you think it would be nice to stumble upon some romance on the road, you better pray you meet twins going in the same direction, because your friend isn't going to want to hang around while you fall in love.

Maintaining your travel relationship

If you do decide to go with another person, give yourselves the option of separating for a while. Even just a morning or afternoon apart every few days can be enough breathing room to sustain a travel relationship. A better bet, however, is to build some solo time into the trip. Perhaps a week or two apart every other month: sign up for different courses or adventure activities in the same region or tackle a city separately. Pick a meeting time and figure out a few fallback ways to get in touch in case one person can't make it, such as email or a note at a certain hostel.

What to look for in a travel partner

First, you want someone with the same budget. If you don't see eye to eye (or wallet to wallet), it's going to be a straining trip. If one is going the comfort route while another is on a tight budget, you won't be staying at the same places, eating at the same restaurants, or doing as many activities together. Or, more likely, you will, but one person won't be having a good time doing it. The one on a tight budget will feel like a scrooge, always getting their budget pushed too far, having to eat plain rice at a nice restaurant or sit outside while the other goes to a string of expensive museums. The one on the bigger budget will be roughing it more than they'd like, yet feel they're shamelessly indulging in front of their companion the entire time.

If your budgets are in alignment, check if your itineraries are too. Talk about what you hope to do during a typical day. Will you get up early and aggressively pound the pavement of a city or sleep until noon, then linger in a café and read a book? Will you be pursuing cultural activities or beaches? Are you keeping things flexible or planning all the details? These are not the sorts of things you want to discover after you've started travelling.

Finding a travel partner

Many people find the prospect of travelling alone so daunting they try to line up a travel partner before leaving. They place personal ads in travel magazines, newspapers and on websites. These correspondence-arranged partnerships may work out, but all too often they don't: heading out on the road together is like getting married after one blind date. There's no need to do this, especially without taking at least one short local trip together first. You'll meet so many travellers during your trip, it's much more natural and sensible to make friends first, travel for a while without commitment and only continue together as long as it's working out.

Travelling with a crowd

With more than two people you're going to find yourself taking votes, which is a fine way to run a democracy but a maddening way to set an itinerary. Whether you leave with a group or simply snowball into an international party on the move, beware: you're going to be about as subtle as a Hare Krishna tambourine parade dancing through a public library. Another potential problem is getting anything done. Before you can all head out to explore a famous museum together, a few people will have to use the bathroom, someone will have to fix a button that's about to fall off, someone else will need to mail a postcard, two others will have to stop at a bank and one will have to bargain for a souvenir on the way. What's more, you're going to have a difficult time finding hostels, buses and restaurants that can accommodate all of you. It's nice to find a social group. But instead of corralling yourself into a tour group, a better idea is to pick a bar or restaurant in the next town and a time and say you'll meet there. Then everyone breaks up and goes their own way.

Travelling on a long organized tour

This locks you in with a group for the duration of the tour, for good and bad. Such trips tend to bring out the best in some and the worst in others. Life-long friendships are common, but so are group conflicts, and you won't be likely to see much about the latter in the brochure. So make sure you ask about the time available away from the group, then take advantage of it when you get the chance.

Costs and savings

hat does it cost to travel around the world? Reasonable question. Unfortunately, a personalized, independent journey doesn't come with a standard price tag, so you're going to have to take a different approach. You can calculate your budget – and this chapter will show you how – but before that's possible you'll need to figure out your level of comfort, where you want to go, and which activities you want to do. Without narrowing down these factors, you'll have a hard time getting within $10,000/£6400 of an accurate figure on a year-long trip. Why? Take a typical budget of $50/£32 per day, plus

---

Starting costs

Backpack: $100–200/£65–130
Travel gear, toiletries, medical kit (depending on what you have already): $100–350/£65–225
Insurance (based on a one-year trip): $300–900/£190–580
Vaccinations: $100–350/£65–225
RTW ticket or other long-range transport: $900–4000/£580–2570
Approximate total: $3000/£1930

$2500/£1600 for a ticket, insurance, vaccinations and gear, and you get a yearly total of $21,000/£13,500. If you stop and work for three months of that, you're down to $16,500/£10,600 plus whatever you earn, which might bring the total down to $14,000/£9000. If you stay with relatives for a few weeks and spend a month in a cheap hangout, you're down to $13,000/£8360. If you confine your travels exclusively to developing countries, that may drop the figure to $10,000/£6400. Cut the trip back to nine months, and you're down to about $7000/£4500.

Daily costs

It's certainly possible to spend anywhere between $3000/£1930 and $100,000/£64,000 on a yearly trip around the world, and with the myriad spending choices you make every day, it's impossible to

Calculating your budget

Within the range of budget travel, the daily costs can vary enormously over the course of a year. Just between the middle and upper levels, there's roughly $18,000/£11,575 of savings to be had. By travelling in developing (read: cheaper) countries you can obviously save a fortune: $4400–18,250/ £2830–11,735 over a year, depending on your comfort level. Put these together and the difference between travelling for a year on a more comfortable daily budget in Europe ($36,500/£23,470) and a tight daily budget in Southeast Asia ($6500/£4180), is pretty significant.

Select your level of comfort, then figure out how many weeks or months you plan to stay in developed or developing countries and add up the costs. For example, if you plan to spend three months in Europe, four in Southeast Asia, and two in Central America all on the lowest budget, that's six months at $300/£190 plus three months at $660/£425, plus about $3000/£1930 for start-up costs. Which makes a total of $6780/£4360 for the nine-month trip. A mid-level budget on the same trip will cost roughly $12,000/£7720.

Lowest

Daily expenses in developing countries: $10/£6; monthly: $300/£190; yearly: $3650/£2350
Daily expenses in developed countries: $22/£14; monthly: $660/£425; yearly: $8030/£5160
Lifestyle: Sleeping in hostel dormitory rooms, sharing rooms in the very cheapest hotels (no matter how bad the guidebook description), camping or

knock out an itemized cost sheet before leaving. Instead, try to look at it like this: you can either make do with what you have or gather more funds before you depart.

Buying a ticket, you can spend ages surfing the Web and calling various travel agents in a massive effort that may save you around $50/£32–$350/£225. It's nice to save money on a ticket, but don't knock yourself out trying: that's not where the real savings are found. With some self-discipline and a few budget tips, you can reduce your daily budget by as much as $15/£10. Over a year-long trip, that saving comes to $5475/£3521. Even on a three-month trip, that's $1300/£836 you can leave in the bank.

How long will your money last? Depends where you go. . . Picking even a slightly cheaper country can save you a fortune on a long trip. Travelling on a mid-level budget, this chart gives you a rough idea how long you can go with $1000/£640.

renting a tent at camping grounds, sleeping on trains and buses. Eating cheap food purchased at supermarkets and the lowest-priced side dishes at budget restaurants or at street stalls. No clubbing and nothing more than the occasional beer. Limited museum visits and no lingering drinks at nice cafés.

Middle

Daily expenses developing countries: $25/£16; monthly; $750/£482; yearly: $9125/£5870
Daily expenses developed countries: $50/£32; monthly; $1500/£965; yearly: $18,250/£11,735
Lifestyle: Cheapest accommodation, occasionally sharing a two-person room, occasional night on a train or bus, and a few coffees at nice cafés per week. Museums are not limited but adventure activities are. The occasional night on the town, but not more than one reasonably priced drink (beer, wine, cappuccino etc) per day.

Upper

Daily expenses developing countries: $50/£32; monthly $1500/£965; yearly $18,250/£11,735
Daily expenses developed countries: $100/£64; monthly $3000/£1930; yearly $36,500/£23,470
Occasional splurge on decent budget hotel, otherwise private rooms in hostels. Unlimited coffee, liberal drinking, two nights out per week, and a decent restaurant once per day.

Spendometer

Days of travel with $1000/£640

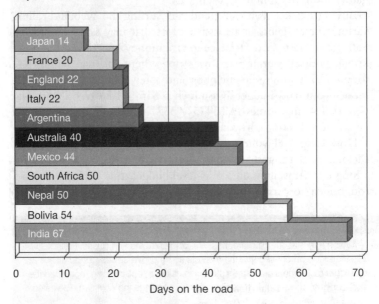

Japan 14
France 20
England 22
Italy 22
Argentina
Australia 40
Mexico 44
South Africa 50
Nepal 50
Bolivia 54
India 67

0 10 20 30 40 50 60 70

Days on the road

How do you travel cheaper?

Without a number of budget tricks, you may end up travelling in a high-end budget while only getting mid-range value. The key to saving money on the road is not to concentrate exclusively on the big expenditures, but to find small savings along every step of the way. Beyond picking countries where your funds will last longer, you want to look for deals on everything from changing money to eating to using pay toilets. Doing this involves a few tricks, some minor lifestyle changes and sticking to your self-imposed budget guidelines, whilst hopefully avoiding full-blown budgetitis (see box on p.56).

Discount cards

There's no magic wand to guarantee savings everywhere you go, but an International Student Identity Card (ISIC) comes close (followed by its sister cards, the Youth Card – for those under 26 – and the Teacher Card). They all cost $22/£14 and provide significant deals, from museums to plane tickets. You may very well make up the $22/£14 on the flight over. The trick is remembering to ask for the discount. It won't help you much in restaurants, but nearly anywhere a ticket is required, be sure to ask. Also, use it as a back-up ID card you can leave behind when renting bikes and so on.

Another popular card is the International Youth Hostel Card ($25/£16; see p.144 to find out if you like the sound of hostelling). Some countries have their own cards that offer discounts on a string of hostels (see individual Regional Profiles for more information). In large cities, local transport and museum cards can add up to tremendous savings.

Beware the leech discount

I went trekking in Nepal in autumn. It was supposedly the shoulder season, but it was a little too early. So I caught the last storms of the monsoon. And leeches. Surprisingly, they're out in force this time of the year in the Himalayan foothills under 9000 ft. They cling to bushes and then latch on as you walk by. Or they get onto your shoe and crawl in through the shoelace eyelet. (At least, that's how I presume one found its way under my foot.) Or they climb up a little higher and get you just above the sock. I'm not exactly sure how they found our skin, but we were pulling them off all day and still finding little bloody spots where others had come and gone. Going to the bathroom was a two-man operation: one person had to – at uncomfortably close range – fend off advancing leeches with a can of bug spray while the other took care of business. This would probably explain why some treks are a little cheaper this time of year.

John Flinn
Travel writer, *SF Chronicle*

Flights

A good basic guideline to follow before booking any flights is to do a little checking on your own so you'll know a good price when you see one. Start looking on the Web (⊛expedia.com, ⊛orbitz.com and ⊛travelocity.com are among the major online booking engines) and check out the lowest published fares for a particular flight. Then, all things being relatively equal, book with a well-informed travel agent and get their email address and phone number. They can point out things you can easily forget while booking on your own (eg a flight that leaves at 5am, before there's any cheap transport running to the airport) and provide access to consolidator fares. Besides, it's nice to have someone to contact in case you're in a jam. Bear in mind that:

- Often, the cheapest tickets are sold far in advance. Call a trusted travel agent or do some Web searches and book the cheapest fully refundable ticket available. Then keep looking. If you find something cheaper, simply cancel the first ticket.
- Whether you're with an agent or surfing the Web, play around with dates. Often just a day or two can make a surprising price difference.
- For Internet booking, consider purchasing the ticket on a Wednesday (when airlines offer special promotions), not at a weekend (when the prices shoot back up).
- Once you find a good deal, check that airline's site directly to see if they're offering any other special promotions to places nearby that are even cheaper.
- Keep in mind the cheapest fares are often less direct, less conveniently scheduled, and may involve an airline you've never even heard of. If you have more time than money, this is a fine way to grab a deal.

Last-minute deals

Again, your best chances of getting a bargain are booking ahead. But if you're caught searching for a last-second flight, here are a few places to look: ⊛www.1travel.com; ⊛www.cheaptickets.com; ⊛www.lastminutetravel.com; ⊛www.travel.priceline.com and ⊛www.smarterliving.com.

Budgetitis syndrome

This is one of the most common budget travel afflictions (followed closely by exaggerated story telling and heavy-pack-induced back strains), and at some point during a long trip, you'll likely suffer from it yourself. With a limited budget and daily expenses that start each day at breakfast and continue until your last beer in the evening, you feel the constant stress of your money belt getting thinner and thinner. The natural response to this relentless stream of expenditure is an attempt to stem the outflow. You begin to realize how quickly costs can add up, so every extra penny has to be justified. Symptoms include: walking an extra twenty minutes to find a bread shop whose loaves are three cents cheaper; full-blown arguments with taxi drivers over the equivalent of 25 cents; and skipping a meal because the local supermarket prices seem a little high.

At some point you have to take a step back and remember why you're travelling. It's fine to save money while you're travelling, but you need to balance this with the fact that you're not travelling in order to save money. Better to come home a week or two early and suffer a little less.

Trains

If you're doing anything more than zipping across a country by rail (and even if that's all you're doing), your best bet will most likely be to buy a rail pass. Most rail passes can only be purchased outside the country where you plan to use them, but with the Internet, this isn't such a problem. If you're already there, or on your way there, you can order it online, have it sent to your parents or friends, and get them to forward it to you. The more difficult task is selecting the right rail pass for you. As a rule of thumb, the less flexible the rail pass, the cheaper it is. In other words, if you know more or less where you plan to go (and you don't feel obligated to hit every single region or country) you can get an excellent deal.

Using Europe's popular train passes as an example, here are a few different ways you could save some money. Let's say you're starting in London, and want to travel for two months in Spain, France and Italy. For starters, you want to get a flexipass. This is a common rail ticket that only allows you to travel a certain amount of days over a given period. There's one for ten days of travel within two months valid for these three countries that would work fine. It costs $352/£226, or $35/£23 per use. If you were to get the full-price unlimited pass, it would cost $910/£585, or about $15/£10 per use if you use it every day. But there's no reason to be on the move every day; travelling every three or four days is more reasonable. And because a few of those trips may only be an hour or two away (eg Florence to Bologna takes one hour and costs about $10/£6), it makes more sense to buy those point-to-point tickets independently and save the rail-pass travel dates for longer trips. Inexpensively supplementing your rail pass this way can provide a total of 15–17 days of travel (which should be more than enough) for just $450/£289.

Also, to reach southern Spain from London, you're going to spend a good two full days on the train. That will knock two days off your trip, two days off your rail ticket, and require a recovery day once you arrive, unless you want to pay for expensive sleeping cabin supplements. With the cut-throat competition and discount airlines such as Easyjet and Ryan Air, it's possible to find a one-way discount flight for as little as $40/£26. It can feel a little odd to start or end your rail travel with a short flight, but if it fits your itinerary, it can be a fantastic saving.

Buses

For bus passes (popular in Europe, Australia and New Zealand), follow the same basic strategy found in the preceding train section. Trains and buses differ in that trains generally have regulated prices, even in developing countries, whereas buses are mostly run by private companies. On most popular routes in developing countries you can haggle for a ticket and get an excellent rate. This can be some of the most intimidating bargaining you'll ever do, as bus touts ofen move about the station in packs, then swarm you with offers, all speaking at once. If you trade stocks on Wall Street, you'll probably feel right at home. If not, it takes some getting used to. The coaches vary dramatically in quality from third-class "chicken buses" to fully reclining sleepers. So, just because you hear someone shout a nice price doesn't mean it applies to the bus you want.

The best approach is to politely but firmly get past the touts, insisting you know where you're going, and make for the ticket windows of the various companies, where you'll hopefully be able play them off one another. A few will be selling tickets to the same location. Get the timetable, information on the bus and the best price from the person at the window. Thank them, then walk off and gather information on the others. Once you have them all (this shouldn't take more than ten minutes), decide on the bus you want and approach the window. Say that it was cheaper with another company, but that their buses didn't look as nice and you heard a tout mentioning a special price with this company (pick a price a little under the one they originally offered) and if that's the case you'd like to buy a ticket. And let the bargaining begin. If they can drop their price they probably will. If they don't, try the next company.

Accommodation

One of the best things you can do to save money on the road is get accustomed to sleeping in no-star accommodations. That means sleeping in dorm rooms when available, trying to share a room with another traveller if there are doubles with lower rates, and not letting yourself be put off by places described in your guidebook as basic, or even grungy. If you're armed with earplugs and a good sleep sheet, you'll be fine. Other money-saving ideas for bottom-end digs are:

- Hostels and pensions in large cities pay the most rent, and pass the costs on to travellers. It's almost always cheaper to stay in small towns and rural areas.
- Ask about sleeping on the roof. In fair-weather climates this is often possible for roughly half the price of a room. Many places provide mattresses.
- Make a point of getting addresses of travellers you meet, and stay with them if you're heading to their home. Try to give a few days' or weeks' notice with an email.
- Head to camp sites just out of town and rent their walk-in tents (with real beds).
- Check out accommodation at universities over the summer. Empty dorm rooms are often rented out at cut-rate prices.
- Hang out around the student union and look for a friendly group. Introduce yourself and ask if you can crash on someone's floor or sofa in exchange for a beer or two, plus free accommodation at your parents' home if they ever get there.

Food

Cosy restaurants and old-world cafés are tempting places to relax, socialize with other travellers, and people-watch. They're also nice places to run down your budget: those double café lattes add up in a hurry. Minimizing these little luxuries is going to be the first unpleasant step. Here are a few others:

- Stick to restaurants that don't take credit cards or have English menus. Places smart enough to do this are usually smart enough to jack up their prices as well. Another approach is to look for places where you don't see other foreigners.
- Look for restaurants near universities. Students worldwide have little money for eating, and there's almost always a cottage industry set up to serve them.
- Sample the street food, find a few favourites, and make meals out of them. Two full days of street vendor-bought meals costs the equivalent of one decent restaurant meal.
- Cook in hostels. Check your guidebook for hostels with kitchen access. It's always cheaper to cook as a group, so don't be afraid to stick your head into the lounge and ask if anyone wants to pitch in and make a communal dinner.
- Single-portion supermarket-dining works. You'll soon learn how to survive on fruit, yoghurt, sandwiches and crisps.

- Try the samples at supermarkets. During weekends and busy shopping times in large supermarkets in developed countries, you can often find a tremendous range of free samples available. With a little luck, you can get an entire meal, as long as you don't mind getting it in fifteen small servings.
- Bring food on trains. Trains throughout the world are united by one common theme: bad food at ridiculous prices. Bring more than you think you'll need, plus water.
- Buffets and salad bars: look for a cheap salad bar or buffet and then stack your plate about a metre high. This may require some advanced engineering skills.
- Pizza gathering is not officially recommended, but it works. Travellers have been known to hang out in franchise pizza joints, order a small salad, then grab the untouched slices from other tables when groups get up to leave.
- Order economically. A restaurant is a great place to rest your feet and socialize, but to keep the bill down consider ordering one appetizer and a few filling side dishes instead of a main meal.

Tipping

In the US, it's 15 percent for respectable service, 20 percent and up for exceptional service and 0–10 percent if you want to make a statement. In Iceland there's no tipping at all. Beyond that, not even Stephen Hawking has successfully unravelled the complexities of global tipping. You can take some comfort knowing that it baffles nearly everyone, often including the people who live in the country you're visiting.

Many restaurants utilize a *service compris* method, meaning a 0–15 percent charge will be summarily tacked onto your bill no matter what you think of the service. You can usually find this information on the menu or bill, but you may have to ask. The thorny part is that, if the service is anywhere from decent to superior, you're often expected to give a little extra, from a few small coins for lunch in a café to 10 percent for immaculate service at an upscale restaurant.

One approach is to simply wait for the bill total, then round up. If your lunch tab comes to, say, $5.60, you might leave an even $6. With a tab of $9.80, round up to $10 for service you could have just as easily done without and $11 for excellent service.

In a crunch, you can always ask a fellow diner or your hotel concierge for some guidance, or play it safe and give 10 percent when service isn't included. But the final decision is up to you. Give what you feel is appropriate and leave the restaurant with confidence.

Changing money

Changing money, even when there is no black market, isn't as straightforward as moneychangers would like you to believe. It's not exactly a science, but there are a few tips that will help you save a bit of money.

- Minimize transactions. Take a moment to calculate what you'll need because every time you change cash, travellers' cheques, or withdraw money from a bank machine, you're paying for the transaction. Cash machines have started tacking on $5 fees in some places. Try to get a card that allows you to take out money fee-free or at the lowest possible rate.
- Use a cash card. In addition to the ATM fees, credit cards hit you with ungodly interest on cash advances. If you're going to use it, try to do so nearer to your monthly payment date so the interest is minimized.
- Avoid changing money at hotels and *bureaux de change*. They're well situated, have great opening hours and charge you a fortune for all that convenience. Don't be fooled by nice rates. They specialize in sneaky transaction fees.
- Always compare before changing money. The rates can differ even on the same street. Check banks or the post office.
- Some countries require official exchange receipts if you want to change your leftover currency back on the way out. That doesn't mean you need to keep every receipt. Just enough to cover your leftovers: one or two is plenty.
- Make deals with other travellers who are leaving the country and have some extra money. By eliminating the third party you can both get an excellent deal.
- Be wary of black-market changers (they're the people who approach you about 30 times a day as you walk down the street to see if you want to change money) and – if you use their financial services – always count your money.
- Change money in larger cities. Rural areas are less likely to give you a competitive price.

Finding the black market

In most places where there's an active black market, this is something you won't have to worry about. Just walk down the street in all your Western-ness and it will find you. In fact, in places like Kathmandu, you'll be convinced that your name has been changed to "Change Money".

Peter Moore

Author, *Wrong Way Home* & *No Shitting in the Toilet*

△ Currency exchange, Bolivia

First-Time Around the World | Costs and savings

Bargaining

Shopping isn't always as simple as bringing an item up to the cash register for purchase. Sometimes you've got to haggle for it. The golden rule of bartering is to keep a smile on your face. It's okay to be firm with your offer, even walk away at an impasse, but if you think of it as a game and keep the atmosphere light and friendly, it's hard to go wrong.

Getting an excellent price on an item, however, is another story. The first thing to do is find out from a local or fellow traveller who's familiar with the market what the real going rate is. Now you've got a goal. You may not get the local price, but if you come close, you've done well. More importantly, this little bit of research will help you recognize any serious swindling. That is, sometimes vendors, just for sport, like to see how much they can get for an item and may throw out a completely outlandish price and see if you'll take the bait.

Take a look at what you're wearing. It's hard to haggle a price down with a ring on every other finger or a watch on your wrist that will tell you the time 300 metres under water. Leave the expensive camera, jewellery and sharp clothes in the hotel room if you know you're heading to a market to do some bargaining. Then go early. Many vendors share the belief that a sale early in the day will bring them good fortune, so they may be more likely to lower their prices than they would otherwise. This also increases your chances that you'll be alone with the vendor, which works to your advantage. With other potential customers browsing within earshot, the vendor may feel pressure to keep prices high.

The next step may be the most difficult: hide the true extent of your interest. That is, you don't want to hold something up to show your travel partner and say: "Look at this. It's perfect!" The vendors may not be fluent in English, but this exchange won't escape them. If you have a salesperson hovering around you, look at the item closely and wait for them to pick it up. Once they do, start to back off. "Why would I want that? I don't even know what it is." Let them try to sell it to you. "It's an X. It does this and that. And I'll give you a good price." If you do decide to pick it up, don't hold onto the item very long, or give any other clues that you're becoming attached to it. Instead, you might start out by lifting it for a moment and casually asking how much it costs. (If you don't know the local word for the item, you might take the opposite approach and use the word "thing", as if you're not sure what, exactly, it is, and therefore have relatively little use for it.)

They'll either respond with an inflated price, a decent price or this question: "How much will you give me for it?" If you've done your research, you're in good shape for any of these. If you get an inflated price, offer a price that's equally below your target price. The vendor will immediately dismiss it as unfair, and you – here's where that smile really comes in handy – can say: "I was just having fun. Maybe we could start the bargaining over again, but this time at a more reasonable level." Your next offer should be just under your target price. On the other hand, if the vendor starts the bargaining at a very reasonable level, don't expect it to go down much. Pick a price just under your target and be prepared to come up in price fairly quickly. They may simply not be in a mood for bargaining much. And finally, if you're asked to start the bidding, you might say: "Actually, I spoke to a few locals who bought these as gifts, and they told me I shouldn't pay more than [insert the local price here]." The vendor will immediately know that you've been doing your homework, but may not be ready to give it up to you at that price. If that's the sense you get, you can say: "Perhaps that's the local price I heard about. As a visitor to your country, I'd be willing to give you a little more." Then offer a price that's one or two percent higher.

Often, sellers like to point out the unique craftsmanship in defence of their inflated prices. To counter, you might say: "I'm sorry, I'm not a professional craftsman, so some of the details are difficult for me to fully appreciate." There's no need to insult the quality of their merchandise during the bargaining. A more subtle way to express your sentiments is to pick the item up and inspect it closely, letting your face show your indifference, then say: "Well, I'd be willing to give you $X for it."

If you'd rather take a more complimentary approach, you might say something like this: "It's certainly a very nice [whatever it is], and I appreciate the time you've taken to point out its features and fine craftsmanship. And I certainly believe you when you say it's worth [his last offer]. In fact, it may even be worth more. Unfortunately, I'm not able to pay that price. I'm embarrassed to say that it's not within my budget. If you'd be willing to grant me a very special price, I would very much like to bring this home as a memory of my journey and our meeting. And I'd be most grateful. If not, I completely understand." Of course, you should be prepared to walk off if you get a no. But if you leave on such a friendly note, there's a good chance the vendor may beckon you back after you've made it halfway down the street. If they don't, and you still want it, you can either return with your tail between your legs or simply buy it somewhere else.

Another more businesslike approach is to introduce yourself to the vendor and tell them that you're considering doing all of your shopping in their boutique. Say that you're familiar with the typical market prices for each of the items and if the vendor is willing to give you a good price on them this could work out well for both of you. You'll be asked to pick out the items you're interested in and then take a seat. After some small talk (and complimentary tea and snacks in Arab countries), the vendor will probably let you steer the conversation to prices. If you're still not close by the second round, let them know that you're sorry it doesn't sound like it's working out and thank them for the tea. They've already paid for some tea and won't want to lose a fairly substantial customer so probably won't let you go that easily.

In the end, it should be a win-win experience. And if you keep the negotiation friendly, keep your cool and only buy at a price you feel good about, it will be. Despite any dramatic claims of losing money, a vendor will never sell you merchandise at a loss, so you shouldn't leave feeling guilty that you obtained an unjustly low price.

5

Working, volunteering and studying

No matter how many museums and handicraft markets you hit, no matter how long you bounce around from bus to train to tuk-tuk, no matter how little you pay for your night's accommodation, you're not likely to get under the skin of a place until you stop and engage yourself. It doesn't matter if you're working, volunteering or studying, all it takes is some ongoing interaction with locals to develop a connection and make some friends. If you've studied, consider the relationship you've had with your closer classmates compared to the one you've had with people you've shared a bus ride with. It's a different level entirely. Some jobs, volunteer projects and courses immerse you in the culture more than others, and it's not always easy to tell in advance which will and which won't, but at least you'll still be earning money, helping others or learning a skill – not a bad way to see the world.

Most wages for travel jobs are firmly set by employers. Therefore, to increase the chances that you'll make some cash to keep you on the road, you'll do well to follow this basic concept: work where the currency is strong and spend it where it's weak. An hourly wage in Japan will get you three nights in a cheap Indian hotel, whereas an hourly wage in India wouldn't cover a tip in a cheap Japanese hotel.

Working

Worried you might run out of funds before you run out of wanderlust? Not a problem. Travellers have gone for years with just a few months' worth of cash in their pockets. Depending on your age, nationality and professional skills, you can get legal permission to work nearly anywhere. If you don't qualify under the country's regulations, or can't be bothered with the paperwork, that doesn't mean you can't work. It just means you can't work legally. Thousands of work-visa-deprived travellers manage to earn money overseas every year, especially in short-term seasonal positions, many of which require language skills that the locals don't possess. Of course, working illegally carries a serious risk that should be weighed carefully.

Many travellers who work abroad needlessly end up in the worst travel jobs. The reason? They take the first one that comes along and never bother to see if it fits with the travel experience they're after. Let's say you want to work in a ski resort. You go to the Alps, search frantically for a job and land one washing dishes. You're thrilled to have work, but the minimum wage doesn't get you very far in a pricey resort. You get by working eight-hour days six days a week (fairly standard). After a few weeks you realize you've only put your skis on once and, as the lone washer, you've been kept too busy to meet anyone at the restaurant. It's not uncommon. In fact, very few jobs in ski resorts pay well (considering the high cost of living) and many don't allow you much time to ski. Eventually, you'll wonder what the point is. If you can't answer "yes" to at least one of these questions, you'd do well to look for a different job:

- Factoring in living costs, does the job bring in enough money to cover future travel?
- Does it make for an interesting experience or provide you with a valued skill?
- Is it a relatively easy workload and/or does it offer a lenient schedule that allows you to partake in local activities you enjoy?

Looking for work

Wake up early, check the classified ads in the paper, check notice boards, put up your own messages, dress smartly, don't wear sunglasses, take off that hat, lose the body piercings, cover any tattoos that may frighten small children, dye your hair back to a colour that could at least pass for real hair, double-check your letters for typos, return calls promptly. In short, don't give them a reason to pass you over.

If you are rejected, take it with a smile, thank them for their consideration, and always take the opportunity to ask them where you might find work. If you've made a good impression, most people won't mind providing a few leads.

Furthermore, don't cross off a potential employer just because they said no a few days or a week earlier. Things change. One of their employees may have quit or been sacked. Or perhaps someone they were expecting never showed up. They might even realize that they needed more help than they thought. And as long as your approach is polite, your perseverance will be respected.

To make a start with your job hunt, try Ⓦ www.transitionsabroad.com, Ⓦ www.jobmonkey.com or Ⓦ www.payaway.co.uk.

Illegal work

If you do illegal work, you could very well – depending on the laws of that country, which certainly worth looking into – find yourself slapped with a fine, thrown out of the country (guess who gets to pay for the ticket home?) or landed

---

Funding a trip

To finance my year-long trip, I spent six months living with my parents while waitressing in a restaurant renowned for its hefty tippers. I managed to save about £5000, even after buying my flight. I chose cheaper countries and budgeted for just under £15 ($23) a day. This worked out fine for accommodation, food and local buses, but to help cover the occasional beers, decent meals and a few once-in-a-lifetime activities (whitewater rafting, hiking to Machu Picchu, etc) I took the odd job I found along the way. I worked in bars in Chile and Peru and taught English in Quito. The wages were in line with the meagre local rates, but they were enough to stop me from dipping into my savings. I ended up renting shared flats in these places, which allowed me to make local friends, improve my Spanish and get an insider perspective on day-to-day living so different from home in the UK.

Claire Southern, Rough Guides

behind bars learning language skills from your cellmates. With that little disclaimer out of the way, there are scores of employers who don't mind hiring unregistered foreign help and, from experience, know that the authorities will turn a blind eye. In fact, you may go to great lengths to secure a work permit only to be paid under the table. They often just like knowing you have a permit in case the police show up requesting documents.

Seasonal work

One of your best chances of turning up and landing a decent-paying job with no previous skills (or a work permit) is going to be taking advantage of the seasonal openings that, at any given moment, are available somewhere in the world. It's a matter of being in the right place at the right time and, if you know what you're looking for, it's easy to coordinate.

Summer-resort work

For summer resorts, you may want to turn up two months before the season begins to beat the rush for jobs, then go travelling regionally and return when the job starts. (Summer season runs from June–Sept in the northern hemisphere, Nov–Feb in the southern hemisphere.) On the hotel/bar/restaurant end, women tend to have a much easier time finding work. Possible jobs include: camp counsellor for kids, bartender, waiter, hotel receptionist, hotel housekeeper, cook, baker, sales clerk, supply driver, DJ, rental shop clerk, cleaner, bouncer, guide, sports instructor, lifeguard, scuba instructor and campsite maintainer.

Winter-resort work

For ski-resort work, either apply in writing for work with a tour company in your country six to eight months in advance or arrive at your desired resort around a month before the season begins (Dec–May in the northern hemisphere, June–Oct in the southern hemisphere). Be especially careful about hiring yourself out as a freelance ski instructor – most resorts keep a keen eye out for unofficial lessons on the slopes and prosecute. Possible jobs include: ski tuner, lift operator, snowmobile guide, ski guide, ski rental shop clerk, chalet cleaner, bartender, waiter, hotel receptionist, hotel housekeeper, cook, sales clerk, supply driver, cleaner, bouncer and DJ. Countries with ski resorts include: Switzerland, France, Italy, Germany, Norway, Sweden, Spain, Scotland, Austria, Slovenia, Argentina, Chile, USA, Canada, Japan, Iran, Lebanon, Israel, New Zealand, Australia and South Africa.

Harvest-season work

If you can eat it, you can probably find work picking it if you turn up at the right place in the right season – from strawberries to dates to apples. The best place for pre-trip research is the Internet: try ⓦwww.pickingjobs.com. Pay is often based on the amount you pick, and it may take a few days to get up to speed. Remember to ask for adequate protection when pesticides and other noxious chemicals are sprayed. Europe, Australia, New Zealand and North America are likely to offer the best rates.

Manual labour

Construction jobs tend to be underpaid and backbreaking. There's often a spot or two in cities where labourers show up each morning and get selected by employers. If no such place exists, or the competition is too fierce, look for large construction sites and ask for work directly from the foreman. There's also plenty of factory work; the nastier tasks usually come with a higher wage. If they don't, don't do them. Possible jobs include: house renovation, road building, landscaping, shrimp peeling and fish packing.

Working independently

Money-making opportunities for the creative entrepreneur are almost endless. You could sell cool drinks on a hot beach or cheap umbrellas on a busy street when it rains. And if you have a trade that allows you to work independently, even better. But unless you have a work permit, find out about the penalties, assess the risk and keep a low profile. If you're looking for a street to perform on, think about good acoustics, an original act and a place where the police are kind (northern Europe tends to be popular in this regard). Often small towns, where there are pedestrian streets and few buskers, bring good fortune. Also, keep an eye out for festivals, which attract ready-to-be-entertained crowds with ample pocket change. Possible jobs include: street musician, masseuse, au pair, private cook, private music instructor, street juggler, house cleaner, gardener, window washer, language tutor, jewellery street-seller, T-shirt designer and pedlar, promotional pamphlet distributor (to other travellers for local bars/hostels).

Teaching English

If English is your mother tongue, you have a university degree of some kind, can dress smartly and carry yourself with confidence, you'll be likely to find a job just fine without a TEFL (Teaching English as a Foreign Language; ⓦwww.tefl.co.uk) certificate. If you do have a TEFL certificate though, you'll probably land a better job or beat unqualified competition, and find it easier in the classroom than if you were winging it. Is it worth $1500/£965 for roughly 100 hours of class work to make that "liveable wage"? Or $300/£195 for a weekend introductory course? Your call. But factor this in:

The classroom versus tutoring

I went over to Korea on a teaching contract for eight months. I had a university degree but no ESL. They took care of my work visa, which was a relief. The experience on a whole was so-so. There was more work than I expected. It's not uncommon to teach a class before businessmen go to work, which is at 6.30am, and your last class for college students and businessmen may be at 10.30pm. You work six days a week and get Korean holidays, plus one day for Christmas and one day for Thanksgiving. The academy did provide supplies or help structuring the classes. On the other hand, I was at their mercy – you can't legally leave that school and stay in the country. Stories of academies withholding final pay cheques, skipping a month's salary or adding up hours incorrectly were not uncommon.

When I decided to go back a few months later, I opted not to go back to the school. I started teaching on my own.

It took a couple of weeks to build up my client list. Some people just ask you in an elevator in a nice apartment complex while you're leaving another student's house. Plus the usual networking. I ended up making more than twice as much per hour as with the programme, saving (with my wife) over $10,000 in six months. And I could take vacations when I wanted – actually I had to leave the country every three months because of a tourist visa. The trick was changing money because they limited the withdrawal for foreigners. There were many foreigners teaching this way so they must have found a loophole. Mine was to have the family I was staying with convert my earnings to dollars. Then I took the dollars and transferred them to travellers' cheques and took them out of the country that way. The other trick was not getting caught – teaching or changing money. You can get fined and kicked out of the country for both, though they're more likely to catch you changing money.

Ken Johnson

TEFL is more valued for the higher-paying jobs in Asia and less valued in Latin America and Eastern Europe. The pay could be anything from $20/£13 a week to $1200/£770. In a country with a strong economy, an elite school or big company might pay upwards of $4000/£2570 a month. However, most require a six- to twelve-month contract to prevent you from skipping out and leaving their students with verbs unconjugated and participles dangling.

Teaching diving

With a Divemaster certification (®www.padi.com), you can find work throughout the world. Landing a job is another thing. Most certified instructors have success making personal contact with dive shops and get paid under the table for their work. Or they return later, once the proper work visa has been processed back home. You might try applying directly to some of the larger, more professional resorts. Among the major diving centres are: Arlie Beach and Cairns along Australia's Great Barrier Reef, Belize and Cozumel in the Caribbean and Sharm el Sheikh in the Red Sea. But you may have more luck at many of the lesser known dive sites you stumble across on your travels.

Journalism and photography

Travel writing and travel photography are very competitive fields, and in both cases, your chances of supplementing your income or supporting yourself while travelling will be greatly enhanced with well-honed skills from a course or formal education, but no matter how much skill you may possess, selling your material without an established track record is extremely tough.

That means if you're serious about writing or clicking your way

Employment in Israel

Israel has traditionally been one of the world's most popular destinations for travellers looking for work. Not surprisingly, the market has been swamped with immigrants and travellers alike, and the wages absolutely stink as a result. Travellers are left trying to raise funds at an abysmal rate after living expenses are deducted. Still, they keep on coming.

On a moshav farm, workers live together and cook together in basic accommodation and put in ridiculously long and hard hours for molecular-size wages ($450 per month, $3.50 per hour overtime). There are generally trace amounts of social life, so the little that's earned is easy to save. On a kibbutz, it's typically less work, less pay and more socializing. You typically "volunteer" seven to eight hours six days a week. In return, you get room, board, some available leisure activities, and an allowance that buys you a couple of Cokes or ice cream cones per week (at the kibbutz kiosk) and probably won't begin to cover your bar tab.

Volunteers and kibbutznicks (kibbutz residents) have increasingly grown further apart as the volunteers have demonstrated their ability to party and the kibbutznicks have responded with more distance and disciplined work conditions. But, again, this is not necessarily the case on the hundreds of diverse kibbutzes. In many places, volunteers are greatly appreciated and welcomed with open arms. Jobs range from milking cows to working in a cement factory to picking fruit to doing dishes to preparing meals. You need a bill of good health signed by a doctor, $250 in cash, an onward ticket and you must agree to stay for at least two months. Placement can be made through a local booking agent, the main kibbutz programme centre (🌐www.kibbutz.org), or by calling or visiting an individual kibbutz directly. Try also 🌐www.kibbutznet.com and 🌐www.argo-navis.com.

around the world, you'll want to give yourself a head start by making inroads in the industry: get some articles or photos published (no matter what the subject), build a relationship with one or more editors, and start putting your portfolio together.

Doing this can enable you to earn decent money for your work once you start travelling. Unfortunately, it can take a long time to develop enough contacts. The other, and far more popular approach, is to document your trip (photographers should use slide film, the industry standard) and try to sell it upon your return. This can certainly bring in some money, but generally very little, and you're not likely to get it until long after you return. Cold-calling an editor just before you leave and asking if you can, despite your complete lack of experience, report your way around the globe is a textbook example of how not to go about it.

Some work practicalities

If you satisfy the requirements of various countries (nationality, age, marital status, student status), you may qualify for a work visa, or a limited version of one. Typically, it's for a set period or for certain job sectors, but it's definitely worth looking into. Just make sure you obtain it before you arrive in the country so you can receive the correct stamps when you pass through customs. Arranging for a work visa once you've arrived is, depending on the country, anywhere between difficult and impossible. You can find just about everything you need online at the immigration or work-visa section of the country's embassy website.

Primarily aimed at students or very recent graduates, international placement organizations (Ⓦ www.councilexchanges.org, Ⓦ www.alliancesabroad.com and Ⓦ www.interexchange.org) help travellers slice through the red tape and find minimum-wage jobs in select countries. The fees range from almost nothing to about $500 – in some countries you may also get insurance thrown in. It alleviates much of the hassle, but you have to decide if that's worth the price.

Once you get a job offer you plan to accept, ask for a few days to fix housing arrangements. Look into family stays, university-room rentals, and enquire at various hostels to see if they'll offer you a long-term deal.

If you work abroad and declare your earnings there, knowing that the amount is too small to be taxed in that country, bear in mind that you might be taxed for the amount in your home country, depending upon reciprocal agreements and any other income sources.

Otherwise, you might apply for work directly with the large wire services (such as Associated Press or Reuters) or, if you plan to stay put for a while, at a small English-speaking newspaper overseas.

Overseas jobs for professionals

If you want to work professionally abroad, you'd do well to set up a job before you go. For most foreign companies to obtain a work visa on your behalf, they need to demonstrate that you have a skill that they can't find domestically, which might include Web-designing, specialized mechanics, commercial diving or language teaching. Or they need to demonstrate that the country is in short supply of your skills, for example in the fields of teaching, medicine, dentistry and veterinary medicine. One of the best places to get information is in your local trade publication or larger national one, where foreign companies may advertise for workers. Or, if you already work for a multinational company, you might start out by enquiring from within. Also try ⊕monster.com, a site that specializes in foreign-work placement.

There's a load of red tape involved in getting this sort of work set up, but much of it is taken care of once you have an employer providing the necessary invitation and paperwork. You should have it all arranged before arriving so that you can clear customs with the correct visa. If you have to travel abroad for an interview for the job, you may need to return home and wait for your work papers to clear immigration before you can re-enter and begin. Many countries have bilateral arrangements that will allow you to skirt much of the process, so it's worth investigating each country's immigration/visa website for the most up-to-date information.

Volunteering

Donating your time can be a tremendously fulfilling experience, but if you're not careful in selecting a project, your time contributed may feel like time wasted. Some organizations' definitions of efficiency and utility may differ substantially from your own. In certain cases, it can be fulfilling for you, but little benefit, if any, to the community. And many of the volunteer ventures are almost identical to English-teaching and labour-intensive work projects listed above, only, as the name implies, you're not getting paid. You might be moving boxes, doing dishes or shovelling cow dung, which is fine, provided you know what you're getting into. Before you sign up, make sure you get an exact description of what you'll be doing and what they expect you to accomplish during your visit. You'll want some local orientation before you're dropped

WWOOF (World-Wide Opportunities on Organic Farms)

Not all WWOOFING experiences are necessarily about farming. My friend and I used it primarily as an enjoyable way to make our budget last a little longer. We chose to spend a week with a couple who had renovated a cottage on a tiny island in the Hawkesbury River, just north of Sydney. Although they had a lovely organic garden, our task was mainly to paint the outside of their house. All our expenses were covered and we • enjoyed some fantastic organic food and wine. After our four hours of daily painting we were able to relax and enjoy the island.

Sally Schafer, Rough Guides

Sample volunteer projects

There are literally thousands to choose from, throughout the year and around the globe. If any of the projects listed below sound intriguing and you want to find something similar, visit a search engine and type in a few of the key words regarding location or the type of work plus "volunteer", "help" or "assist". Meanwhile, here are a few volunteer sites to get you started:

ⓦ www.yearoutgroup.org/organizations.htm
ⓦ www.travellersworldwide.com
ⓦ www.volunteerinternational.com
ⓦ www.workingabroad.com/organis/international.htm
ⓦ www.worldwidevolunteering.org.uk

Nature conservation

Repair forest pathways in Spain • Survey Australia's Great Barrier Reef • Aid forestry conservation near Japan's Mount Fuji • Renovate hiking paths in the Black Forest of Germany • Construct mountain footpaths in Italy • Work on an organic "Wwoof" farm in New Zealand • Develop ecotourism in Ecuador • Build an "eco house" in Belgium • Maintain parks in Argentina

Wildlife

Patrol beaches to protect turtle eggs in Mexico • Catch lemon sharks in the Bahamas and tag them with transmitters • Catch kangaroos in Australia and attach radio collars to them • Swim with and collect data from playing dolphins in New Zealand • Track killer whales off the west coast of Canada • Bring wintertime food to reindeer in Finland • Dive to examine ghost shrimps in Papua New Guinea • Locate groups of howler monkeys in Venezuela • Record octopus behaviour in the waters of Burma • Track orang-utans in Borneo's rainforests • Monitor wildebeest migration in Kenya

Human aid and development

Build simple water and sanitation systems in rural Nicaragua • Teach and assist at an orphanage in Malaysia • Meet with medicine men to discover medicinal uses of plants in Nigeria • Assist at a camp for children with learning disabilities in Australia • Volunteer at an orphanage with an organic farm in Cambodia • Build city parks in Turkey

Archeology

Excavate dinosaur bones in southern Australia • Restore fortified castles in France • Catalogue dinosaur remains in America's Mojave Desert • Excavate Mayan remains in Belize • Analyse mummies in Chile's Azapa Valley • Preserve an unearthed town from 1537 in Mexico • Restore archeological and architectural sites in Italy • Sort and catalogue unearthed pottery in Fiji

off with your project and a safety net (local contact) for emergency support, supplies, and advice. You can ask for these things because you're not just going to be working there for free; you're helping finance it. And it ain't as cheap as it sounds. First, there's the air fare. Then you often need to pay a fee that covers your lodging, food, insurance and the entire screening and orientation process. You might be looking at costs in excess of $400 a month. As a guideline, the more exotic the project the more you pay to assist.

Most projects have specific dates for training and transporting new volunteers. Plus, the organizations prefer to screen applicants.

So showing up to lend a hand, though well intentioned, can actually backfire. Your best bet is to make arrangements well before you leave. If you're already on the road, your best shot might be online contact at a nearby Internet café. With a more Web-advanced organization, you may be able take care of all the details before you arrive.

Rewards of volunteering

- Live and work in a remote community where it's easy to make friends.
- Learn customs and language skills.
- Get to know volunteers from around the world.
- Get hands-on practical experience.

- Put your professional skills to use to make a tangible difference in peoples' lives.
- Feel that you're striving to leave the world in better condition than when you arrived.

Studying

Taking a course is one of the most enriching things you can do on your trip: it's a chance to learn a new skill that will remain with you long after you've returned. Education aside, many offer a nice break from the travel scene and provide a chance for you to meet up with some locals or other foreigners with similar interests.

Many courses can be arranged at the last minute, especially if you're travelling alone. But most often, the better programmes require some advance booking. Look into this well before you arrive. In fact, well before you arrange any flights. Unless you're absolutely sure about the soundness of a programme, don't pay the entire fee in advance. And pay with a credit card to help protect yourself. The courses listed below are not "recommended" by Rough Guides or the author, but are meant to provide a sample of some of the activities out there, and are only intended to be used as a starting point.

Studying a language

"Hello", "please", and "thank you" won't take more than five minutes to learn, no matter what the language. If you want to move beyond a few words, a language course is a great way to start your travels in a new country. Aside from tools that will help you unlock the cultural codes of the country, you'll meet more locals, be able to get assistance when needed, keep your grey matter active and make your travels far more meaningful. You'll need at least three weeks to make real progress, no matter how intensive the course is. Two months should provide good conversational skills, depending on your study habits.

Many of the better-known language courses take place in towns loaded with English-speaking students – great for your social life, but lousy for language discipline. It's better (and cheaper) to select a smaller place where you'll get an experience far more intensive than the more expensive "intensive" courses offered in major language-learning centres. If you're set on a specific course, you may need to sign up in advance. Otherwise, you can walk in off the street and usually start the same day. And, naturally, you can find inexpensive private tutors to teach you in nearly any city. Put up a notice near a university and you'll have a few offers within hours.

Studying photography

Even if you're just taking a pocket camera, learning how to compose your photographs is going to get you a lot further than expensive film and an overpriced lens. You may not learn anything more valuable than the tips on p.208, but you'll need to practise them and develop an eye for what works and what doesn't. That means taking oodles of photos, getting them developed immediately and having them critiqued. You can find community photography workshops for less than $100/£65, but the upper-end instruction doesn't come cheap. It does, however, often include a trip to India, Morocco or some place you may not feel comfortable venturing to on your own.

- **Close Up Expeditions** ⓦwww.cuephoto.com. Workshops in over forty countries concentrating on nature, landscape and traditional cultures; 7–21 days, $185–250/£120–160 per day including lodging, meals and ground transport.
- **Ralph Paonessa Photo Workshops** ⓦwww.rpphoto.com. Specializing in birds, nature, landscapes, and travel, these 5–9-day programmes cost around $1275/£820 with lodging, some meals, and ground transport.
- **Traveller's Eye Photo Tours** ⓦwww.lisldennis.com. Tours to international locales selected for their architecture, culture, customs and cuisine. On-location demos, one-on-one sessions and evening photo discussions; 10–17 days, $3450–4995/£2220–3210 including lodging and meals.

Outdoor survival

You don't need one of these courses to navigate the planet, but it certainly wouldn't hurt. Most survival schools are run by Americans these days, but many of the programmes take place around the world. You can study general skills or take a specific course in jungle, desert, mountain, marine and Arctic survival. Some, such as NOLS and Outward Bound, place more emphasis on the group experience while others are more technically oriented. Make sure you ask plenty of questions before making your decision.

- **Australia Outdoor Training and Tours** Fingal, Victoria, Australia ⓦwww.aott.net/training_and_courses.htm. Two-night basic $196/£126, 4-night advanced $333/£214.
- **Boulder Outdoor Survival School (BOSS)** Boulder, Colorado, USA ⓦwww.boss-inc.com; $965/£621 for 7-day field course to $3075/£1709 for a month-long course. Most courses are in Southwest USA.
- **LTR (Learn To Return) Training Systems** Anchorage, Alaska, USA ⓦwww.survivaltraining.com. Mostly two-day programmes on a variety of topics for $300/£193 each. Specializes in aviation-oriented survival, but also offers courses in Arctic survival, water survival and international travel survival.
- **NOLS** Wyoming, USA ⓦwww.nols.edu. Roughly $800–1200/ £515–770 per week with courses typically lasting two weeks to one month. Courses mostly in USA and Canada, but also around the world. Transferable educational credit is possible with some universities.
- **Outward Bound** Garrison, NY, USA ⓦwww.outwardbound.org. Roughly $1000/£640 per week with courses of 1–11 weeks. Focuses on wilderness training and team-building. Courses in the US, Caribbean, Europe and South America.
- **UK Survival School** Hereford, England ⓦwww.survivalschool .co.uk; $78/£50 for one-day courses to $622/£400 for five-day courses. Courses are taught in the UK, but expeditions to Africa and further-flung locales are also available.

Mountain survival

If you're more interested with staying alive in the mountains and summitting in the process, check out this list of International

Mountaineering courses, ⓦhttp://dmoz.org/Recreation/Climbing /Guides_and_Schools, or one of the following:

- **Australian School of Mountaineering** ⓦwww.asmguides.com /enter.html. Guiding and training in the Blue Mountains.
- **Bob Culp Climbing School** ⓦwww.bobculp.com. Rock and ice climbing trips to the Alps, Italian Dolomites and in the USA; 5 days in France/Italy/Switzerland for $1000/£6431 (air fare not included).
- **Colorado Mountain School Boulder CO** ⓦwww.cmschool .com. From first snow school to extreme alpinism, and from starter rock climbing to Big Walls.
- **Swiss Association of the Mountaineering Schools** ⓦwww .bergtourismus.ch/e/schulen.cfm.

Learning to cook

Learning how to make one great local dish could very well be the best souvenir you bring home. Cooking schools can be found almost anywhere. If you find you're really enjoying a local cuisine, talk to the local tourist office about courses available. Most last from a day to a month, with widely varying prices. As well as the listings below, try ⓦcookforfun.shawguides.com.

- **APICIUS Cooking School** Florence, Italy ⓦwww.apicius.itclasses. Taught in Italian (recipes can be translated, individual courses can be held in English). One-day wine class (in group): $50/£32; 1-class individual course $220/£141; 1-week summer workshop: $1500/£965.
- **Chiang Mai Thai Cookery Course** ⓦwww.thaicookeryschool .com; $20/£13 per day.
- **Konishi Japanese Cooking Class**, Tokyo ⓦwww.seiko- osp.com/kjcc; $35/£23 for a two-hour class.
- **Le Cordon Bleu French Cooking** ⓦwww.cordonbleu.net /contact/index.htm. Schools in France, London, Australia, Tokyo and Canada.

Martial arts

Most of today's traditional martial arts come from China and Japan (with other popular disciplines in Korea, Thailand, and Brazil) and it can be particularly inspirational to study and train with masters where the craft was developed. If you're already trained in one or more of the martial arts, then it's likely you'll already have a decent grasp of the working vocabulary. And what you can't follow verbally, you can certainly pick up by watching, as most explanations are accompanied by demonstrations. This does apply to newbies as well, though it can be particularly helpful to have English instruction if you're just getting started. If your local training centre doesn't have such contacts, they can usually point you to someone who will, as it's always nicer to arrive with a personal recommendation.

Otherwise, you'll just have to find your own way in, either through website contacts or by poking your head in the front door and making enquiries yourself. Be forewarned: while you may be welcomed with open arms, some locals may be reluctant to spar with you. They may be afraid to lose face if beaten by a foreigner or find it boring if your level is too low. In other instances, locals may try to demonstrate their superiority by giving you a sound beating. Keep in mind that some dojos practise rougher training than you may be used to: it's better to observe before you participate. A few courses cater to international students:

- **Boxing** Kronk Gym ⓦwww.kronkgym.com. A classic American boxing gym in Detroit, USA.
- **Capoeira schools of Brazil** ⓦwww.capoeirista.com. A list of various training centres around Brazil, where you can try this rhythmic martial art.
- **Kick boxing** Jitti's Gym, ⓦwww.thailandroad.com/jittigym.
- Learn Thai kick boxing in Bangkok from the trainer of national champions.
- **Shao Lin Martial Arts Academy** ⓦwww.shaolins.com. Learn kung fu straight from the monks who've passed it down for generations.
- **Taekwondo** Kukkiwon ⓦwww.parandeul.co.kr. Kukkiwon is the world Taekwondo centre in Korea, and has training and competition facilities.
- **Tai chi** Hong Kong ⓦwww.hktaichi.com. Hong Kong's Association of Tai Chi can steer you towards courses and practice venues.

No one says you have to learn something you'll ever use again. So long as it perks your interest, it'll be a nice addition to your collection of experiences. Here are a few less conventional programmes:

Chinese Acupuncture ⓦ www.cscse.edu.cn/laihua/gaoxiao/zjxy.html. Take a stab at this, and hang out in Beijing for a while.

Ikebana, also known as Kado ⓦ www.ohararyu.or.jp.The art of Japanese flower arranging. Learn how to make a living sculpture in Japan.

International Car Racing Schools ⓦ www.racingschools.com. Here's a chance to burn rubber with someone else's car, from F1 racing in France to drag racing in the USA.

Marcel Marceau's Pantomime School Paris, France ⓦ www.ecolemarceau.com. More than just finding your way out of an invisible box.

Taiko drumming ⓦ www.asano.co.jp Bang a drum in Japan.

Wat Pho Thai Massage School Bangkok, Thailand ⓦ http://bangkok .thailandtoday.com/leisure. Get the lowdown on sore muscles and pressure points.

Windsurfing school Hood River, USA ⓦ www.hoodriverwaterplay.com. Big wind plus big water equals big air. Hold on tight.

World Champion Bullriding and Bullfighting School ⓦ www.rodeoattitude .com/rodeoresources.htm. Learn how to stay on a bull's back or, make it angry, or just get out of its way.

Meditation

This is perhaps the ultimate remedy to fast-paced travel. Whether you're spending a week in total silence or taking a series of Yoga classes, getting back in touch with your mind and body can be an invigorating pit stop – just what you need to continue on your physical and inner journey. Many courses are offered in English around the world, so a simple online search including the name of the country where you plan to take a break and "meditation" should yield numerous listings. Try also ⓦ www.dhamma.org, ⓦ www.kopanmonastery.com and ⓦ www.yogadirectory.com.

6

Hanging out

I t's been said that one of the most problematic aspects of doing nothing is that it's hard to know when you're finished. Hanging out, though, is hardly doing nothing. There's an art to this inertia, not to mention a history. This chapter traces the roots of modern budget travel, addresses some of the developments in hanging out, and the places where it's being put into practice.

Hippie hangout history

The original Hippie Trail grew out of the 1960s the same way just about everything else did at the time: with a search for spiritual enlightenment, or at any rate, drug-induced enlightenment, or at any rate, drugs. Throw in sex, rock'n'roll, adventure and a VW bus and what self-respecting beatnik could possibly refuse? The word Kathmandu had a magical ring to it. And, more important, it had cheap ganja. The clothing was just an added psychedelic bonus: baggy leggings from India, embroidered Pakistani vests covered in little mirrors, Afghani sheepskins for evening wear and Nepali prayer beads for all occasions metaphysical. By the early 70s, a multi-hued stream of near-penniless travellers had created a pulsating road to Kathmandu.

The most common route passed from northern and central Europe through Croatia and the Dalmatian Riviera, Sarajevo,

Montenegro, Macedonia, Bulgaria and on to Istanbul. Until the mid-60s, the trail just stopped in Istanbul: most hippies were content to drift to Marrakesh or Mediterranean havens (Tangier, Ibiza, Greece). But gradually Istanbul developed into a major launching pad to the East, with travellers passing though (or out) in droves. They stayed at "The Tent", a corrugated iron and canvas shelter on the roof of the Gulhane Hotel next to the Blue Mosque, while they gathered information at the Pudding Shop, the closest thing to a guidebook. Travellers swapped tips and directions to private homes with rooms for rent. From there, The Trail went across Turkey, northern Iran (with a stop in Tehran) and into Afghanistan. A major crossroads formed on Chicken Street in Kabul, which served as the halfway point (and halfway house) of the journey. With a fresh stash of hash, travellers traversed the breathtaking mountain passes and proceeded on to Pakistan, then over the border and into India. After paying homage in Manali, the supreme supply centre of marijuana, and Dharamsala, the seat-in-exile of the Dalai Lama, it was over to Varanasi for a toxic splash in the Ganges river and north to Kathmandu.

Meanwhile, back on the other side of the Atlantic, American hippies had worked their way down to a charming Guatemalan volcano-surrounded lake town called Panajachel. Before long, there was a virtual stockpile of stoned foreigners wearing mismatched Guatemalan outfits, and the town was dubbed Gringotenango.

The orally swapped travel information found its way into guidebooks, which helped pave the way for other travellers. More families turned their homes into guesthouses, and cafés started popping up to accommodate visitors reluctant to give up their Western eating habits. The quest for enlightenment, chemically induced or otherwise, has not diminished completely, but has been diluted by a newer breed in search of famous attractions, adventure excursions and passport stamps.

Contemporary hangouts

Travellers who used to visit hangouts for weeks and end up staying for months or years are now more typically coming for days and leaving after weeks, or coming for days and leaving in days. They have tighter itineraries, more energy, and are about as politically

△ Hang out in a hammock

Breaking through the travel bubble

When you're caught up in the excitement of travelling in a foreign land for the first time, everything you see seems so different and wonderfully exotic, it's possible to miss the travel bubble. But after you notice it, you'll wonder how it ever eluded you.

Look around the traveller trail and you'll notice the Westernized biosphere, with cafés serving up banana pancakes, brownies and muesli on demand. Don't like to dine alone? No problem. You can watch the latest Hollywood movies on video while you eat. When it's time to shop, you can find a complete range of pirated products, from designer clothes to DVDs, at a fraction of their normal prices. There are reasonably priced laundry services that specialize in taking two months worth of stink out of your clothing in one wash. There are henna artists, hair braiders with nimble hands and countless beads, discount body piercers, and tattoo artists who can apply the most popular indigenous designs to any curve you offer up, and they're all anxious to help you look like a hardened traveller who has been changed by a rigorous journey on the road. In other words budget travellers aren't as far removed from the hair-drying, luggage-wheeling, tour-guide-following, videotaping crowd as they once were.

You're not likely to escape this bubble by travelling longer or further or faster. Instead, go deeper. Learn a language, communicate with the locals, spend time with them (a lot of time), and form your own firsthand perspective.

One of the best ways to do this is to work for them or alongside them. Volunteering is another excellent path (see p.75). Joining a local sports club or choir will also create inroads. Since there's no membrane on this bubble, it's impossible to say when you've burst it. But there are a few signs. Can you describe the character of the local people to someone back home? Do you have the phone numbers and addresses of local friends you've made? Have you been invited over for dinner? These are certainly more worthy things to strive for on your trip than passport stamps.

active as Bart Simpson. You can still hear Pink Floyd tunes wafting through café terraces, but what is increasingly common is thumping techno beckoning travellers to nightclubs or outdoor raves.

In popular hangouts, it's rarely just enough to find a beautiful beach with palms jutting out over cheap bungalows; they more often come equipped with traveller cafés and offer "adventure" activities, from diving to camel safaris.

Returning hippies may only recognize a few traits left on the Trail (namely, the funkadelic outfits derived from local handicraft), though the new batch of hangouts still serve as gathering points for gaggles of travellers in search of an escape from the very countries they came to see. The places may not be the bargains they once were, but they're still relatively cheap ($3–12 for barebones accommodation). And the police seem to be employing the same law-enforcement techniques: a blind eye coupled with the occasional bust.

Ten current hangouts

Kathmandu's Freak Street isn't that freaky any more, but some of the old haunts are still going strong. Yet it's the crop of new relaxing and revelling refuges that seem to dominate the trail.

Goa

Where is it? Southwest coast of India, about 17hr by bus south of Bombay.

What's the attraction? Once known for its status as the crown jewel of do-nothingness on the Hippie Trail, it has turned into one of the world's largest rave scenes. Despite rising opposition from the locals in this former Portuguese colony, thousands of techno-loving revellers (many over from Europe on a two-week holiday charter) continue to arrive and decorate the forests with fluorescent orange and lime paint. Groups of travellers rent dumpy cottages for weeks or months at a time, but short-term accommodation can be scarce. The beaches are spread out and each has its own scene with the exception of two common seaside roamers: hungry cows and hawkers.

Byron Bay

Where is it? Australia's east coast, 12hr north of Sydney by bus.

What's the attraction? Originally the surfing was the major pull in this otherwise sleepy town with 30km of unbroken sandy beaches. For some, it still is. The surfies were followed by the hippies, who brought with them enough crystals, herbs and tarot cards to transform it into Australia's New Age centre. It was then discovered by the backpack set, who have been slowly pushing the once enchanting small community the way of Times Square, with mainstream developers licking their chops. If you don't mind the rather intestinal sound of Westerners trying to learn the didgeridoo, it can be extremely relaxing.

Gili Islands

Where are they? In Indonesia, east of Bali, just northwest of Lombok.

What's the attraction? The major draws are beaches, beer and bongs. There's also diving, snorkelling and nightly beach bashes. Most of this just occurs on the party island of the three, called Trawangan, with a ring of cottages and restaurants that stretches nearly all the way around the shore to house and feed all the merry-makers. Depending on the island you're headed to, it takes 20min to 1hr by *jukung*, a small outrigger that leaves from Lombok's Bangsal Harbour.

Ko Pha-Ngan

Where is it? Thailand, 15hr by bus/ferry south from Bangkok.

What's the attraction? Drawn by the pill-popping, fire-eating, breast-exposing rave parties on the island's Haad Rin beach, about 5000 people show up every month to sacrifice their cerebellums under a full moon. Naturally, you need to get there a little earlier to secure accommodation, then stay a little longer to recover. The beaches and tranquil waters are likely to lure you into lingering.

Dahab

Where is it? Red Sea coast of Egypt's Sinai Peninsula, 8hr by bus from Cairo.

What's the attraction? Travellers coming from Israel are typically burnt-out kibbutz and moshav workers who have been picking fruit or milking cows for months. But wherever you've come from, the cushioned and carpeted Bedouin tents right on the shoreline with sweet-tobacco octopus-shaped water pipes offer a welcome break. Sadly, there's not much snorkelling any more. The coral reef, or what's left of it, has been trashed over the years and fished out by local restaurants. New "mini-Dahabs" are popping up all along the coast.

Pokhara

Where is it? Nepal, 6hr by bus west of Kathmandu.

What's the attraction? Trekkers these days gearing up for or returning from the Annapurna Circuit can't seem to resist the charms of this serene lakeside town. It has one of the world's most spectacular mountain backdrops. You can rent a canoe, shop for excellent used climbing gear or just munch fresh brownies and play Battle Ship in a café.

Cape McClear

Where is it? Lake Malawi, Malawi 5hr by bus from Blantyre, plus a 20km lift in the back of a pick-up truck.
What's the attraction? It's a classic backpacker watering hole on the shores of the 570-kilometre-long freshwater Lake Malawi, serving up cold beer, thatched tents and a dreamy selection of hammocks. For the less lethargic, there's a full range of water activities, from kayaking to scuba diving.

Dali

Where is it? Southwest China, 5hr by bus northwest of Kunming.
What's the attraction? It's said to be the best place in China to get away from China. Even among the Chinese in the region, it's known as a backpacker's paradise. Travellers are inclined to stay in the centre of the ancient city on Yangren (foreigner's) Street, which isn't more than a short stumble away from the town's popular cafés. Pagodas, temples, lakes, mountains – it's a visual delight.

Vang Viang

Where is it? Northern Laos, 6hr by bus from Vientiane.
What's the attraction? In a word, drugs. This hangout, a modern-day Manali, is one of the budding centres of narco-tourism. Discount opium and weed beckon travellers (over 35 guesthouses full of them) to this otherwise easily missed hideaway. Muang Sing, another Laotian centre for delirium, gets plenty of narco-traffic as well.

Lamu

Where is it? An island just off the northeast coast of Kenya, 7hr by bus north of Mombasa.
What's the attraction? The donkey sanctuary isn't a big draw. It must be the sloth-like pace of life (aside from the initial barrage of hustlers trying to help you find a place to stay) and dawdling dhows sailing travellers up and down the blinding beaches and off to distant islands. Zanzibar's sleepy northern cousin has Kenya's oldest

functioning town (also called Lamu) and possesses much of the same medieval pulling power.

Drugs

Whatever sort of cerebral journey you're after is usually cheap and easy to find, and you'll see plenty of travellers partaking. If you plan to use any drugs during your travels, there are two things you should do: rent the movie *Midnight Express* and read the following paragraphs.

There's almost nothing your government can do to help if you are caught transporting, using or in possession of an illegal substance abroad. In most undeveloped countries, your chances of a fair, innocent-until-proven-guilty trial are just fractionally above zilch. Each year more than 1000 Americans get incarcerated overseas for drug-related crimes. Right now, there are about 100 Australians, 240 South Africans and 1200 Brits rotting in foreign prisons on drug charges. Many are students, husbands and wives – recreational users on vacation.

Just to give you an idea, in Thailand carrying 190 grams of heroin will probably get you a life sentence, though you could get it commuted to 25 years. In Malaysia, it'll get you a death sentence. In Indonesia, possession of 40 grams of hashish is worth about seventeen years behind bars.

Never ever take any narcotics across international borders, and keep an eye on your pack to make sure you don't become an unwilling mule for traffickers. Refuse to carry anything for anyone – even as small and innocuous as a flashlight or postage stamp – through customs. Never buy more than the tiniest amount (the difference of a few grams can mean years in jail or losing your head, so check local regulations). Never sell any drugs (which might trigger local suppliers to report you) and keep in mind that even in crowded rave scenes with thousands of users, busts have been made. Sometimes travellers are carted away and sometimes they're asked to produce outlandish fines, which may entail having funds wired in from overseas (imagine making that phone call back home at 3am).

What about Amsterdam? Drugs are not legal there either. But the Dutch police do tolerate personal consumption of hash in small amounts, provided you stick to the coffee shops, which have been zoned for recreational use. If you're caught trafficking, kiss your tail goodbye.

Because much of the supply in developing countries is produced locally, there's a lot of talk about getting the purest or best while you're in the area. You could also end up with soap powder, rat poison or other undesirables in the mix, which can be especially difficult to detect in pills. There are travellers sitting in popular hangouts at this very moment who popped a tab or two and never came back down after the experience. Every so often, officials from an embassy, dispatched by worried parents who have not heard from their children in months, show up and pass photos around the hangouts. It's chilling to witness.

7

Documents and insurance

etting your documents in order for a long trip isn't
nearly as much of a hassle as it sounds – just a case
of sorting out your passport, any necessary visas and
travel insurance. Many countries either don't
require visas or make it easy for you to pick them
up in neighbouring countries. But take a look at the box on
p.100–101 for the all-important departure countdown.

Passports

A passport is a document issued by your country of citizenship that
establishes your identity and allows you to exit and re-enter your
country of citizenship. That is to say, without a passport, you're
looking at a short trip. Probably to the airport and back. Here's
how you get one.

Two or more passports

The important thing for dual or triple passport holders is that you
pick one passport – the one that grants you the most visa-free access
into other countries – and only use the other for emergencies (leave

the third one at home with your document copies so it can be mailed to you if a crisis should arise) or to get around work-permit issues. It may be tempting to swap when you can save a little money on a visa, but, especially when travelling among neighbouring countries, this isn't a good idea as you need to be able to demonstrate a clear travel history to customs officials. Any gaps will raise suspicions. To keep the customs process at borders moving smoothly, it's best if you avoid bringing up your multiple citizenship.

Visas

Visas are essentially stamps (but sometimes stickers or entire documents) inserted into your passport by immigration officials or embassies or consulates acting on their behalf, that grant you permission to enter their country for a specified period of time. There are other conditions that can be included as well – such the right to work, the right to re-enter the country multiple times and the right to extend your visa – which may require special approval. Much of this depends on which passport you hold. Each country has its own set of agreements with other countries, with fees yo-yoing (with diplomacy) in the region of $25–60.

Many countries require no visas for some passport holders, or simply hand out visas at the airport or border crossing for free or for a small fee. Otherwise, they can take anywhere between a day and a few weeks to process, but they can usually be taken care of within a few days if you opt to pay an additional fee to expedite the application.

The big question is whether you should arrange for these before you leave or at embassies and consulates along the way once you've started travelling. For shorter trips, you should try to get it all taken care of in advance. For longer trips it may simply not be possible. Some visas are activated the moment the stamp goes into your passport, and may expire long before you even set foot in the country.

Getting visas at home

If you're planning to work legally in a country, apply for that visa first since it must be arranged from your home country. Next on your list should be the first country or two you plan to visit, if a visa is required at all. Then look at the country/ies you

Obtaining a passport

Australia

Regular service 32-page passport: $A144, 64-page passport: $A216; 10 working days

Expedited Additional fee of A$60 to process in 2 working days (case-by-case basis ☎ 131 232)

Photo info Two identical photographs taken within the last 6 months, between 35 x 45mm and 40 x 50mm, good-quality colour, full-front view of your head and shoulders in front of a plain, light-coloured background. The back of one photograph should be correctly endorsed by the person who identified you with "This is a true photograph of (your name in full)" and signed, in black ink, by the identifier. Exhaustive guidelines are given on their website – best to check it out.

Valid for 10 years

Website ⊛ www.passports.gov.au

Canada

Regular service 24-page passport: C$85, 48-page passport: C$90; processing time: 27 days by mail (not including mailing time), 10 days in person, no renewal available, new passport must be purchased

Expedited Express: 2–9 days; C$30 Urgent: same day or next day (only available on case-by-case emergency basis); C$70

Photo info Two identical passport photos, black and white or colour, taken within the last year.

Valid for 5 years

Website ⊛ www.dfait-maeci.gc.ca /passport

New Zealand

Regular service 10 working days; $NZ80

Expedited 3 working days; $NZ160. Call-out service, when urgent delivery falls out of working hours, $NZ360; ☎ 0800 22 5050

---

may plan to use as hubs, since extended and multiple-entry visas can sometimes be more difficult to arrange at borders, but only pursue these if the visas are activated upon entry. After that, go for as many visas as you have time for, looking at the more "exotic" countries first (again, only if the visas are activated upon entry). It's uncommon but not unheard of for some developing countries to issue 48-hour visas at the border that have to be extended in the capital, which may mean some unpleasant backtracking, depending on your itinerary. And those who are winging it with their travel plans should watch out for visa applications that require itineraries, with specific ports of entry and exit. If you want to keep your dates and itinerary loose for the moment, take care of the visa when you're in a neighbouring country and have a better idea about your intended route. Plus, if you're turned down for a visa at home, you can certainly try again at a neighbouring embassy.

Photo info Two identical photos must be less than 12 months old, clear, sharp, and in focus, approx 40mm x 50mm, with a light-coloured background (not white), without hats or head covering or sunglasses, full-front view of face, head and shoulders, on photographic paper. The witness identifying you must write your full name on the back of one photo, then sign and date it

Valid for 10 years

Website ⊛ www.passports.govt.nz/

United Kingdom
Regular service 2-week service at post offices and select travel agents; £30
Expedited 1-week service at passport offices; £60. Same-day service at passport offices £75; appointments must be made on ☏ 0870 521 0410
Photo info Two identical photos taken against a white background, clear and good quality, printed on normal thin photographic paper, unmounted 45mm x 35mm, and full face.

Valid for 10 years
Website ⊛ www.ukpa.gov.uk

United States
Regular service 6 weeks, $85; $55 for renewal
Expedited $145 plus overnight shipping both ways
Photo info Two identical photos 2 x 2 inches (between 1 inch and 1 3/8 inches from the bottom of the chin to the top of the head), colour or black and white, taken within 6 months, full-face front view with a plain white or off-white background. Uniforms should not be worn, just normal street attire. No dark glasses or non-prescription glasses. If you normally wear prescription glasses, a hearing device, wig, or similar articles, they should be worn for the photo.

Valid for 10 years
Website ⊛ http://state.gov/travel

Getting visas abroad

Picking up visas at neighbouring countries (or even distant countries, provided there's an embassy) is a fairly straightforward affair, but one that should be well thought out. Arrive before the office opens to secure your place at the beginning of the queue, which will invariably develop. With a small staff, all it takes is one person with a complex case in the queue ahead of you to delay the entire process for hours. Remember that granting visas is not compulsory, and appearance counts (more at some places than others), so dress as smartly as your limited wardrobe allows. A clean button-down shirt and trousers should be fine, though you'd be advised to subtly cover any startling tattoos and remove conspicuous body piercing for the visit. Also, you may be asked about where and when you plan to exit the country, so you should arrive with some idea: bring along a guidebook to help you figure things out if you need to make some last-minute decisions. Bring plenty of photos as well. It's likely you'll be asked to provide two to four identical photos. Most don't mind if they're colour or black and white, but bring both just in case. Every major city has such photo facilities, but it's better to have plenty taken in advance, so you don't need to hunt them down for every application.

Entry requirements

Some countries require you to have an onward ticket and substantial funds to support yourself while in the country. A credit card or two plus the crisp notes of your emergency cash (see p.117) are generally sufficient for the financial aspect. It also helps if you look presentable. In fact, you should make a point of pulling out your backpack's best for border crossings and flights because officials can, even if you're holding a valid visa, deny you entry. As for the onward ticket, it may seem a little problematic if you're travelling overland or buying plane tickets as you go. There's an easy solution. As noted in the section on one-way tickets (p.28), you can simply make a fully refundable booking using your credit card on the Internet at a reliable site, print out the confirmation of the ticket and booking, and then cancel the ticket without penalty once you've entered the country. You can also do this at a major airline office, which can issue you the actual tickets. Just make sure to confirm (ask for it in writing) that they can be cancelled without fee from the city where you plan to cancel them.

Other considerations

- Some countries will not allow entry if you have a certain stamp in your passport. Israeli stamps, for example, may mean refusal into some Arab countries. In such cases, consider getting the stamp on a separate sheet of paper, which can be temporarily taped to your passport. The other two options require substantially more effort: obtaining a new passport or altering the order you visit countries to avoid stamp conflicts.
- Be aware of local holidays, as visa-issuing offices at home *and abroad* are likely be be closed.
- Some countries don't have embassy representation. In such cases, find out if it was a former colony, and of which country. Then

contact that embassy or high commission instead. They many not be able to offer you a visa, but they should certainly be able to point you in the right direction.

Insurance

Here's the single most important thing you need to know about travel insurance for an extended trip: get some. To find out why, what makes a good policy and what it costs, read on.

Why get insurance?

All it takes is one mishap – a drowsy bus driver, a patch of sand when you try to brake your rented scooter, a knee twist during a trek, a bite from a malarial mosquito – and your family might be stuck selling their home to cover your rescue by helicopter, air-ambulance ride home, surgery, plus ongoing treatment (which may not be covered by your home insurance policy). All this could easily top $100,000/£64,000 not including any ongoing medical expenses. A comprehensive health-insurance plan may cover some of your medical expenses, even those incurred overseas, but it's not likely to pick up some of the major rescue and repatriation costs. Even among countries that have reciprocal health agreements (such as the EU), you will not be fully covered, and certainly not for repatriation.

If, at the last moment before your trip, you get terribly sick, called up for jury duty, robbed or whatever, you don't want to get stuck with cancellation fees on top of it. A good policy will cover this, which is why you should book some flight insurance at the time you book your ticket, provided you're booking more than a one-way flight to get an overland journey started. Also, if your trip is disrupted for an emergency, they should assist with arrangements to continue your trip once you're ready.

Also, no one plans on defending themselves in court while abroad. But if it happens, it's unlikely to be cheap. Say you hit a local cyclist while driving a rented car on a difficult-to-navigate road. Or scuff a Mercedes. Travel insurance is about the only way to prepare for such an unfortunate event.

△ You never know when you might need cover

Finding an insurance policy

You need to find out what you're covered for already so you can pick out an insurance package that covers the gaps. Without this knowledge, you'll most likely waste your money on double coverage. Unfortunately, this means digging through the fine print. You might start with your homeowner's insurance policy to see if it covers lost luggage (even your parents' policy, if their home is still your official residence, may have you covered). Airlines generally reimburse travellers for up to $20 per kilo, but the process is time-consuming and potentially exasperating. Second, check to see what kind of travel insurance your credit-card company offers, and whether it is solely for tickets or goods purchased using the card. Some credit cards offer flight insurance in the event of a plane crash or other transportation accidents. Then take a look at your medical policy. Will it cover you for illnesses or accidents incurred overseas? If so, photocopy the list of activities it will cover you for (or ask your insurer to send you the list). Finally, check out your life-insurance policy. Will it still pay out if you die bungee-jumping in South Africa or mountain-climbing in the Andes?

Not all travel insurance is created equal. Most of the best policies aren't cheap, but that doesn't mean the most expensive policies are the best. One sign of a good insurer is a featured list of what they will and won't cover – most prefer to bury this information, knowing you'd rather hack off your arm with a rusty knife than dig through the fine print of their policy. (Instead they pad their list of benefits with things like "money transfer referrals" and "embassy referrals" – which is nothing more than a referral you could find in half the time with a search on the Internet, or in this book.) No two lists of activities seem to be the same. One requires a supplement for an activity that another policy includes in the most basic package. And some policies won't cover you if you get hurt or injured in countries that appear on your foreign office's travel-warning list. Some provide excellent emergency assistance, but little medical coverage. Best to get a few brochures or websites and compare (start with ⊛www.insuremytrip.com or ⊛www.worldtravelcenter.com). If you're checking the Web, be aware that some policies only apply to certain nationalities. STA Travel's insurance, for example, has a strong package for UK citizens, but their policies for Americans and Australians are rather feeble. Find out who the underwriter of the insurance is (it's almost never the travel agency issuing it), and try to contact that company directly and make a deal. Again, check what you're covered for already.

Many policies provide 24-hour emergency assistance – a reverse-charge phone number you can ring from anywhere and get access

Departure countdown

You could theoretically get everything together in less than a week. You might pick up an ulcer in the process, but you could do it. You'd also pay more, not be fully vaccinated (you'd have to look for places along the way to get the additional shots), and miss out on valuable pre-trip research. Better to start six months in advance.

Six months before departure

Get a passport. If you have a passport, make sure it has several blank pages left, and will still have six months of validity left by the end of your trip, as some countries require this cushion for entry.
Starting thinking about the things you'd like to do and see.
Figure out what sort of jobs, volunteer programmes, or courses you'd like to do (see p.66) Gather applications and apply for those that require advance submissions.
Consider your budget (see p.51). If you don't have the funds for the trip you want, perhaps pick up some extra work before you leave.
Start surfing the Web for plane tickets (see p.295).
If you want to get a Hepatitis A and B combination vaccination that's good for ten years, you'll need six months to get the injections (see p.183). If you plan to travel for more than a year and hit many developing nations, this is certainly worth considering.

Four months before departure

If you're going by yacht, check ideal times and places to start your trip (see p.30).
If you're going by cargo ship, try to book passage (see p.34).
If you're flying, book a plane ticket and take out insurance (see p.97) at the same time to cover you in the event of cancellation.
Arrange visas for any extended stays due to work, volunteering or study, plus the first country of entry (if necessary) and any countries with complex visa requirements.
Make arrangements for your apartment rental (see p.104).

Two months before departure

Get a medical checkup.

to an English-speaking operator, who will keep you on the line while you sort out your troubles. With standard inexpensive travel gear, you needn't bother with protection against theft unless it's either included already in the policy you want or you're carrying something expensive (very nice camera, watch, etc). But such items may be covered in your homeowner's insurance. Besides,

Check the CDC website to see which vaccinations you'll need, then call around to find the best rates (see p.18).
Get credit cards and bank cards (see p.122) and meet with your banker to set up your finances (see p.122) so they can be handled while you're away, either with help from your parents or via Internet banking. Try to set up a line of credit.

One month before departure

Buy your travel gear. If you're bringing or sending ahead new hiking boots, start breaking them in (see p.111).
Get any discount cards (ISIC, Teacher Card, Youth Card, HI Card) you need (see p.54).
Arrange for a communication card or kit (see p.158) if you plan to use one, and a mobile phone, if you plan to take one (see p.165).
Visit a dentist.
If you need to get more rugged glasses, order additional contact lenses, or determine your prescription, visit an optician.

One to two weeks before departure

Start taking anti-malarials if you're heading directly to a malarial region (see p.194)
Leave parents or friends an envelope with photocopies of your documents (credit cards, passport, etc) that can be sent to you in case of an emergency.
Take care of any veterinary needs your pet may have before dropping it off with a caretaker.
Arrange for your mail to be forwarded if your parents or room-mate aren't willing to handle it.

Two to three days before departure

Pack
Reconfirm flight

Day of departure

Run over this checklist one last time.

in the event of a theft, replacing your backpack, some clothes, toiletries, and a pair of sandals with items available locally is going to be quite cheap and a lot less hassle than trying to get reimbursed for every little well-worn item.

Find out if your insurance provider will pay your expenses directly or reimburse you. In either case (but especially the latter), ask for and hang on to receipts for everything.

In addition to the comparison sites above, here are a few other insurance providers worth checking out. Rough Guides offers travel insurance – it's one of the easiest policies to understand and offers an upgrade for more adventurous types. For a quick online estimate, see ⓦwww.roughguidesinsurance.com. Another good policy for UK residents, also with an upgrade, is STA Travel: ⓦwww.statravel.co.uk For a strong yearly rate (if it fits your criteria), take a look at SOS International: ⓦwww.sosinternational.com.

Insurance for specific activities

It's hard to anticipate what opportunities may come your way while you're travelling. Even timid travellers work up considerable nerve to try new things after a few months on the road. Remember to check the fine print for the activities you hope to do, but also try to give yourself as much leeway as possible, in terms of your policy, to try new things. Here are some of the activities you should look for. In fact, a quick way to find the relevant section of your policy is to scan through the fine print until you see a list of activities grouped together. There's a good chance you'll have to call and enquire about some specific activities they've left out. To get an idea of what the insurers deem most risky, and also which things to ask about, take a look at the following lists.

Rarely included

Base jumping, boxing, cliff diving, competitions, crewing on vessels between countries, cycle touring, endurance tests, free climbing, heliskiing, horse jumping, hunting, ice caving, ice hockey, martial arts competition, motor sports/rallying, mountaineering (free climbing), open ocean yachting, parachuting, piloting a private aircraft, polo, scuba diving (below 30m), ski acrobatics, ski jumping, skydiving, solo sea sailing, stunt flying, using weapons, yacht racing.

Sometimes included

American football, bouldering, bungee-jumping, canyoning, caving, football, glacier crossing, gliding, hang gliding, high diving from platforms, horse riding, horse trekking, jetskiing, marathon running/triathlon, martial arts training, mountaineering with ropes, mountain-biking on trails, motorcycle touring, rock climbing with ropes, rugby, skiing (off-piste may require a guide), sledding on bobsleigh/skeleton/luge, snowboarding, snowmobiling, snowshoeing, snowcat skiing, speed skating, tobogganing, trekking (over certain altitude), waterskiing, white-water rafting, yachting in territorial waters.

Usually included

Abseiling, baseball, canoeing, cricket, cycling, deep sea fishing, elephant trekking, fencing, go-karting, hiking, hot-air ballooning (commercial tour), ice skating, kayaking, mopeds, motorcycling up to 125cc, mountain-biking, overland expedition, paintballing, parasailing (behind boat), passenger light aircraft/helicopter, quad-biking, safari, sailboarding, scuba diving (above 30m), sea canoeing, cross-country skiing, soccer, surfing, on-piste skiing, walking high altitude, weightlifting, windsurfing.

8

Before you leave home

I f you have any possessions, it's always nice if they're still around when you return. Keeping plants green and pets alive is another trick, one you'll certainly have to face. This chapter will help with the arrangements you'll need to make before you can head out. For information on arranging your finances before you leave, see p.122.

Renting out your property

The two best ways are renting to a trusted friend, who can take care of things for you while you're away, or to a company, who will probably be willing to pay more, and provide a guarantee of payments and the safe keeping of your property (of course, not everyone has an apartment that would appeal to an executive).

To avoid the hassles of dealing with tenants, you may wish to work out an arrangement with an estate agent or property manager, who will not only lease your place, but also collect the rent and handle any problems that may arise. This service isn't cheap, but if you're less worried about turning a profit than having to deal with day-to-day problems, this could be the way to go.

Otherwise, you can take out an ad. Ask around before ringing your favourite newspaper. Often there are much cheaper alternative publications that attract a much better-targeted group.

If you do rent your place to previously unknown tenants, it's worth taking the following precautions:

- While you are with your tenants, take a video camera and walk around the property, videotaping everything with running commentary ("There's a small mark on the table already and one spot on the wall . . .") so that they're protected against minor damage you may forget about during your trip, and you're protected against anything new that appears. If you are going with an estate agent, you may wish to do this before you leave anyway so you can prove any damage upon returning.
- Agree on anything that requires maintenance, such as plant-watering or garden care.
- Show the tenants that things are in working order (refrigerator, washing machine and so on) and make sure as many of these points as possible are listed in the contract.
- Remove and store personal treasures and anything that would cause the lightest emotional stir were it to break or grow legs and walk off.
- Have some family member or friend keep an eye on the tenants and deal with any emergency situations that may arise. And let your tenants know that someone will be watching them. For minor issues, let them know you should be emailed. Bring the number and email address of a trusted electrician and plumber with you, so you can take care of things that pop up with minimal effort.
- Arrange for your mail to be forwarded to parents or friends, who can sort out the junk and send on what you need to your next port of call.

Leaving an empty apartment

If you're leaving your flat empty, unplug appliances, cancel your newspaper subscription, cancel the cable TV, have your phone turned off, clean out the fridge and made sure someone is coming by every so often to check on your property. If you do leave your phone switched on, change the message on your answering machine, although "Hi, I'm out of the country for five months, leave a message and I'll return your call in July," is probably not a great idea.

Plants

Don't just hand over your plants to a good friend, unless you happen to know they have an excellent track record with their own plants. It's more important to find someone who's good with plants. Just about anyone with green fingers will be happy to find some space for your horticultural assets, and possibly take better care of them than you would.

Pets

It's not always easy to find someone who will love your pet as much as you do. Your best bet is going to be leaving your canine, cat or fish with a friend or family member, which may involve some carefully chosen endearment opportunities. Think of your pet's most attractive qualities and try to coordinate those with visits from prospective pet guardians. If you have a dog who can catch a frisbee, play catch with the friend who would find that most appealing. If the pet is cute and friendly and successfully helps you line up dates, let your desperate friend see this in action. If it cuddles up on your bed and keeps you warm, ring your friends with poor heating. If it's sweet, but looks menacing, perhaps some security-minded women living alone might find this useful.

Packing

I f you open ten different guidebooks, you'll find ten different packing lists. Naturally, this is a matter of personal preference, and the only one that really matters is yours. The problem is it will take you a good six months to get a good feel of what you actually use and what you can do without. Until then, it's better to bring less, not more. This may sound like twisted logic, but it's much easier to pick up additional things you realize you need than to throw away stuff you don't. In this chapter, you'll get the lowdown on selecting a pack, what to do with souvenirs, how to handle your film developing, which clothes to leave at home and which medications come in handy.

Why take less

As Henry David Thoreau once said, "Even the elephant carries but a small trunk on his journeys. The perfection of travelling is to travel without baggage." The bigger the pack:

- the bigger the sweat stains, the more odour you emit, the more often you have to wash.
- the more difficult it is to run for a train, the harder it is to lift the pack over your head into a luggage rack.
- the more gear you have to lose, the bigger target you are for thieves, the harder it is to run away from them.

△ Heavy load, Simla

First-Time Around the World | **Packing**

- the harder it is to walk around, the more desperately you need to find a place to leave all your stuff, the bigger the locker you'll need everywhere you go, the more you'll need to pay to leave it.

The test

You should be able to wear your pack for two hours without suffering spinal compression. You should be able to pack it in five minutes. And you should be able to easily lift it over your head. Someone (maybe you) is going to sit on it, step on it or drop it, so don't pack breakables – or pack them well. Go ahead and toss your pack across the room and then step on it to test your setup. And count on the fact that it may get stolen, so leave your mother's pearls, your snakeskin cowboy boots and your collector's edition silver-plated backgammon set at home.

Sending souvenirs home

The best way to get your souvenirs home is to send them as you buy them. They have a better chance of getting lost, broken or stolen in your backpack. Check the local postal regulations first. Sometimes there's a certain weight or box size that's extremely cheap, and you can divide your purchases into a few separate parcels accordingly and save a mint. Overland shipping takes a few months but it usually gets there. If you'd rather not take the chance, try registered mail. If you plan to stock up on trinkets on your last stop before heading home, simply buy a cheap duffel bag for about $5.

Solving the film problem

This can be a real pain. If you develop film on the road, the prints

What travellers are carrying

I spent a few days walking around Stockholm's central train station last summer with a survey and a scale. I interviewed every traveller I managed to stop, and weighed their packs. The average weight was just over 20kg. Some of the heaviest packs (over 25kg) belonged to women who weighed less than 55kg. It looked like they were going to be crushed at any second, Wile E. Coyote-like, under their packs. Everyone I asked had something they wished they hadn't brought. The general consensus on the least used item was formal shoes for going out. After that came textbooks and extra novels. The most used items were sandals and a rain jacket. I asked a few people to open up their packs so I could have a look. If you're wondering what people with large packs are carrying around, here's what's taking up about seventy percent of that space: shoes, sleeping bag, souvenirs and dirty laundry.

Doug Lansky

become heavy to carry and can get ruined. Plus, you're taking your chances with a local developer who may not have the best equipment or have fully understood the directions that came with it. If you don't develop it, the film can go bad collecting mildew in the bottom of your pack. The best ways to handle film are to either avoid it altogether with a digital camera or send it to a mail-in Web developer. Both have their pros and cons.

A digital camera is handy because you can see immediately if the photo turned out as you hoped. Then you send images from the nearest Internet café (bring the software on a disk) with captions. However, the camera costs more, breaks more easily and has a ferocious appetite for high-performance batteries, which aren't always easy to find or cheap (and lugging a bulky recharger kit isn't much better).

A traditional camera is significantly cheaper, usually takes better quality photos, but comes with film and developing costs, plus the shipping and waiting. The best bet with film is to mail it to an Internet developer (Australia ⊛www.extrafilm.com.au, ⊛www.fujicolor.com.au or ⊛www.metrophoto.com.au; UK ⊛www.kodak.co.uk; NZ ⊛www.extrafilm.co.nz; US/Can ⊛www.ofoto.com, ⊛www.snapfish.com, ⊛www.shutterfly.com). They'll place all the photos online, which allows you to access them from the road and create a digital photo album for others to view, send photos as email attachments, or have glossy prints made and sent (along with the developed film) home. If this is what you plan to do, bring along some aluminium foil to wrap your film (inside the plastic canister) to protect it from postal X-ray machines. A large sheet of foil can be neatly folded and kept flat between the pages of your journal. For more on film and photography, see p.208.

Resupply on the road

There may not be toilet paper in every stall or ice in the drinks, but you can get sweaters, T-shirts, socks, toothpaste, soap, band-aids, superglue, film, hats . . . nearly anything almost everywhere you go. Just take the smallest tubes and bottles, plan on buying supplements, and stop at an Internet café and special-order something to your next destination if you can't find it.

Sending gear ahead

If you're going to be trekking every other week of your trip, bring your favourite hiking boots. If not, they're going to take up thirty percent of your pack and make the other seventy percent smell. Tying them to the outside of your pack may be even worse: the dangling Christmas tree look makes it tricky to run for departing transport, knocks people in the head as you enter and leave trains, and lets people smell you from a remarkable distance. It's better to send your boots ahead to the place you'll need them, or simply rent boots when you get there. All major trekking centres have boot rental and cheap used ones for sale.

Picking a pack

No matter how big your backpack is, you will always manage to fill it. The single best thing you can do is start off by buying a small rucksack: 40–55 litres. That's just slightly bigger than a day bag. Once you do this, it's pretty hard to go wrong. The stuff you don't need simply won't fit. Be forewarned: that's not likely to be the advice you'll get from the shop assistant. The bigger the pack, the more it costs, and the more stuff they can sell you to put in it.

This is not the time to try to save money. Take an internal frame model for support. Couple that with a major brand name and you're looking at prices in the range of $65–130. There are a few bells and whistles that are nice to have, but skip the zip-off daypack, since these don't make the best daypacks and they tend to unbalance the main pack when attached. Check out the rucksacks used by climbers. They keep the gear closer to your body for a fuller range of motion and better balance. Packs that extend wide with side pockets make it extremely difficult when you're getting on and off trains and buses. Packs that extend straight back (such as those with attached packs) force you to lean forward to counter the weight. There should be some kind of alternative opening that allows you direct access to the inside or bottom of the pack so you can grab things like a rain jacket or first-aid kit. Make sure there are compression straps on the outside (usually, the sides) to keep the stuff on the inside from jiggling while you walk and to make the pack smaller if you use it for a day-hike. Look for a top compartment that's completely detachable, because if you can raise and lower that, you can stuff things under it more easily. If you need to carry a bag of souvenirs to the post office, for example, the pack can temporarily accommodate the extra gear. Also, you could detach it completely, clip on a camera strap, and you've got a shoulder bag that makes an ideal daypack.

The most important feature is that it fits comfortably. This is not something you should buy over the Internet unless you've tried it on first. The waist strap should not dig into your hips and the straps should be easily adjustable when you're on the move. Sometimes there's one strap that's meant to be sized to the wearer, and it's not that simple to find or adjust. Have the sales person adjust it for you and drop something heavy in before you try it out. Every pack feels great when there's nothing in it. There are now a number of special packs for women that are worth checking out, especially if you have a more curvy or petite body type. These feature narrower shoulder straps, a shorter frame, more cant on the waist strap and a pack mounted lower on the frame.

Think twice about packs with wheels. You can roll them in some places, but in just as many you can't. In most airports (where they work best) you can find trolleys. For hiking trips, the extra weight of the wheels and plastic suspension isn't worth it. At the risk of sounding like a drill sergeant, if you can't carry it, you don't need it.

Clothes

Most people have probably experienced packing for shorter trips: a week in Mexico, Bali or Gran Canaria. On these trips it's perfectly fine to bring along a suitcase or two the size of an early model Cadillac. They only have to be dragged into and out of the airport. The problem, you're thinking, is that it was difficult enough to figure out how to get a week's worth of stuff into just two enormous suitcases. How on earth are you going to get a year's worth into a tiny backpack?

To figure out what to bring, there's a question you need to ask. What clothes do I need to survive a day: go from swimming in the ocean to tanning on the beach to a cool evening walk in the rain to a moderately nice dinner at a place where there's dancing, and be able to wash it all in the sink afterwards?

Let's start with the swimsuit. For guys (and possibly women), make sure it's quick drying and has pockets you trust enough to put car-keys in while you swim – probably some kind of zipper-Velcro combination that will foil pickpockets as well. The shorts should cover your legs modestly so they can be also used for city exploring in appropriate countries – they're the only shorts you have along. Women, it doesn't matter if it's bikini or one-piece as long as you can use the top as a top in a casual setting (again, in appropriate countries). You'll also want a beach towel. It should be fairly thin, but long enough to stretch out on comfortably and wrap yourself modestly. Later in the day, you'll want a hat and T-shirt to help ward off the sunburn after you've been on the beach for a while, and to cover yourself when you run over to the café for a snack.

Just one outfit?

There are two basic approaches to dressing: stay in the same town and change clothes every day; or wear the same clothes and just change towns. When you travel you just have to accept that your general standard of cleanliness is going to be lower than you're used to. Also, you're going to have to wash your clothes daily, or tri-weekly – if you try doing it monthly, you're in for some strange looks, not to mention rashes.

Once you get the hang of this, you'll see you don't need more than one set of clothes. If you wash the clothes before you go to bed, hanging them on a clothes line outside, they'll be dry by morning. If you wash the clothes before taking a siesta in the afternoon and hang them in the sun, they'll be dry in about forty minutes.

Clothes pack list

- [ ] 1 T-shirt – women, if the T-shirt is a little longer, it can double as a nightshirt
- [ ] 1 long-sleeve polypropolene shirt
- [ ] 1 micro fleece – if it's fairly stylish, it can be worn as a pullover in a nice setting
- [ ] 1 rain jacket – expensive Gore-tex doesn't help much when it pours
- [ ] 1 plastic poncho – this covers your pack as well
- [ ] 1 thin beach towel or sarong
- [ ] 1 swimsuit – doubles as walking shorts for men and a casual top for women.
- [ ] 1 pair trousers – not black, but a good dark dirt-hiding colour is ideal. Also, make sure they're lightweight, wrinkle-free, comfortable, fairly stylish and easily washable, with good deep pockets.
- [ ] 1 wrinkle-free travel shirt – short- or long-sleeved is fine
- [ ] 1 pair socks – for cool overnight bus rides and cold hostel floors
- [ ] 2–4 sets of underwear – special travel underwear dries quicker and lasts longer
- [ ] 1 pair of sports sandals. You don't want to skimp on these: they should be reasonably stylish (smart enough for a decent restaurant), have good support, stay on during a swim, not rot when they get out of the water and allow you to run for a train.
- [ ] 1 collapsible hat
- [ ] 1 bandana – soak it with water to keep you cool on warm nights. Cover your mouth to protect your lungs from dust. Use it to dry off in the shower when you don't have time to let your towel dry.
- [ ] 1 wrinkle-free travel skirt (women)
- [ ] 1 pair shorts (women)

For a cool evening walk, you can get by with sandals or sandals with socks. You've got long, comfortable walking trousers. They should have deep front pockets that will deter thieves and not spill your valuables if you need to make a pit stop in the woods. On top you've got a long-sleeved polypropylene shirt that wicks away sweat, a micro-fleece pullover (not cotton!), a nylon rain jacket, and a bandana on your head to absorb any sweat. You're carrying your plastic poncho in your small daypack in case it really starts to pour.

For dinner, you can still get by in sandals, especially if they're black or brown solid colours. You've got a smart, short-sleeved or long-sleeved lightweight, wrinkle-free shirt/blouse. If it's still a little chilly inside, the micro-fleece should be stylish enough to wear. Men, your walking trousers will suffice, provided you didn't get those "adventure travel" ones with more zipped pockets than 80s breakdancers. They should be dark enough to hide any dirt you might have picked up on your walk. Women might also elect to go with a long wrinkle-free skirt.

Wash and repeat.

Winter gear is too bulky to travel with and too easy to pick up on the road to merit carting it along. A cheap pair of warm shoes, gloves, hat, long underwear and a wool jumper can all be snatched up for about $50/£32 at a secondhand shop or handicraft market. Then give it away or send it home before you head on to warmer climes.

All of your clothes, minus what you need to wear, should fit nicely into a compression sack: one that holds a mid-weight sleeping bag will do nicely. With a few yanks on the cords, your clothes will be compressed to the size of a football. Crumpling is unavoidable unless the clothes are wrinkle-proof, and even then they won't look perfect. To minimize creases, try rolling your clothes first.

Toiletries

Start out by buying a toiletry kit with a built-in mirror and hanger since you may not have as much counter space in the bathroom as you're accustomed to. You could transfer perfume/cologne from a heavy, breakable, chic bottle to a small plastic or sturdy glass one with a tight, screw-on lid. Extended sandal-wearing takes its toll on your feet, so bring a foot file to help shed unwanted calluses and keep people from smelling you before they see you.

Major-brand contact lens fluid can be found at supermarkets, opticians and pharmacists in most cities and towns around the world. Bring a pair of glasses along just in case, plus your prescription in case something happens to your glasses. Pity to travel the world, then have to check your photos back home to see what it looked like in focus.

Outside the major cities in developing countries, tampons and pads can be hard to find. Even in the larger cities, they're likely to be low quality and expensive. Everywhere else, finding them shouldn't be a problem. To avoid being caught without, consult your guidebook.

Again, only buy the miniature travel containers and restock as you go. Local toothpaste is especially interesting to sample and – there's at least one traveller doing this – collect.

Toiletry pack list

- ☐ Toothpaste
- ☐ Toothbrush
- ☐ Dental floss
- ☐ Cologne/perfume (in plastic bottle)
- ☐ Foot file
- ☐ Contact lens fluid (if needed)
- ☐ Lip balm
- ☐ Comb/brush
- ☐ Lotion
- ☐ Razor
- ☐ Sunscreen
- ☐ Mosquito repellent
- ☐ Mirror
- ☐ All-purpose soap
- ☐ Conditioner (if needed)
- ☐ Deodorant

Miscellaneous gear

There are a few tiny items that, when you need them, you need them immediately. And they're not always easy to find. Keep the following items in a separate bag (preferably transparent):

- Ear plugs – don't leave home without them. Hostels have a nasty habit of occupying the space above nightclubs and next to busy streets. Plus, every dormitory seems to come with at least one snoring champion.
- Permanent marker – for making hitchhiking signs and other notices.
- Superglue – this fixes just about everything (keep it in its own plastic bag).
- Duct tape – this fixes nearly everything the superglue doesn't fix (wrap it around the marker to save space).
- Guitar string/wire – fixes whatever's left.
- Sewing kit – okay, that's a lie. This fixes whatever's left.
- Candle – power cuts are common. Here's a romantic way to save batteries.
- Lighter – you don't need a $60 lighter that works on top of Mount Everest.
- Power adapters – you can pick them up at major airports as you go (see ⓦwww.kropla.com for country requirements).
- Pocket knife – you can leave the Rambo survival blade at home.
- Spoon – just grab one for free on your first flight. It comes in handy for supermarket-food dining.
- Clothes line – you'll need about 10m of nylon cord.
- Mosquito coils – only carry when in malarial or buggy areas. They should be easy to find and cheap in those areas.

- Sleep sheet – you can sew a sheet in the form of a sleeping bag, or buy a pre-made model. The nicest are silk, which cost a fortune, but can be worth it, as they keep the bed-bugs out. In Southeast Asia, you can have one custom-made for about $10. Get it in white, so the cheap dye doesn't ruin your clothes.

Optional extras

Here are a few extras that you might want to bring along.

- Books: see the Regional Profiles for suggestions.
- Small travel games: backgammon, chess and cards are the most popular. They can keep you sane on a forty-hour bus ride across the outback, and can be a nice way to meet locals.
- Instrument: a guitar can be worth the effort, especially if you're good and plan to earn money playing it, but a harmonica is better suited for transport.
- Frisbee: doubles as plate and soup bowl.

Extra stash

Consider keeping an extra stash of money separate from your passport pouch. Perhaps keep it in a pocket in your address book or taped to the inside of your backpack – $50–100 should be fine, just enough to spend a night in the hostel, get some food, or take transport to the nearest embassy.

Travel with a seatbelt

Admittedly, it sounds like a warped idea. It sounds like something Kramer is trying to push on Seinfeld. But if you value your life and plan to travel by bus in developing countries, this is probably the single best thing you can do for your health (besides not trafficking narcotics across international borders). Buses crash. You'll see them flipped on their backs, tanning their rusted underbellys at the bottom of a ravine or bear-hugging the trunk of a tree.

For less than $10/£6 you can get about a metre and a half of webbing (the same material as the hip-strap on most backpacks) and a plastic clasp at any outdoorsy shop. It rolls up to the size of a ice-hockey puck. Then wrap it around the back of your bus seat and clip in. Will the people around you think you're nuts? Probably. But then again, you're a foreigner living out of a backpack and travelling around the world. They probably think you're a little nuts already.

First aid

Most prepackaged first-aid kits sold in outdoor stores are almost worthless. Make your own. Start out with a Tupperware container large enough to hold about four muffins. Those nylon sacks don't keep your bandages and pills from getting wet or crushed. You should be able to resupply all you need – see the box below – on the road.

A lot of travellers like to take antibiotics along. And if you're whacking your way through a rainforest for weeks or in a similarly

Medical packlist

- ❏ Band-aids – take a box worth, but put them into a clear plastic sleeve that holds photos or credit cards
- ❏ Compeed – modern science has created the wonder blister cure
- ❏ Elastic wrap bandage – vital for twists and big cuts
- ❏ Lidocain cream – works well on stings and bites
- ❏ Antihistamines – you never know what will spark an allergic reaction
- ❏ Hydrocortisone cream – cures most rashes and skin irritation
- ❏ Aspirin/Paracetamol – for minor aches and major hangovers
- ❏ Laxatives
- ❏ Anti-diarrhoea medicine
- ❏ Iodine – for sterilizing cuts and your drinking water (a few drops). If you can't deal with the taste, then water purification tablets are a good idea
- ❏ Rehydration sachets – about four is enough to get you started (in a crisis, make your own mix: 1 litre water, 1 teaspoon of salt, 8 tablespoons sugar, dash of juice if available)
- ❏ Condoms – bring some from home, and try to use only major brands purchased in developed nations
- ❏ Motion sickness pills – stale air and curvy roads make a lethal combo
- ❏ Malaria pills – if you need them; see p.194 for more info
- ❏ Thermometer – electronic rather than glass and mercury

If these don't fit in the first-aid container, toss them in the gear bag:
- ❏ Tweezers – find a good pair with a sharp point for removing splinters
- ❏ Vaseline – prevents chaffing and blisters during long hikes
- ❏ Sports tape – it's mostly for blister prevention, but helps hold plasters on
- ❏ Iodine – works for both water purification and cuts
- ❏ Nasal spray – undeniably one of the world's great inventions (plastic bottle)
- ❏ Antiseptic wet wipes – a great refresher when you're stuck in a bus seat for two days, trying to clean up before a meal, or helping clean up a wound
- ❏ Tiger balm – the all-purpose sports cream that also clears up clogged sinuses and soothes headaches

remote location, it's probably not a bad idea. But the vast majority of travellers are never that far from a local doctor or hospital. If you get sick enough to require antibiotics, you should be going to a doctor, who can prescribe the best ones. Plus, antibiotics don't travel well. They expire, don't hold up well in heat, and are often not handed out by doctors, who are understandably trying to prevent their misuse. If you do take antibiotics, take the full course, even if your symptoms abate after just one or two days. Otherwise, the few microbes that don't get killed off tend to mutate and come back stronger.

Daypack

Even a small, eight-kilo internal-frame pack is not a joy to lug around the entire day while you explore ruins, museums and cities. Something smaller is a more sensible way to carry the few necessities you'll need.

Most travellers opt for small daypacks, such as the detachable ones that come with packs. If that's your preference – and for women who are getting repeatedly touched in crowds, wearing the pack on their front is an excellent idea – you can simply empty the laundry and toiletries from your main pack, tighten the compression straps and that should work fine. While it's on your back,though, it can be hard to protect from quick-handed thieves. Some prefer the comfort of a waist pack, but this is something of a thief magnet. A better idea is a shoulder bag. It's easy to tuck under your arm to protect from pickpockets, can be accessed more quickly while you're on the move and doesn't peg you as a tourist, especially in bars and nightclubs. If the top compartment of your backpack detaches, a camera or guitar strap can turn it into a decent shoulder bag.

What to keep in your day bag

- Water bottle
- Guidebook – you can lighten the load by ripping out unneeded sections
- Sunglasses – don't skimp on these as sunglasses without UV protection allow your pupils to widen and expose your eyes to more damaging rays
- Journal/address book/pen – a necessity. Some photos of home and friends are also nice to include for letter-writing inspiration

- Reading matter – for more info on books and swapping, see p.131
- Pocket knife – you don't need the Swiss Army knife with all sixty functions
- Flashlight – the little LCD key-chain ones work well
- Pocket camera – you can get a good one for under $100/£60
- Cell phone and charger – this is optional, but a triple-band phone works almost everywhere these days, and can be easily worth the one emergency you need it for

Camping gear

If you plan to camp the entire time, bring what you need. If you're not sure, don't take anything. The gear will more than double the size and weight of your rucksack. You'll be forced to spend more on transport: getting in and out of cities on local trains and buses becomes a real headache. And you may worry about your belongings when your tent is unattended. If you're not dissuaded, make sure you have the right gear:

- Light, rainproof tent
- Cooking stove
- Pot with lid
- Cooking utensils
- Sleeping bag
- Sleeping pad
- Headlamp
- Tarpaulin to lay under tent

What you don't need and why

- Shoes – this may come as a shocker, but with a decent pair of sandals, you can get by without them. If you find you're going out clubbing regularly or need shoes for work or it's just getting too cold, buy a cheap pair for $10–25/£6–18 and ditch them when you're done.
- Sleeping bag – nearly every hostel can produce a blanket for you as long as you have a sleep sheet. Beyond that, if you layer on all your clothes for a rare chilly night on a train or bus, you should be fine. If you're worried about a particular train ride, pick up a cheap hat and blanket before boarding.
- Walkman/discman – this is a great way to tune out and relax. However, you're also cutting yourself off from the sounds of the

country, which, though often aggravating, are part of the experience. More importantly, it discourages locals from making contact with you. Besides, it's something else that can break, get stolen, take up space in your pack (with CDs) and chew expensive batteries. Read a book instead.

- Electronic language translator – just try to have a conversation with one of these! The most common words and phrases can be looked up in nearly all guidebooks. Better yet, take twenty minutes and learn a few words and phrases before you arrive.
- Currency converter – your primary-school maths skills should get you by nicely.
- Pro-camera set up – if you're a serious amateur or professional photographer, bring what you need. If not, this is probably not the time to start. Forget the SLR, lenses and tripod. Stick with a pocket camera and you'll get more use out of it.
- GSM – if you're charting new territory, fine. If not, leave it at home.
- Jeans – resist the temptation to pack your favourite pair, no matter how good you may look in them. They're too warm in hot weather, too difficult to wash by hand and take too long to dry.
- Sweatshirt – the comfort is alluring, but it will take up far too much room, offer no warmth when wet, and require about two days to dry on it's own. Microfleece is the way to go.
- Compass – the sun rises in the east and sets in the west. That sentence should get you by. If you feel better having a compass along, take a tiny key-chain model. If you depart without one and regret it, you can always buy it along the way.
- Mosquito net – if you need one for a specific journey, you can pick one up on the spot. Otherwise, most hostels are equipped with them in malarial areas. If there's no net (and even if there is) use any combination of bug spray, clothing and mosquito coils – all of which are easier than carrying a net and stringing it up everywhere you go.
- High-absorption "travel towel" – a bandana will do just fine, even if you have to wring it out a few extra times.

10

Carrying valuables

Passport pouches, also known as money belts, come in a variety of styles. Some go around the waist, just under the trousers, some hang around the neck and still others fasten to your leg. It's a combination of personal preference, how it works with your clothing, and how easy it is for thieves to spot. Try a few on before you make a purchase since this is something you'll be wearing round the clock.

Before you leave, remember to photocopy the contents of your money belt (except the cash), leave a copy with your parents or trusted friends and take a copy with you and store it separately from your money belt or with your travel partner. To save space, try to get all the vital information onto the front and back of one piece of paper.

Carrying money

Once upon a time, travellers' cheques were a great idea. Today, with more vendors accepting foreign currency, most accepting credit cards and cash machines almost everywhere, it makes more sense to carry cash (US dollars or euros), two credit cards and a bank card.

Cash

You'll want to carry your US dollars and euros (by bringing both, you can take advantage of the best exchange rate) in a variety of denominations. The €100 notes are nice space savers and fine for changing at banks, but for an emergency stash ($300–500), as well as some bills for hard-currency shopping, a good number of 20s, 10s and 5s are far more practical. If you've got a cash card and credit card, you can use those as your primary tools to pay for rooms, food and tickets and get local currency, but you'll want some dollars/euros available at all times, which means either taking a large stack of bills or replenishing your hard currency along the way. If you can arrange to meet a trusted friend or relative just leaving home, perhaps they can carry some over for you. Or try a priority delivery service. More likely, you'll just have to take cash out in a local currency, then exchange them for euros/dollars and take a bit of a beating with the exchange rate.

With an Internet banking account, you can transfer money to yourself at a local bank on the road, but there are drawbacks. Making an international money transfer is unreliable in developing countries (even with a major bank) and may take weeks or fail entirely, possibly resulting in the loss of your money. It may still take two days to two weeks to clear in a major bank in the most developed country. Try to get a time estimate from the bank manager before you decide to make the transaction. The next step is to get the bank's transfer information, go online and wire yourself the money. Keep your banker's number just in case, plus your account number, the bank's address, and its routeing numbers.

Credit cards

Don't leave home without one of these. Two is even better. Visa and Mastercard are the most widely accepted. You should have codes for both to access cash machines, but in the event a cash machine can't be found, most banks will still allow you to use them for cash advances. That is, you can go to a bank window, let them swipe your credit card and buy cash (for a fee, of course).

The benefits

- You can access emergency funds and cover many daily expenses without carrying a thick bundle of cash.
- You can track your finances easily.
- Parents, relatives, friends can send funds to your account, which you can quickly and easily withdraw anywhere in the world.
- Cards can be replaced quite easily if stolen.
- You're entitled to additional insurance when you use the card to make purchases (see p.99).

The drawbacks

- Merchants who accept credit cards pay a small percentage fee to the credit-card company for the right to accept their card. Although they're not supposed to do this, many smaller companies make no secret about passing that percentage on to you (it's still often cheaper than withdrawing money from a cash machine, especially for one purchase).
- Some credit-card companies have started tacking on little surcharges for foreign purchases.
- You not only pay a fee to withdraw money from a bank machine (or bank), but you may have to pay interest on that withdrawn cash until your next bill is paid.

Choosing a credit card

- Not all credit cards are alike. They depend on the bank or financial institution behind them. When deciding on a credit card, make sure you ask about the surcharges for foreign purchases. More and more cards are adding a three-percent conversion fee. Try to find one that doesn't.
- Try to max your spending limit before leaving. Simply call the credit-card company and ask if you can get your limit raised. You may have more expenses on the card (or cards) than you're used to, and with an emergency purchase, such as a plane ticket or hospital bill, you might be quickly out of funds.
- Many credit cards or bank accounts can be set up for "Auto-pay". Each month, your credit-card bill will be automatically paid from your current or savings account. That way you don't have to worry about missing any payments and getting hit with high interest rates. Of course, what you may have to worry about is having enough money in your bank account. To be safe, meet with your

banker and set up enough credit (\$2000–10,000/£1300 –6400) to cover you in a pinch. If you get Internet banking, all this can be easily monitored from any Internet café.

Bank cards

These bank-issued cards can't be used for purchases, but they can be used to withdraw cash. You'll still be slapped with a withdrawal fee, but you won't have to pay interest on the money withdrawn, which makes them better than credit cards for this purpose.

Travellers' cheques

Many people still like the comfort of travellers' cheques, which do provide more security than the other options if used properly. Here's how they work: you buy the cheques (for a small fee), keep track of the serial numbers of the cheques you use, then, if they're stolen or lost, you can report which ones are missing. Of course, in order to do this, you need to have a current list of the ones that were used, keep that list separate from your cheques, and hope the bag with that list didn't get stolen or lost as well. Some places do accept travellers' cheques as cash, but they're few and far between, and you're likely to have to encash them. Sometimes you can do this for free – you can cash American Express cheques at AmEx offices for free for example – but you may not be anywhere near the relevant office. So, you're more likely to be paying a fee to cash cheques in addition to the cost of exchanging the currency. Understandably, some people find this to be a hassle – one that outweighs the security factor.

In general, places that take travellers' cheques also take credit cards (or are not far from a cash machine or bank that allows cash advances). However, if you plan to spend an extended period in a rural area, and have read in your guidebook that cash cards and credit cards are of limited use, but that travellers' cheques can be cashed, you can always pick some up in a major city if you're uncomfortable carrying the amount of cash you'll need to get by.

Visa, Thomas Cook and American Express issue the most commonly used travellers' cheques. There are no real advantages in terms of acceptance (though AmEx does allow clients to collect mail at some of their offices, and AmEx and Thomas Cook allow

Giving to beggars

You learn a lot about yourself when you travel, and being confronted by beggars twenty times daily will certainly flex the bend of that learning curve. It's a vexing issue. You're walking around with more money than these beggars may ever possess, yet you'll have to return in less than a week if you start handing it out as you may like. Even if you give money to five people a day, you might be refusing it to fifteen. Or you give some coins to a starving woman and her two starving children and you walk off thinking that you could have easily done so much more.

It's common to feel callous – to the extent that you neglect to broach the subject with other travellers, including the ones you may be travelling with. Imagine you're walking beside a traveller who is emotionally touched by a beggar when you're not. They give and you don't and when you continue walking there's suddenly a little gap between you.

There's no right way to approach it. Some people hand out tiny coins to everyone they encounter. Some never do, but may contribute to a charity that can (hopefully) better distribute the funds. Most fail to adopt any sort of policy and just end up giving when they can no longer refuse, when they need an emotional lift (giving can be extremely rewarding), or when they've just spent too much on a meal and feel the pangs of guilt. Some try, with a look, to figure out if the funds will be used for alcohol or milk, and if they will be helping support the truly bereft. For this reason, many people prefer to carry tiny gifts or snacks to hand out (although this is not always appreciated).

Begging can get aggravating at times, so aggravating that it's possible to lose sight of the bigger picture: that they're the ones with a life harder than anything you can imagine. Instead, you begin to feel like the victim. You feel like you're viewed as nothing more than a walking money machine. You think: "I'm spending my money in your country, trying to learn about you, and if you don't plan to get to know me in a genuine way, I'd really prefer to be left alone once in a while. Come to my country and see how you like getting hassled for change all day." Needless to say, try your best to keep things in perspective.

two people to sign the cheques). Remember to make sure the assistant is watching you countersign the cheques. Don't let them walk off while you're busy scribbling your name, or the whole thing may be void. And shop around when buying travellers' cheques.

AmEx also has a "travellers' cheque card", which you can load up with money, then use to withdraw funds from bank machines. When it's empty, simply toss away the card. However, if you've got a cash card from your bank or a debit card, this is unnecessary: you don't need both.

Debit/bank cards

These work like credit cards, often issued with major credit-card names, and can be used to withdraw cash and make purchases. The difference, as the name implies, is that there is a fixed amount of money behind them that can be reloaded. For those who don't trust themselves with the spending limit granted on a credit card, this can be a good alternative, but the drawbacks are clear-cut: there's no credit, which is no good when you're faced with unexpected, urgent expenses. And if the card is stolen and used, charges aren't protected as they are with credit cards, so the money is as good as gone. If you can't arrange a credit card, or want to use this as a second card, ring or meet with your bank.

Other items for your money belt

Passport

Goes without saying. To find out how to get a passport, see p.92.

Driving licence

It's helpful to have an official photo ID besides the passport, especially since there's a good chance you'll end up driving a car at some point. The International Drivers' Licence (should you decide to pick one up) won't easily fit in your passport pouch, and you won't need it for many rentals, so before you pick one up, check if you'll be visiting many of the 50 countries where it's required. See ⓦwww.theaa.co.uk for country listings.

Student ID card/under-26 youth card/teacher card

If you qualify for one of these, it's probably best to keep it close by. It's not as valuable as the other items in your passport pouch, but its size makes it easy to lose. For more information on these cards, see p.54.

Ten extra passport photos

This seems like a lot, but there's a good chance you'll be using at least that many during a long trip. When you apply for visas and such, you often need three photos just for one application. Local transport cards sometimes require them as well.

Insurance card

If you've got insurance, carry the card. If you're just issued a large piece of paper, make your own card with your account number and emergency telephone number and laminate it. See p.97 for more on insurance.

Phone card

These cards list the local access numbers you'll need, so you have them handy in case of an emergency. You can get them for free from the phone service you plan to use. You can find the numbers online if you misplace the card.

Other licences

If you're a trained scuba diver or pilot, or hold other such licences that easily fit into a passport pouch, bring them along.

One anti-diarrhoea pill

It's hard to predict when dysentery is going to strike. Inevitably, it'll happen while you're out wandering around town or on a long bus ride with your medical kit stored in the luggage hold below. Best to keep one pill handy for such emergencies.

11

Guidebooks and other reading

This is precisely where you might expect to find a few sentences of Rough Guide propaganda. Happily, you won't. Not much, anyway. Naturally, the editors and writers at Rough Guides are proud of the guidebooks they produce, but they also understand it comes down to individual taste, trust, and how you like your information gathered and presented. For that, you'll have to head to a bookstore and compare. Better yet, you might even "test drive" a few different guides out on the road and see which suits you best.

Specialists in the independent market are Rough Guides, Lonely Planet, Footprint's Handbook Series, Let's Go, Time Out city guides and (for French speakers) the Guide Routard. For more mainstream travel, there's also Frommer's, Fodor's, the design-intense city guides by DK and Rick Steves' self-guided tours.

At a bookstore, pick up a few guides on the same country and compare a few paragraphs on the same topic. Start with a city or town you're particularly interested in. Is the layout and writing easy to follow? Are the maps clear? Also take a look at the author bios. You'll want someone (or several people) who has spent considerable time in the country they're writing about. It's always helpful if they speak the language and have been able to get information by conversing with the locals.

How to use your guidebook

For most, it's a revelation to find there are books that tell you every-thing you need to know to get around: where to stay, where to eat and what to do while you're there. However, this does more than just remove some of the adventure. It sends everyone to the same places. Not just the same towns, but the same cafés, hostels, bars and scenic spots. Ask nearly any guidebook writer and they'll tell you the book is best used as a reference, not a bible or substitute tour guide. The little maps are great for helping you navigate your way from the bus station to a hostel at 3am or finding a vegetarian restaurant in Scandinavia, but your best guide is still your own nose. Find your own unlisted restaurants and lodgings, and it's likely you'll have a much more memorable experience.

Here's another common misuse. The temptation is to sit there on the bus or train approaching the city and scrutinizing the hostel descriptions. Then you read them over and over until you get them into your head, and before you know it you've got the experience largely mapped out before you've even done it. Save yourself the effort. It's not worth it. There's not that much difference between four recommended hostels. And if you don't like it you can either change the next day after you've had a chance to look around, or just crash there at night and spend your waking hours elsewhere in town. You'll eventually find a system that works for you, but mine is something like this: if I'm tired out or staying a bit longer, I'll pick a place further from the centre. If I'm just staying a day or two and feeling fresh, I'll go for the best rated of the flea traps in the centre. If there are a few decent choices in these categories, I'll typically go for the ones that are the easiest to get to. But, whatever the case, I won't spend more than five or ten minutes deciding.

How many guidebooks to bring

Here's some good news. Just because you're planning to hit twenty countries on your trip doesn't mean you need to pack twenty guidebooks. Just take the one for the country or region you're heading to first and buy or trade for the rest as you go. Relevant guidebooks (those for that country or city, plus surrounding ones) can be found in hostels, hotels, bookstores and airports – virtually everywhere. Ideally, you'll be able to locate someone who's heading in the direction you just came from and make a straight swap. If you're trading with a hostel or second-hand bookstore, you may have to throw in some money or a novel to complete the deal.

Putting the guidebook down

One day me, my wife, and her sister decided to drive near the Swiss border to explore the countryside and find a small-town, mom-and-poppa restaurant for lunch. But for some reason, we couldn't find a place to eat. Hard to believe, but it was true. We were ravenous, but our timing was off – it was late afternoon, and we'd managed to miss the opening hours of what a few rural restaurants we could find. The troops were getting restless.

Out of desperation, I pulled onto the deeply rutted driveway of a farm and drove a quarter of a mile to the main house where I asked in broken German if there was anywhere nearby to eat. Maybe the farmer and his wife who answered the door could see the hunger, for they invited us in and cooked up an unforgettable meal of ham (that I bet was squealing out back the day before), sauerkraut and boiled potatoes. Some sharp mustard completed the feast. I still remember the meal, as well as our host and hostess, fondly.

It was the kind of event that could never have been planned.

Rudy Maxa

TV & radio host
(ⓦ www.rudymaxa.com)

What to read along the way

One of the very best ways to add richness to your trip and bring the locales to life is to read up on them. This entails getting beyond the brief guidebook descriptions and finding stories that explore cultural nuances and history easily missed while searching for your hostel or a better exchange rate. The Travellers' Tales series published in San Francisco offers diverse and well-crafted anthologies on the most popular destinations that do just this. And if you can find room (or manage to lift) any of the country-themed James Michener tomes you're in for a treat with folklore and fiction woven into the locales named in the title.

But it would be a pity to miss out on some of the classics, especially in the regions where they are set. Reading books like *Midnight's Children* in India, *Seven Pillars of Wisdom* in Syria, *On the Road* in America, and *Ulysses* in Ireland is one of the great joys of travel. These are among the most popular titles along the appropriate routes and can be bought or traded for quite easily. So, when you're starting out, one paperback will do. Pop fiction authors like Clancy and Grisham tend to serve as the strongest currency, but start with something you like and let your continuous swaps serve as a reading adventure that runs parallel to your trip.

Your city, country or regional guidebooks will provide a more complete reading list with descriptions; see also the Regional Profiles at the end of this book.

12

When you arrive

One of the best ways to take advantage of your time on the road is to vary the way you travel down it. How you get around, whether it be in the air, through the water, on wheels, or on the back of an animal, will shape the memories you bring home. And that doesn't just apply to transport. You can be adventurous or timid in your choice of accommodation, what you eat, even the bathrooms you decide to use. It's always going to be easier to travel in the style you are accustomed to at home, but making the choice (often several times a day) to try the local alternatives will ultimately enrich your trip. This chapter will provide you with a little taste of what lies ahead.

Transport

After a lifetime of domestic, business or short holiday travel, it's easy to get caught up in the industry's lingo: "arrivals", "on time", "quickly and comfortably", and "perks". You simply can't apply these words and phrases to most overland transport. And you shouldn't try. The key is to remember that on this type of journey, travelling is just as much about getting there as arriving, or maybe even more. This may not be apparent when you're sweltering on an Indian train that has broken down for twelve hours, so it's important to remind yourself regularly.

One way to do that is to take unusual transport. When you're sailing down the Nile on a felucca, it's a little easier to relax with the fact that you're moving barely faster than driftwood. The frustration comes when you're trying to get somewhere quickly, so the slower you try to go the less frustrating it is likely to be. In fact, the level of frustration may be directly linked to the difference between the speed you should be going and your actual speed. A four-hour delay on a nine-day trip up the Amazon by cargo ship won't faze anyone in the slightest. Sit four hours on an airport runway, and peoples' ulcers start to bleed.

If you have the chance, skip the air-conditioned bus and try… well, anything. Here's a guide to getting yourself around.

Aircraft

Confirm your flights by phone or email 72 hours in advance. You won't be automatically bumped if you neglect to do this, but it's nice insurance and more important in some places than others. Most carriers will have English-speakers manning the phones, but have the hostel receptionist or tourist office help out if you experience a language barrier. And remember to confirm your in-flight meals if you have any special dietary considerations.

On long flights, request a seat by the window if you plan to sleep, preferably near an emergency exit, and take anti-jetlag precautions so you don't sleepwalk through the first week of your trip (see p.194). Contact-lens users should either switch to glasses during the long flight or bring extra solution to combat the dry cabin air.

With local carriers, you may not experience the sort of professionalism you get on flights at home (if, indeed, you get such service at home). And the planes may not look that professional either. If you're nervous about flying with these companies, that's normal, but remind yourself that it's statistically safer than the other modes of transport, including walking. Flying during daylight may help with some of your worries.

Bicycle rickshaws

You can't ride in one of these and not feel like a hardened traveller. The problem is you may also feel like a slave-driver. Propulsion never looks easy for these malnourished pedallers, but they often throw in a few extra grunts to help justify the price. There's no meter, so always fix the price before you depart.

Bicycle

Bikes can be rented nearly everywhere. And where they can't be rented, you can pick up a low-tech model for a trifle. Take advantage of this. It's an ideal way to get to know an area, particularly the ones set up to accommodate cycles: you can stop whenever you get the urge yet you're more inclined to venture further, well off the main tourist routes, which will afford you some of the most interesting views. For longer bicycle journeys, see p.43.

Buses

You'll find some buses are as aerodynamic as Concorde, have spacious, fully reclining seats and attendants serving almost-edible food. If you need to cover some ground and get a good night's rest, it's worth the extra few bucks. When boarding older buses, choose your seat carefully if you can. Try to get a window seat near the front (but not at the very front) on the side that's not getting direct sunlight (take a moment to figure this out before you step onto the bus). That way you can control the temperature with the window, minimize the greenhouse effect, get a view of where you're going, and still have a few rows in front of you to cushion any collision.

Camel

Camels, though they conjure up Lawrence of Arabia adventures, are about as tempting to ride over long distances as they are to French kiss. As Jacqueline Kennedy said on her trip to India, "A camel makes an elephant feel like a jet plane." Sometimes there is just one rein, fashioned to a nose ring on one side, affording the rider an easy pull to go that direction, but rendering it near impossible to make it go the other without a 359-degree rotation. In other words, be sure to ask for two reins.

Canoe

A convenient step-up from their dugout brethren, the modern canoe can be affordably rented in an astounding number of countries, and provides an easy way to leave just a few footprints while you travel. From the Boundary Water Canoe Area in North America to the hippo-packed Zambezi river, you get the best possible views of the area with little more than a guide or a good map.

Car

See p.40 for general information on transport, and the Regional Profiles at the end of the book for specific tips on buying, selling and renting cars as you travel.

Hitchhiking safety

In some countries, it's relatively safe to hitch, in others it should never be done. Your guidebook will help explain where it is and isn't an option, but there are several things you can do to minimize the risk, starting with your choice of hitchhiking spot. At petrol stations near the highway, you can simply approach the drivers that look most trustworthy – families, couples, and single women drivers. Of course, to get rides with these people, you'll have to look presentable and trustworthy yourself, which means a shower, clean clothes, no sunglasses, and a smile.

If you do have to stand on the side of the road, don't just hop in a car because it pulls over. That's only how it works in the movies. You want to go to the driver- or passenger-side window (you may have to open the passenger-side door) and ask them where they're going. Use these few moments to see if the person looks, well. . . normal. Scan for open alcohol containers and smell for alcohol on the driver's breath. If they look rough or drunk, just say thanks, but that you're actually headed to a different place and walk off.

Once in the car, if you sense that the driver may be drunk, over-fatigued, dangerous, or is driving too aggressively, ask them to let you out at the next petrol station. If there aren't any around, have them drop you at an intersection (where cars are more likely to slow down), or just get out as soon as possible. If the driver turns off the interstate and starts heading in a new direction without telling you, ask to get out of the car immediately. If you feel you are in serious danger and the driver won't stop to let you out, try hopping out at an intersection when the car stops or slows down. Hitching is never a good idea for women travelling alone, but especially so if you can't find a ride with a family, couple, or single woman driver. Simply put, make sure you're never the only woman in the car.

Cruise ship

This doesn't fit the traditional traveller image. The cabins aren't conducive to drying hand-washed laundry, the staff don't appreciate people walking down the corridors in just a towel, and body art and piercing may frighten some of the other passengers. But this can be a way to connect certain legs of your trip at a decent price. See p.34 for more information.

Dhow

These wooden sailing boats are very similar to feluccas, although they're slightly more seaworthy. They're usually found hugging the coast of eastern Africa: trips are common in Lamu, Kenya, with camping along the surrounding islands, and near Zanzibar. They come in all shapes and sizes, from three-person dinghies to commercial fishing vessels. The faster ones employ a counterbalance beam. If you're allowed, crawl out onto it for an exhilarating ride.

Dugout canoes

They look and sound exotic, but most tip or take in water easily, and they're about as convenient to portage, weight-wise, as an automatic cash machine. Best if you have someone along who knows how to balance it and avoid crocs.

Elephant

You can ride these oversized beasts in Thailand, Vietnam, India and other selected tourist haunts. If you can get over the smell and bargain your way to a decent price, it's a pretty comfortable and regal ride. Unless, of course, you're riding bareback.

Felucca

These ancient wooden sailing boats are most commonly associated with the Nile. Most travellers book tours in Aswan for three-day trips north, sleeping on the boat's cushioned decks. They're among the slowest sailing boats you'll ever encounter, but the tranquillity is unsurpassed. Don't forget to bring a good book.

Ferry

You may have a hard time trying to circumnavigate the planet by ferry, but they do connect a rather substantial part of the earth's shorter shipping lanes. Some are barely afloat and others are nearly as luxurious as their cruise-ship cousins, with hot tubs, saunas, movie theatres and discos, and all are more expensive if you try to bring along a car. For a web listing links of ferry lines around the world, try ◍http://routesinternational.com.

Horse

Equestrian travel can be incredibly romantic and exciting. You can take an African safari by horseback, cross mountains in the saddle or canter along the beach. But, in the words of Ian Fleming, "A horse is dangerous at both ends and uncomfortable in the middle." Make certain, therefore, you get a little practice before you head out on a longer journey, and spend some time getting to know your steed's signals before you need to interpret them in an emergency.

Jeepney

These converted 1940 US Army jeeps are a little too unique to be lumped together with the other minibuses; they have become one of the Philippines' most recognizable symbols. The Filipinos stretched jeep bodies to three or four times their original length, added rows of cushioned seats and about 20 kilos of glitz and paint.

Minibus

Better known, depending on the location, as a **beemo**, **dolmus**, **matatu** or **songthaew**, these privately owned small vans or pick-up trucks function as city buses and inter-city transporters. They aren't always cheaper than city buses, but they run more frequently and can be much easier to locate. It's not uncommon to find eighteen people crammed into one designed to hold seven, with the tout still trying to take on passengers. Your best bet is to grab a window seat near the front, opposite the sliding door, just in case the oxygen levels start to drop. Too close to the sliding door and you'll have a buttock in your face for the duration of the journey, most likely that of the designated fare collector (also charged with the task of corralling as many people as possible aboard) who generally prefers to stand and hang out the open entry.

Motorcycles

There are probably two hundred safer ways to navigate the planet, but few that offer the opportunity to do so in leather. Helmets and protective clothing are a must as road conditions and other drivers are often completely unpredictable. See p.42 for overland Carnet information and for the lowdown on buying an Enfield in India.

Motorized rickshaw

Mate a scooter with a golf cart and then drive it across Asia, and you'll get something that looks like a motorized rickshaw. You may recognize these yellow and black mini-transports from James Bond's *Octopussy*, and you'll certainly hear them coming. The mosquito-sounding engines get them going quick enough to somehow enter the flow of traffic. Meters exist, but they don't always work, or must be cross-referenced to some indexed price list. So consider learning the going rate and making a deal for the ride beforehand.

Ocean-going cargo ship

They come in all shapes and sizes, but few are appealing to the eye from the outside. The cabins can be another story, as more state rooms are being refitted for travellers. Getting on board is usually no small feat, but advance planning and fees are generally involved. See p.34 for more on travel by cargo ship.

On foot

There's no better way to get around than with your metatarsals. Pounding the pavement gives you the pulse of a place. According to author Wendell Berry, "Our senses were developed to function at foot speeds." Put another way, if you move though a new place faster than a few kilometres per hour, your eyes, ears and nose won't be able to register all the information they're getting. There are two classic variants of hoofing it: pick up a map, or simply wander until you're lost.

Overland trucks

See p.40.

River cargo ship

Smaller than their ocean-going sisters, and generally much easier to get passage on, river ships are a far more casual affair. On Amazonian ships, you string up a hammock on deck and sleep elbow to elbow. Thanks to an extensive canal network, much of Europe can be navigated by inland boats as well. Some are over-hauled luxury vessels for tourists, some are private mobile homes, and some are commercial barges. Look for passage on all three.

River kayak

These are short, rugged, and they tip easier than a toddler on rollerblades, so it's best to take a course when getting started. Because handling is so sensitive, most kayakers prefer their own boats. However on a long trip, you'll probably just have to make do with what's available on site. If you stick to the rafting epicentres, you'll find there's good equipment on hand and, depending on your skill level, you may be able to catch free rides with rafting trips working as a safety kayaker.

Sea kayak

Both the hardshell and the collapsible variety have merits, depending largely on how you're able to transport them. They're increasingly available for rent, so enquire before you drag yours halfway around the globe. You'll also need to check with airlines to see what additional fees are involved for taking them on board.

Subway

No matter how little there is to see out the window, make an effort to try out the subway once or twice. It's an integral part of any big city's character. Some offer incredibly high-speed and efficient transport, some are overdue for repair, and some are simply underground marvels. The lines in Moscow, St Petersburg, London, Tokyo, New York, Washington DC, Singapore and Stockholm are particularly worth a look.

Taxis

At home you might order a taxi or flag one down for a personal and usually short ride. You can do that on the road as well. But in developing nations, some taxis function more like minibuses, and the driver will commonly supplement his journey by giving as many people rides as possible along the way without deviating from his course. These are known as shared taxis or collectivos.

In other cases, you may (particularly if you can arrange a group of three or four travellers) decide to hire a taxi for an entire day, maybe longer. It's surprisingly cheap, and may make the most sense if there's a border crossing where the alternative is to take a bus followed by a long walk, or if there are a number of interesting sights located just outside the city centre. Arrange a price before starting out, but don't pay until it's over. Fuel should be paid separately to keep your driver from cruising along at an energy-efficient 10kph, refusing scenic detours, and trying to convince you that the air-con doesn't work.

Taxi thrills

A fight breaks out between the taxi drivers outside of my hotel in Cairo when they see me exiting. Eventually, I decide on one. I meticulously set the price before entering, though I still know I'm getting ripped off. The taxi takes off like a springbok with a bum full of dynamite. The drive is reminiscent of a computer game, only with bad smells. There are wall-to-wall beaten-up cars, five lanes of traffic (at least five) on a two-lane road. I can actually hear the taxi sucking in its breath as we pass between two other cars. Green means go in Cairo. Apparently so does red. And pedestrians are fair game. The driver tries to sell me a hubble-bubble pipe, demonstrating how it works as we hurtle through the city centre. I find it difficult to pay, as my hands are shaking so much. I find one aspect settling, and I try to cling on to it as I count the bills and coins: a bungy jump would have cost fifty times the price.

Craig Ayre

Trains

Remember to check that the train car you are boarding has the name of the city you are going to posted on the side, especially in Europe. If the individual car says "Hamburg" on it, that's where it's going. But that doesn't mean the entire train is going to Hamburg. In fact, there's a good chance it isn't. Trains drop off some cars and pick up others along the route, so you can easily end up someplace you hadn't counted on – and many do. It's tempting, especially with rail passes, to save money with a few nights on the train. See p.170 to find out why that's not a great idea, and the Regional Profiles at the end of this book to learn about supplementing your pass with other cost-effective travel.

Old locomotives are wonderful, if you can find any that haven't been turned into tourist rigs. They make you feel like a traveller, assuming they eventually get you where you're going. Some, like second-class Indian trains, give an excellent taste of the culture, while others, such as the rooftop rides in Ecuador, provide jaw-dropping vistas you can't get from the road.

With the most recent models (Japan's Bullet Train, France's TGV, Germany's ICE), it hardly feels like you're moving, never mind travelling. Until, that is, you catch the 250kph blur out the window. When high-speed trains are involved, it's almost always cheaper to get some type of railpass. (It may even be cheaper to fly.) There's a monopoly on the food, so plastic-wrapped sandwiches are priced like Michelin-star meals; fortunately, though, the rides don't last that long, so a few pack-along snacks should see you through.

For world-wide rail links see ⓦwww.routesinternational.com.

Tuk-tuks

Thailand's answer to discount taxis. These enlarged high-powered golf carts appear to have been decorated by someone on an acid trip: judging from the typically rapid lane changes and high-speed U-turns, it's probably the driver.

Water taxi

Found everywhere from Venice to Stockholm to the Bahamas, they're usually priced for vacationing millionaires, so make sure it's a special occasion before you flag one down.

Accommodation

Bolivia is a little too far to travel to stay at the Hilton. And your budget is likely to suffer from even one night's plush rest. It may take some time to get used to staying in budget digs, but it's more rewarding than it might initially seem. There's a sense of camaraderie that you simply won't find at the Ritz. You can swap tales at breakfast, make dinner together, play backgammon – it's a nomadic commune of sorts. The atmosphere changes from place to place, even day to day if enough new travellers pull in. You can also seek more interesting places from time to time: a hostel in a cave; a bed in a backyard tree house; an underwater hotel. Even if these unconventional digs cost a little more, it's usually worth the experience.

Camping

Traveller camping falls into two categories: free camping, which is usually illegal but pretty easy to do outside of big cities; and paid camping, at designated campsites with tickets and other amenities. If you plan to go down the free camp route, you'll probably need to give big cities a miss. Many of the city parks are too dangerous to sleep in, or too likely to be patrolled by police. Either way, you're in trouble. In smaller towns, you can usually find a field, perhaps even a remote part of a park, if you're discreet. Some designated campsites are quite extravagant, with a restaurant, supermarket and pool, but even the smaller ones can be surprisingly expensive – especially in Europe. For just a little more, you can often hire a walk-in tent with a "real" bed.

Farmstays

The name conveys the gist. You stay on a working farm where the family has made a few rooms available to those who are willing to pay for the experience. There's a significant range in comfort and price, but many of them dip well into the budget range ($30/£19.50 including breakfast). Some offer courses in riding or gardening, many provide family-style meals, and you can sample everything from grape-growing to a full cattle ranch. They're typically available in Australia (⊛www.heartlandfarmstays.com.au), New Zealand (⊛www .farmstay.co.nz), Europe (⊛http://pro.wanadoo.fr) the US (⊛www .mass.gove/DFA) and Argentina (⊛www.argentinatravel.com).

Guesthouses/pensions/B&B

These are typically private homes or apartments with a few spare rooms or bungalows in the backyard. They're often run by older people whose children have moved out, and who are looking to earn a little extra money by letting travellers into their private living space. This means showing a little more respect and courtesy than you might employ at a hostel. Even if it is rather lacking in services, keep in mind you're living in someone's home.

Homestays

Like farmstays, these are run by people who have opened their homes to paying visitors. They're often very reasonably priced – sometimes better than hostels – and give you a little insight into the way people live. You typically receive a private room and breakfast. You'll get your host's personal take on the country or city, which (for better or worse) is at least genuine and often interesting. It can otherwise be challenging to make contact with people who live in the country you're visiting. Some stipulate that they only accept women, couples, or enrolled students.

Go to a search engine, type in the name of the city you're heading to plus the word "homestay" or "homestays" and you'll probably get a selection to choose from.

Independent hostels

Independent hostels come in as many different shapes and sizes as rocks, which, coincidentally, is what some of them seem to use to stuff their mattresses. You'll find some setups extremely professional, particularly in Australia and New Zealand, where they've either been taken over by franchises or all read the same youth-hostel-starter-kit handbook. Some have great bar scenes with cheap food and people dancing on the tables in the evenings, others feel like giant, anaesthetized dormitory-type buildings with concierges. Others are blissfully charming and serene with hammocks and sofas and a chance to dine with the owners. They can be both centrally located and fiendishly remote, with little commonality other than being the cheapest digs in town. See p.54 on discount cards.

International youth hostels

No, you don't have to be a certain age to stay at a youth hostel. Being young at heart is enough. Official IYHs (all 4500-plus of them in more than 70 countries; ⓦwww.hostelbooking.com) are part of an organization, which means there are certain standards, although it does not mean the standards are terribly high. Nearly all of these are well cleaned, some practically sterile, with dormitory-style rooms and separate quarters for men and women, self-service kitchens, common rooms, and lockers, and a cost of $10–30/£6.50–19.50 per night. Some are equipped with pools, hot tubs, and barbecues while others are about as basic as their tree-and-hut logo. Even though they like to tout their lighthouse property in California and the tall sailing ship hostel in Sweden, IYHs don't usually earn many points in the architecture, cosiness or roaring-social-life departments. Most are located a little way out of the centre of town and come with a curfew (during the day and/or night). There are almost always budget alternatives, but if this sounds like your cup of discounted tea, pick up the $25/£16 membership card. If not, you're still welcome, but will pay slightly more. Try to book in advance if you know when you're arriving, especially in high season.

Sleeping rough

Ah, the last resort of the traveller, the safety net that leaves your back out of alignment, the experience that will help you overcome whatever was annoying you about hostels. At some point, it's likely you'll spend the night on a park bench or in a train station or airport lounge.

Even if you never do, it helps mentally to brace for the possibility. You probably won't be the only one doing this, so when it looks inevitable, start trying to secure a good spot. What's a good spot? You'll know it when you see it, if there is one. Not too hidden, not where people have to step over you, not right under bright lights. Corners are usually quite nice, and frequently coveted. You may be inadvertently borrowing the resting place of a "regular" – so be forewarned that many of them don't take kindly to this. Look for newspaper or cardboard to place under you; a cold marble floor will drain your body heat and make it difficult to rest. If you've got a travel partner, take turns staying awake. If not, make sure you're bear-hugging your backpack while you sleep. Alternatively, look for an all-night snack shop or bar and sip tea or coffee until the sun creeps up, then find a more comfortable place to sleep at a park or beach.

Eating

No matter what level of comfort you choose to travel in, you don't want to circle the globe without sampling local cuisines. Check out the markets, or follow your nose into a tiny restaurant and discover anything from Brazilian moqueca stews to hand-rolled pastas in Sicily to tongue-sizzling Indian curries. There's no need be paranoid about what passes your lips. If it looks truly vile (greenish drinking water), you might want to give it a miss. And, in developing nations, shellfish for sale anywhere but right off the fishing boat should probably be skipped. Otherwise, eat, drink, be merry, and see p.192 on lightning-fast cures for diarrhea.

Hostels

They know the budget of their customers better than anyone. Many hostels offer extremely cheap stews, sandwiches and plates of pasta. The ones that don't may offer cooking facilities. Team up with another traveller, or an entire group, head to the supermarket and make a meal together.

Restaurants

Eating at restaurants can run up your expenses quicker than almost anything else you do, so choose where you eat with care. As comforting as it may be to dine with other travellers, you'll often get a better deal ditching the guidebook, heading to the poorer parts of town and checking out places packed with locals that don't take credit cards. Here's one good tip: ask a construction worker for a recommendation. They're usually experts on cheap, filling meals.

Street vendors

Don't believe the intestine-quivering rumours. Not every street snack leads to a week in squatter solitaire. In fact, buying food from street vendors is a wonderful way to supplement your diet: some travellers manage to exist entirely on these often-exotic snacks. You can get fried grasshoppers and scorpions in China, which have more crunch than taste; delicious fried bananas with cinnamon in Indonesia; luscious pineapple on a stick in Thailand; salted cucumbers in Turkey; and warm and spicy bhajis in India.

McDonald's

On one hand, there's simply too much wonderful food out there to justify a trip to the Golden Arches. On the other, *McDonald's* has some rather exotic (albeit processed and chemically enhanced) dishes in addition to the old classics. For example, in New Zealand there's the Kiwi Burger, a quarter-pound cheeseburger with beetroot and eggs. In Uruguay, there's the McHuevo, a hamburger with a poached egg and mayo. India has the Maharaja Mac, a lamb burger. Turkey has the Köfte Burger, a spiced patty inside a bun enriched with yoghurt mix. The point is, if you absolutely must get your McFix while you're on the road (and these places are packed with travellers), you can at least give yourself a push to try something new.

Traveller cafés

You can't miss them. They're filled with travellers, plus the ubiquitous banana pancakes and mango milkshakes and toasted cheese sandwiches served to the beat of a Van Morrison song. These oases for the Western palate are what keep many travellers sane. They also keep many travellers from venturing into more interesting dining and drinking establishments.

Personal hygiene

Staying clean on the road is a challenge at times. The times it becomes particularly rough are during the back-to-back long-transit rides (an overnight bus ride followed by a long plane trip); walking in hot, humid cities; and when you're not feeling well. If you can't handle the toilets, that can be a problem as well. Either way, relief can be found.

Airports and buses

Many airports now have showers available for a small fee. Some have a sauna and gym as well. You may have to hunt around a little, as they're not as well situated as the duty-free items and postcard vendors. Even if you have to put your yet-unwashed clothes back on, a refreshing shower ($1–4/65p–£2.50) can be an enormous boost. And you probably have some spare coins to get rid of anyway. If you don't take the opportunity during a long haul, the smell is only going to get worse. The budget route, of course, is simply to wash in the toilet, perhaps with a paper-towel shower, and swing by the duty free and take a squirt of perfume before the next leg of your journey.

On nicer bus rides, particularly around Turkey and the Middle East, don't be surprised if an attendant comes by and offers you a splash of unisex perfume or some fragranced towelettes. They're not as nice as the warm flannels distributed by many airlines, particularly considering they have the olfactory properties of toilet-bowl cleaner, but it's still better than being trapped beside someone with nuclear B.O. The individually wrapped moist tissues function better since they also remove the dirt and odour rather than simply masking it. Bring some of your own just in case.

Turkish bath

A perfect remedy for travel grime – the accumulated film that covers your body after weeks with low-pressure showers. These medieval bath houses are mild steamrooms with washbasins, sometimes a hot pool and a steamier section, and most offer, for an additional fee, a joint-cracking, back-popping, skin-blasting "massage" that will leave you feeling like a boneless chicken. Upon exiting, you can cool down wrapped in towels with a refreshing yoghurt drink.

Japanese bath

No trip to Japan is really complete without a dip at a "sento" or its outdoor cousin, the "onsen". These public baths are sometimes as elegantly crafted as temples – or as commercial-looking as shopping malls. They offer scalding water, some with herbal mixes or stimulating electric shocks. It's as cultural as it is therapeutic, relatively inexpensive (the outdoor ones are often free), and will keep you clean in a country that practically demands it.

Toilets

Alert readers may notice this section is slightly longer than the ones above. That's because using a foreign toilet is rather more complex than catching a taxi or finding a traveller café. To find out how to avoid visiting the toilet too often, see p.192. Meanwhile, here's a look at a few of the more common models you may end up facing.

Squatter

The idea with these is that you are supposed to squat over the hole and, like a B-2 bomber, hit the target. Place your feet on the small foot-size platforms provided and align your hole with the one in the floor, which usually means facing the way you came in as you would on a Western toilet. There's rarely anything to hold on to, or anything you'd want to hold on to, so the obvious danger is simply losing your balance and falling backwards. The less apparent danger is that squatting causes your pants pockets to become somewhat inverted, so your valuables may go sliding irretrievably down the hole. And if this doesn't sound challenging enough, remember you may have to hold a flashlight in your mouth since these lavatories often don't have decent lighting or, sometimes, any lighting at all.

Don't know squat

What gets lost, I think, amid all the fretting and complaining about toilets in the so-called Third World is this: it's just a hole.

A hole, and nothing more.

It's an undeniably elegant design, brilliant in its simplicity – a place to poop, I posit, that far surpasses anything we have in the United States.

This notion is reinforced on almost all my trips. Usually, the last place I use a bathroom in the US is at the airport. You know the type of stall – one where you have to place a sheet of what looks like deli paper on the seat, and then lower yourself gingerly down so the paper doesn't become a slip'n'slide, and then sit there while the electric-eye flush mechanism is triggered three or four times for no apparent reason, often dampening your nether regions, and then, of course, with all this careful hygiency, you have to grab the lock on the stall door – the one spot you can be certain that every unwashed hand has been placed – and then head to the sinks and hope the electric eyes work there, and then, finally, dispense yourself a paper towel by grabbing a lever that, once again, everyone has touched, thereby negating your hand-washing.

After I land – in Africa, in Asia, in Central America – my toilet facilities usually consist of this: a hole.

A hole, and nothing more.

A place where no fleshy parts make contact with any toilet parts.

Why it's not common knowledge that Third World toilets are superior to all other toilets comes down to one notion – we don't know squat.

That is, we don't know how to squat. We come from a baseball land – we squat like catchers, up on our toes. This is wrong. Proper hole-squatting technique demands a flat-footed stance. It's difficult at first, I'll confess, but if you work on it at home it'll soon become second nature.

So, first get the squat down.

Next, go travel.

And then you, too, will learn to love the hole.

Michael Finkel, National Geographic Adventure contributor and author of *Alpine Circus*

△ Be open to new experiences

And by the way, there's no toilet paper. Most of the world goes without. If you look closely, you'll see there's a little plastic bowl and a water tap in every stall next to the hole. The idea is you wipe with your left hand (no, I'm not kidding) then wash it off under the water. There's probably no soap, so you can choose to wash with soap later, bring your own, or do like the locals and just use the right hand for eating and shaking hands. Or just bring your own toilet paper. How to flush the hole is not entirely apparent. There's no little handle to push. No knob to turn. You have to fill up the plastic bowl a few times and dump the water into the hole and let water displacement take care of the rest.

Almost-Western

This one looks like a Western model, but it was installed by someone who may not have fully understood the directions that came with the assembly kit. Or lacked the necessary tools. If you're lucky enough to find one with a seat, you'll notice it's usually secured by something with the strength of chewing gum, so if you don't sit down exactly straight, the seat detaches and you slide right off the porcelain rim, which – take it from me – can be pretty painful.

More commonly, however, the plastic seat is missing altogether. This means that you're back to squatting again. Only now it's more difficult because you can't do a regular squat; you have to do a "standing squat" so you can clear the rim of the toilet. This usually entails bracing yourself with one hand on the wall behind you, which is highly exhausting for your arm and leg muscles and often makes them cramp painfully.

A few of these bathrooms do come equipped with paper, but it's usually the sort that Rambo would be afraid to use. Some provide strips of newspaper or a glossy magazine on a nail. So, while you're sitting there (or semi-squatting) use your time wisely by crumpling and uncrumpling the paper until it's almost tolerable. This takes about twenty minutes with the glossy stuff, so you may want to start working on it before you actually get to the toilet. (In an emergency, simply employ this technique with a few of your guidebook pages.) Whatever you use, if there's a little waste bin beside the toilet, put your used paper there. Don't even think of throwing your used paper into the toilet. These loos, though they may look vaguely like ours, have a violent reaction to toilet paper: even one square of proper loo-paper brought from home can clog it for about a month.

Japanese toilets

Most of these models have more wires than Keith Richards' guitar, more features than a scientific calculator and the comfort of a beanbag chair. These commodes do just about everything but brush your teeth, although I'm sure technicians are working on that now.

The control panel is sometimes built in next to the throne and sometimes on a remote-control device attached to the wall with a Velcro patch, so you could conceivably remove it and flush the toilet from across the room. It automatically raises and lowers the seat with the press of a button. Another button creates natural, camouflaging noise when you need it. A quiet vacuum under the seat continuously pumps any noxious emissions through an air filter and a dial controls the temperature of the seat. There are three separate

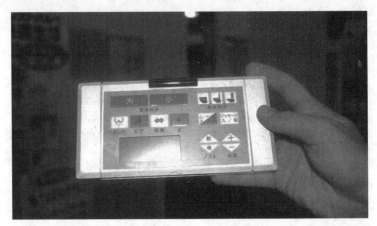

△ All this, just to flush – Japanese toilet control

buttons for the rinse cycle: one is exclusively for women, the second creates a gentle rinse of the backside and the third calls up a power spray. When you push one of these, a small plastic spigot creeps out from underneath the rear of the seat and commences cleaning. You can, of course, adjust the temperature to your liking.

Are you a tourist or a traveller?

Why on earth should you go out of your way to try some sport or activity you've never heard of and will probably never do again? Why bother with the slow, less comfortable modes of transport? Why go anywhere near a squat toilet or, for that matter, a Vietnamese ear cleaner armed with what seems to be shish-kebab skewers?

Because if you're not doing something new, you're doing something you've done before. If you're not taking local transport, you're taking Western-style transport. If you're not using the local language (or hand gestures and phrasebooks), you're probably speaking with professional guides and concierges. If you're not staying in places with local standards, you're staying in places with Western standards. If you're not eating local food, you're probably eating food you know from home. If you're not using the local toilets, you're using Western ones. The creature comforts (and language) of Western life are now available virtually everywhere, and if you don't go on a creature-comfort diet, you'll be getting a Disneyfied view of the place you're trying to see. It's often the inconvenient and uncomfortable elements that give travel its extra dimension, and separate the Sphinx in Las Vegas from the one in Egypt, the gondola ride in the Epcot Center from the one in Venice – and the tourists from the travellers.

Higher-end models also feature a pulsating "massage" spray. Then there's the built-in blow-dryer to complete the treatment. Whatever you do, don't jump up if you push the wrong button or the whole bathroom might be doused with water. Most are equipped with some kind of emergency stop button. Make sure you can find it before you begin your journey.

13

Culture shock

Culture shock is simply a dramatic way of saying that things aren't quite the way they are at home. It sounds dramatic precisely because it can be. When you change everything you eat, say, do, smell and hear at the same time, the effect can be overwhelming. Especially if amplified by sadness or apprehension about leaving home, fatigue from the journey or illness. The natural tendency is to return home immediately. But if you give yourself time, it will almost certainly pass.

Combating culture shock

Researchers in the 1970s and 1980s developed an idea that the individual traveller didn't need to embrace all or even most aspects of the society, just some key features to be able to operate within the culture. By reading this and simply being aware of the phenomenon, you're already a step ahead. Here are several practical things you can do to minimize culture shock:

● Recognize it for what it is: a reaction to sensory overload and unfamiliar surroundings. (Oh, that's just a bout of culture shock – I'll be fine soon.) Look at the upside of what it represents: you're getting new experiences, new insights, and a new perspective. How bad is that?

- Start your journey in countries similar to your own.
- Read up on the place before you arrive. You're going there to experience what that country has to offer, but a little knowledge can decrease the number of cultural surprises. It can be enough for some to just buy the guidebook a day before departure and start reading background information, but reading a novel set in that country will do far more to get you in the mood.
- Get some sleep on the plane (see p.194). Jetlag gets your trip off on the wrong foot.
- If you are making a large cultural jump early in your trip, you can do a number of things to ease into your new location. Start by staying in a Western-style hotel for a day or two, and looking for cheaper, local digs after you've had a chance to acclimatize. Or simply spend some time just relaxing in a nice hotel lobby free of charge and don't return to your hostel until you're ready to examine the back of your eyelids.
- Speak to other travellers. Compare observations.
- Keep a journal.
- Allow yourself to get excited about your trip. It's natural to be a little nervous about what's ahead, but focus on converting that into positive energy.

Four stages of culture shock

Everyone has slightly different reactions, so this may not provide a complete blueprint for your adaptation. The speed of the process also varies, and many people go through different phases more than once.

1 Honeymoon
Cultural differences are intriguing and the new sites are fascinating. You are still comforted by the close memory of your home culture.

2 Crisis
After some time abroad, differences begin to affect you. Differences in language, concepts and values begin to create feelings of confusion and anxiety. (This is normal. It's a sign you're reconnecting with your own cultural values.)

3 Recovery
You begin to accept the differences and feel comfortable in new situations. Often the crisis dissipates as language skills improve.

4 Adjustment
Despite occasional bouts of strain, you're enjoying the new culture and able to make choices based on preferences and values.

Your travel philosophy

What you take with you on your trip will, to a large extent, determine the experience you take away from it. And in this case, I'm not referring to the dual-current hairdryer that you should probably leave at home. I'm talking about your travel philosophy: your approach to dealing with the cultures you encounter.

You'll face this the moment you begin your journey. People you meet off the "beaten track" tend to be more genuine, as they haven't been hardened by years of loud tour groups and tough-bargaining backpackers. If you're well off the trail, a situation common among independent travellers, you're in a more culturally fragile environment and should thus move about and interact with deliberate care.

Here are a few concepts to keep in mind:

- You are a guest in a foreign country. Be a gracious guest. Travel with an open mind and a desire to learn.
- Familiarize yourself with local customs and make an effort to learn at least a few words of the local language. Your efforts will make an impression on those you meet. (How would you react to someone who came to your country and asked you for directions in another language, then spoke louder and more slowly when you didn't understand?)
- Be a sensitive photographer. Be discreet or ask permission. And consider the long-term implications before paying someone in cash or sweets to take their photograph.
- Bargain and resolve conflicts with a smile.
- Look beyond the tourist streets and resorts. Make an effort to meet and spend time with at least one local who is not trying to sell you any goods or services.
- Pay attention to the local dress. Shorts, vest tops and other revealing items often aren't appropriate. Better to choose styles and colours that help you blend in rather than display the latest fashions from your own country.
- Don't litter or waste electricity and water.

Tourism impact

How about the "shock" of your impact on other cultures? Last year alone, the World Tourism Organization reported 699 million international arrivals. In other words, over half a billion people took a trip abroad. With high-speed trains connecting jumbo jets to quick-check-in rental cars, the world is now more conveniently, comfortably and cheaply accessed than ever before. With a few clicks of the mouse and a valid credit card, travellers can send themselves around the planet. Yet just ten of the richest countries account for nearly sixty percent of all international travel. And hundreds of millions of these trips are short, packaged vacations to beaches and quaint, picturesque towns in comparatively poor lands, where visitors can enjoy comforts they couldn't or wouldn't pay for at home.

The travel industry obliges by creating an easy-to-navigate infrastructure complete with parking lots to handle dozens of tour buses; view-blocking, shadow-casting luxury hotels right on the beach; colourful costumes for evening cultural dance programmes; light shows with multilingual recorded voice-overs; and air-conditioned restaurants. The locals that travellers are most likely to encounter have been trained to accommodate: they speak the tourists' languages and sell items they desperately need (film, sun lotion, beer).

But is contact with visitors and their money making the lives of local people better? For some, yes. At least by Western standards. You see many driving more comfortable cars and living in nicer homes as a result. The money can also bring better drinking water, better schools and better medicine, but it doesn't always. How it affects the social fabric of a place is difficult to calculate.

Especially when you meet teachers who gave up their jobs to earn more selling postcards or bracelets. Oddly, the people who don't seem to benefit are the ones tourists are most interested to photograph: rug weavers, cloth embroiderers and donkey cart drivers. They seem to be working like mad with little to show for it.

With good reason, travel publications have long asserted that mass tourism destroys the very things – quaintness, genuine hospitality, serenity, unique culture – that attracted visitors in the first place. Truth be known, we independent budget travellers contribute to this as well, probably more than we'd care to admit. Simply by being aware of your impact though, you'll probably make more thoughtful decisions about where you spend your money and how you interact with people.

14

Staying in touch

Not long ago, staying in touch was a reasonably straightforward affair. Unreliable mail services, expensive telegrams and uncooperative pay phones that ate coins by the fist-full were your only options. Now, perhaps the most difficult aspect of staying in touch is choosing how you want to do it. On a bare-bones budget you can get by with a free email account and the occasional reverse-charge call.

Communications kit

This is the long-awaited phone plan designed for travellers that's actually useful. For a fairly complete communication package, eKit (⊛ekit.com) provides a discount phone-card account that works in eighty countries, a voice-mail account that allows you to listen to messages by phone or for free over the Internet, an email account with 50MB storage, access to a Web service that allows you to send and receive faxes as easily as email and an electronic vault where you can securely store backups of your passport, travellers' cheque numbers, credit cards and other essential documents. The vault is free and you're essentially just paying for your calls and faxes – an account you preload by credit card. The calls cost around $1.5/£1-$5/£3 for four minutes of international chatting. They also provide a 24-hour customer service operator in English, German, French, Spanish and Portuguese. If you're somewhere you can't access it, you'll have to use one of the other methods listed below. And for local calls you're best off buying a local phone card or buying a local SIM card for your mobile phone.

Email

With time zones and long-distance charges, email is going to be your best ally for almost-immediate contact. You can knock off one letter then send it in bulk, or alter it for specific people with a little cutting and pasting and save yourself (not to mention your metacarpal ligaments) the hassle. Unless you're writing a novel along the way, there's no reason to bring a laptop. You can get Internet access virtually anywhere. And by anywhere, I really mean anywhere. Nearly all hostels are now equipped with a connection, and if they're not, you shouldn't have to walk more than five or ten minutes to find an Internet café. Expect to pay anything from $0.50/£0.30 to $3/£2 for fifteen minutes, although libraries, universities and many hotels offer free access. Just make sure you're set up with an account you can check from the Web. If you have a digital camera, you can easily include photos as you go. Some cafés are equipped with a scanner, so developed film can be sent for a slight additional cost. (For other photo options, see p.208.)

Over communication

I spent my first thirty minutes in Asia standing outside an Internet café waiting for my friends to finish writing to people back home about the trip over. Even in remote areas, Net access was cheap and easy to find, making it a painless way to stay connected to home... and with the nearest familiar place an ocean away, feeling connected became something I found myself wanting more and more.

From Internet cafés in Northern Thailand, I was moderating room-mate disputes, checking sports scores and typing out relationship advice to friends back home more often than I did when I lived there. Pretty soon I was less focused on my adventures in Asia than I was on finding a high-speed connection. And I wasn't alone. Internet connectivity has become a common addiction on the travel trail.

Eventually, I learned to check once a week, limit myself to one good mass email a month, and cheerfully neglect the day-to-day stuff, which gave me enough distance to experience the culture I came for. No one back home seemed to mind. When you're living in villages and sleeping on trains, nobody expects you to be plugged in 24-7.

Jonathon Werve

Snail mail

Sadly, letter writing is becoming a lost art. There's still nothing quite as nice as receiving an actual letter from abroad: the stamps, the smell and knowing it had to travel around the planet to get to you. The proliferation of email simply makes the occasional postcard or letter all the more special. It's easy to forget this while you're on the road hopping from one Internet café to the next, but it's worth the effort and is likely to strengthen friendships and ensure you'll be getting mail from your travelling friends in years to come.

Sending packages

Depending on the place, sending a package can take anywhere from five minutes to five hours. There are a few tricks you can use to simplify the process, but they all revolve around the same concept: scout out the requirements before you try to mail something. In some countries, there are special postal boxes you can buy that will speed up the shipping process. More often there are package weight limits in various price categories. (It's a drag to show up with your carefully wrapped package, only to learn you're 20 grams over a price cut-off, which will cost you an additional $15/£10.) Sometimes you can get good bargains within a lower weight range, so if you divide up a larger package you can actually save money. Before you start wrapping, swing by the post office and find out about the rates and any wrapping requirements. Quite possibly, you'll need string, cloth, forms and a wax seal, but bear in mind that you may end up having to open packages for inspection. Consult your guidebook for local tips.

Surface mail

Surface mail is fairly reliable, cheap and slower than a snail with a hangover. It's perfect for sending home items you realize you no longer need (or never did), inexpensive souvenirs, worn-out clothing you simply couldn't part with, and so on. Just about the time you've forgotten you sent it, it'll arrive, prodded and shaken by countless customs officers, like a gift from the heavens.

Registered mail and major couriers

If you're sending anything of value, such as jewellery you purchased, a filled diary or film, don't use the regular mail service. Spend the extra money for registered mail to make sure it arrives. If the local mail service has an especially shoddy track record, go straight for a private delivery company such as DHL or FedEx.

Sending film

To protect your film from the strong postal X-ray machines, make sure you wrap it in aluminium foil. Tear off a long sheet of foil before leaving home and fold it neatly into a flat rectangle that can easily fit between the pages of your journal or address book. Then rip off palm-sized pieces to wrap each film roll before putting it into its little black plastic canister. The question is where to send it: to your family for (hopefully free) development; or to an online photo-developing service that will put your pics on the Web before sending the negatives or prints to your family.

Receiving mail and packages

If you're organized enough to plan an itinerary, you could send it off to your friends and relatives with a note trying to encourage some letter writing. Mail and packages can be sent to you marked with the city, country, and the words "Poste Restante, Central Post Office". If you have an American Express card or at least one AmEx travellers' cheque, you can also pick up your mail at their global offices found in nearly every major city. Addresses can be found on the Web at ⓦwww.americanexpress.com. Note that most AmEx offices do not accept parcels, just letters. If you don't have an AmEx card or travellers' cheques and don't trust the main post office with a valuable delivery, you could, for a small fee (or perhaps nothing if you find a kind clerk) make a delivery arrangement at a top-end hotel.

Forwarded mail

Check with your national mail carrier to see if your post can be forwarded for free or an additional charge. The Royal Mail (ⓦwww.royalmail.com) charges £13 for one month, £42 for six months and £63 for a year if you know where you'll be. The catch is you have to stay in one place for at least a month. For up to two months, they'll hold your mail for £15.75. Canada Post (@www.canadapost.ca) offers international redirection for C$54 for three months and C$18 per month thereafter. Holding mail services cost $6 for the first 10 business days and $3 per additional week. In Australia (@www.auspost.com.au), a year of forwarded mail costs A$66.00 (not sent internationally) and mail holding rates are A$9 for the first week and A$4 for each additional week. In the US (@www.usps.com), they'll only hold your mail for up to 30 days, but won't charge for it. New Zealand Post (@www.nzpost.co.nz) will hold mail for an unspecified period of time at no cost. Best, of course, is if you can have a friend or relative filter out the junk mail and send stuff on.

Phoning

There's not much that can make up for a loved one's voice, even if the signal does sound like it's being bounced off Mars. The rates on different types of call differ dramatically. Making the right choice could save you over $20/£13 on a single five-minute overseas conversation. Much of this depends on if you're on the move or staying still. Plus, bringing a mobile phone is becoming an increasingly viable option, and with the right approach you won't feel shackled to it.

Callback

This is a relatively new concept, but works well for those who are staying in one place for a while (for work or study for example) and

Learning the local rates can save you a fortune.

Sample: **Sweden to the US, four-minute call**

From private phone: $0.50/£0.30
International prepaid card: $1.20/£0.80
eKit phone service: $2.20/£1.40
Monthly billed card: $3.20/£2
US mobile phone (not including minimum $20/£13 monthly fee): $4/£2.60
Satellite phone (not including minimum $25/£16 monthly access fee or $50/£32 activation fee): $8/£5
From hotel room (with hotel charges): $14/£9
AT&T calling card: $18/£11.50
AT&T collect call: $19/£12

△ You toucan stay in touch

have access to a private phone they're not supposed to use for international calls. It may sound a little complex, but really it's quite simple. Once you've set up an account by contacting a callback service and providing a billing address and credit card number, it works like this: you dial a special number, let it ring once, then hang up. This part doesn't cost a thing. In a few seconds, you get a call back. When you pick up the receiver, you get a dial tone. Then you just dial as if you're in your home country. You can make several calls without hanging up by pressing a few designated keys after each call (such as # three times). The phone bill is automatically paid by credit card and sent wherever you'd like it. This is likely to be around 30–40 cents a minute, but depends on the call.

Collect calls

Many of the major national phone companies have set up special numbers in nearly every country so that you can be connected directly with an operator back home. This allows you to reverse the charges – otherwise, you'll have to use a local operator. Check your guidebook for local numbers. This service is convenient but it's not cheap, and works best in emergencies or if people back home are so happy to hear from you they won't mind the charges.

Fax

Email hasn't rendered these machines obsolete just yet. In remote locations where you need a document quickly, can't access email, or can't afford the local calls, it's an ideal alternative. Keep those fax numbers handy just in case.

International phone cards

There are two basic types: prepaid cards and monthly billed cards. Of the two, prepaid cards tend to provide better rates, but they can expire after one to three months (some last longer), so any remaining unused funds on your card are lost. Also, surcharges may apply when using the card at a payphone. To check out the prices and purchase a card, try ⓦwww.besttelephonerates.com. Bear in mind however, that an international prepaid card will not necessarily get you better rates than a locally bought phone card; it differs from country to country. For the monthly variety, there's a wide range.

Most of the major phone companies have their own international calling card programmes. The charges can be added to your or someone else's existing phone bill, but it's not likely to be the cheapest option, especially with discount services set up, many of which are offered by the callback companies or travel services such as eKit.

Local phones

You'll still encounter the money-eating coin phone, but it's much more likely you'll be using a phone card (available at most kiosks) that can be inserted into the phone. These come in a variety of values and often offer a good deal, provided you end up using the entire amount. Try to find out how much you'll need before buying the card, then keep an eye on the clock once you start talking. Usually, you can see the units tick away as you speak, so you'll have a good idea when the conversation is going to be cut off. Sometimes there are special overseas phones that offer better rates; your guidebook should advise you on that.

Mobile phone

Carrying a mobile phone is a decision worth thinking about. In that one emergency situation, it could save you, or make life much easier. But it may feel like an expensive ball and chain for the rest of the trip, unless you leave it turned off and have the calls diverted to your eKit voice-mail service, a family member, or simply leave a message instructing people to email you. First, you'll want a triple-band phone. These start around $150/£96, not including monthly fees. If you plan to stay somewhere for a while and want to make use of your mobile phone locally, buying a local SIM card makes the most sense. These cost $30–60/£19–38 and can be refilled easily. Or stick with a subscription back home and pay the steep surcharges for each international call. Remember, you'll have to pay these surcharges for accepting calls as well, so if you use your phone for anything but emergencies, the bill will be frightening, not to mention making you a target for theft.

Satellite phone

This isn't really a viable option for travellers. For field researchers on a corporate budget, it can be ideal (Globalstar makes a 12oz model that uses 46 orbiting satellites). But the $800+/£500+ heavy phones and high per-minute rates make it impractical at best. Besides, it doesn't work indoors.

Telephone centres

These old phone centres can be charming: there's no reason to be intimidated by them. You simply fill out a form stating who you want to call and the number where they can be reached. When the operator gets them on the line, she points you to a phone cabin and connects the call. You pay after the call is completed. It's often possible to make reverse-charge calls this way.

Webphone

If you're on the move, you'll need a headset and special software installed in the computer, so it's not a realistic plan as long as it's not offered at most Internet cafes. But that could change in the near future. A webphone allows you to dial from a PC to a phone and pay a fraction of the best rates (1.9 cents a minute, on one plan). It's a great idea. The downside is that audio quality is not yet up to par, so you're likely to hear an annoying echo. If this doesn't seem like such a bad trade-off for the savings, try ⓦwww.net2phone.com or ⓦwww .iconnecthere.com.

Keeping up with current events

When you're in travel mode, it can be easy to feel too removed from current events to bother with a newspaper. Some distance can be wonderful, but keeping an eye on things can also keep you safe. You don't want to unwittingly walk into a war zone or riot. Don't neglect the local press, provided you can read the language; besides, there's often an English edition. These are usually the cheapest newspapers and magazines and are most likely to tell you about local security issues as well as events, sales and performances you may not want to miss. For a taste of home, you'll be able to find most major international newspapers in big cities. They're expensive, but sometimes provided for free in nice hotel lobbies. And there's always the Internet. Check out your home-town paper on the Web from time to time; there are usually things going on that your family and friends forget to tell you about.

15

Security

Most of the world is extremely peaceful, though this can be hard to tell from the media. Television coverage of riots, wars, terrorist incidents, volcano eruptions, hurricanes and famines may keep you up to date with unfolding world affairs, but won't do much to awaken your wanderlust. Nor will it convey an accurate picture of the level of danger abroad. When Prague's Vltava River flooded in 2002, it made front-page news around the world, as it should. The floodwaters subsided soon after, but the images of Prague underwater didn't. In this chapter you'll find out where to get good information, how to determine if a place is actually dangerous, how to take precautions as you go, how to avoid scams and what to do if things actually do go wrong.

Is my destination safe?

Start by getting the official position of state departments. But keep in mind, a country can be very safe but for a single, remote border dispute. The UK Foreign Office website (✆www.fco.gov.uk) is more likely than the others to specify the volatile area when they place an entire country on warning; cross-check with Canada's Consular Affairs department (✆www.voyage.gc.ca), Australia's Department of Foreign Affairs (✆www.dfat.gov.au) or the US State

Dept (@http://travel.state.gov). Syria, for instance, has a consular warning as a "terrorist-supporting nation", but travellers have been visiting safely for years. So a travel warning does not necessarily mean you should not go – it just means you should investigate a step further. That step is checking your guidebook. Nearly all the major guides have security information. They may very well explain that the country has had a strong travel advisory for years, yet remains extremely popular with travellers and is quite safe but for a single easily avoidable region. However, even recent editions get out of date quickly, especially in terms of political unrest, so check guidebook websites as well.

If you're still uncertain, surf the Web for tourist bureaus. You can almost always find an email address of a specific office within that country. The people who staff the counters meet travellers all day and generally have a good feel for travel conditions. Tell them your nationality, when you're planning to travel and roughly where you hope to go. Ask if there are any security issues you should be concerned about. Lastly, check with other travellers. Visit Internet chat sites so you can hear directly from travellers who've been there in recent weeks, or are still in the country: try Rough Guide's message board, Travel Talk (@http://roughguides.atinfopop.com); Let's Go's Forum (@www.letsgo.com/forums); or Lonely Planet's Thorn Tree (@http://thorntree.lonelyplanet.com).

If the political climate changes

If the political conditions take a turn for the worse, you probably don't want to stick around to check out the mass riots, no matter how exciting it may seem. And if you're American, you probably don't want to go to the US Embassy either (often a prime target, so they shut their doors when the going gets rough). The Australian embassy, Canadian embassy, New Zealand embassy, UK embassy and others should be fine – even for American citizens. The other option is to get out of town immediately (it's rarely a country-wide riot). If you hadn't picked up some discreet local clothes yet, this would be the right time. Keep an eye on the local news, and head to an Internet café if necessary to find English updates.

How to avoid being robbed

The trick here is to blend in, keep out of areas where you're likely to become a target, stay alert, carry your valuables securely and provide yourself with a quick exit when you need one.

Start by removing all jewellery (if necessary covering a wedding or engagement ring with a band-aid or tape). Wear a cheap digital watch or no watch at all. Keep your camera well concealed. Then you'll want to wear clothing that blends in, the more discreet the better. A little tip: safari pants with zip-off legs and a photo-journalist vest are generally not what the locals are wearing.

Show that you don't have much to steal – or that you have less than other potential targets. With just a backpack and no carry-on bag, you have both your hands free and can remain mobile for a quick get-away or to give pursuit, so robbing you looks like more of a challenge. Finally, consider disguising your pack in developing countries. The small padlocks and wire mesh pack-covers will do little to protect your pack, but they will draw attention to the value of its contents. Plastic rice bags are easy to find, dirt cheap, decrease the perceived value of the pack's contents, and make great rain covers. It takes five or ten seconds more to access your pack's interior, but it can make you less of a target. Cut two slits for your shoulder straps, then sew or use duct tape to fasten.

Packing for safety

Don't keep your money and passport in a handbag or daypack, or even in a wallet. Use a secure travel pouch. A waist pouch kept under the waistline of your trousers is quite effective, and similar pouches that hang around your neck (under the shirt) or fasten to your ankle are also available. Just make sure you don't access it in busy areas like train stations and markets. Walk over to a more discreet spot and, if you have a travel companion, you can make a privacy shield if you stand between them and a wall so that your actions are hidden.

To protect your slightly-less-valuables, wear your backpack on your front in crowded places and don't use a backpack for a day bag. Because it's inconvenient to wear a day backpack on your front all day for city exploration, use a shoulder bag and keep it tucked tighter under your arm in crowded places. Try to find a model with Velcro flaps, which are difficult to open without you noticing, or a double-entry system (eg a zip plus a clasp). "Bum bags" (waist packs) are thief magnets and as such are best avoided — at least avoid keeping your valuables there.

And finally, don't keep all your money in one place. Stash some emergency funds in the secret compartment of a belt, or tape some (in a small plastic bag) to the inside of your backpack.

Avoiding dangerous areas

Often a hundred metres can be the difference between a completely safe street and a dangerous one. And these boundaries may change after dark. Ask your hotel clerk or tourist office staff to mark the dangerous areas on your map (both day and night). No matter where you are, get in the habit of checking over your shoulder and across the street every now and then. Even in crowded markets, you can see if you're getting followed after a few turns. But be particularly aware after dark. Muggers can easily hide in doorways, so the closer you are to the street, the less chance they have to surprise you. If you spot one or more suspicious characters in a doorway up ahead, cross the street. Or hop in a taxi if you've got a bad feeling about the area. Trust your gut feeling and always keep enough change ready to pay for a short cab ride. For less than $1, you can quickly get yourself back to a safer area. Otherwise, walk with confidence. When you're in an area you're not sure of, resist the temptation to pull out your map on a street corner. Keep up a brisk pace and duck inside a coffee shop or store to study the map or ask directions.

Take a few extra precautions in bus and train terminals, where many pickpockets lurk. If you need to pretend you're a secret agent to stay alert and pull this off, so be it. One simple method is to walk around the perimeter of the station instead of crossing it so you can keep a wall on one side and your eyes on anyone approaching. Another trick is to keep a decoy wallet in your pocket. Empty your wallet except for $5–20 and a non-essential ID and a few random photos or business cards. Use your pack as a pillow or hold it while you sleep. Once in transit, it's not enough to put your pack up on the luggage rack overhead or beneath your seat, where any thief could get it without waking you. Use it as a pillow or bear-hug it while you sleep.

Also, get in the habit of avoiding the tables near doors or bordering sidewalks in cafés. A quick thief can grab your gear and run. Keep your bag under your table while you eat, with the strap around your leg. If you need to use the toilet, take your bag along. You can't expect someone else to guard your bag as closely as you do.

Accommodation safety

It's not just local thieves – travellers steal as well. Sad, but true. There's much threat to your dirty laundry, but your

continued.....

Lebanon Army stepped aside. I walked into Israeli-occupied territory.

I had no idea what to do next. Then I realized that, on a hilltop about fifty yards away, there was an Israeli gun emplacement. A .50 calibre machine gun was pointed at my chest. The Israeli soldier behind the machinegun made a "come here" motion. I had to walk up the hill. The machine gun was trained on me the whole time. I was thinking, "Wait a minute. My tax dollars paid for that machine gun. That is my machine gun." But of course I didn't say so.

I asked the Israelis if anyone spoke English. The company commander certainly did. He was from Santa Barbara and had gone to UCLA. He said, "What the f—— are you doing here?"

I said, "I'm on vacation."

And he began to laugh. He said, "Actually, I'm a reservist, and as a matter of fact this is my vacation. Have a good time." And he let me through. I walked away from the Israeli military positions and found a taxi cab. I told the cab driver, "I want to go to the ruins."

The cab driver stared at me. "Lebanon," he said, "is all ruins."

P.J. O'Rourke, author of *Eat the Rich, Holidays in Hell, Give War a Chance* and others

valuables still need to be guarded. At night, cameras and suchlike are better left at the reception desk in a safe, in a hostel locker if provided, or behind the counter if there's someone keeping an eye on it. Some places also offer the reception safe to travellers who need a place to keep their passport pouch while at the beach – which is better than taking it along. Otherwise, treat your passport pouch like your spleen: sleep with it (or put it in your pillow case) and take it along when you shower – you can hang the pouch on the hook, just under your towel *inside* the shower stall.

Some hotels require your passport for a few hours to gather information. They should not require it any longer than that. Ask for it back as soon as they're done.

If you have everything stolen

Fortunately, this is not as much of a hassle as it used to be (except for Americans, who are now required to return to the US for a new passport). You could very well have everything you need – credit cards, passport and cash – in one to ten days. But act immediately to get the process started. Your first job is to file a police report. Go to the nearest police station, report the robbery and ask for a numbered copy of the police report. Presenting this at your embassy will speed up the issuing of a new passport. Your insurance company will also want a copy.

You may be waiting a while at the police station for the forms to be processed, so use this time to make phone calls. Try a guidebook, local operator or the back page of the *International Herald Tribune* for reverse-charge numbers. Start with a call to your travel insurance company (assuming you have one). Most good insurers accept charges and keep you on the line while they cancel your credit cards and have new ones issued. Otherwise, you'll have to cancel them yourself by phone or email. If your insurance or credit-card provider doesn't supply emergency cash, Western Union (UK ☎0800-833833; USA ☎1800-325-6000) can assist, if you have someone at the other end put money in. They can even provide this service online (☻www.westernunion.com). Expect to pay a fee of 4–7 percent, depending on location. So sending $1000/£650 will cost around $50/£35.

If you don't have copies of your documents stored in an eKit online vault (see p.158), you should scan and leave copies of your credit cards, passport, tickets, ID cards, a list of the contents of your backpack with photos of any expensive items (camera, laptop, tent) and insurance papers with your parents and/or trusted friends. Give it to them in a FedEx envelope that can be dropped in the mail in an instant or on a disk that can be emailed. Sending documents by email is not secure, but if you decide to do it, give the attached file a vague name (eg "travel stuff"). Do not label it "Visa card" or "Passport number" or include any of that info within the email.

Then call your embassy, tell them what happened and that you'll be on your way over as soon as you get the report. Ask for an appointment or a specific name you can request at the gate. Make sure you have a few passport photos before you show up at the embassy.

If you have no copies of your documents or any cash, throw yourself on the mercy of your embassy. If you're travelling with another citizen from your country with a valid passport, have them come along and vouch for you. And have your friends or parents fax any documents they have (old photo ID, pictures, birth certificate etc) directly to the embassy.

How to avoid sexual harassment

Most harassers get information direct to their libido via their eyeballs, so let's start with appearance. Dress conservatively. Even if your clothes aren't racy by your own standards, they might (coupled with the general loose image many Westerners have) send out the wrong signals. Shorts, short skirts and tight-fitting clothes are likely to denote you as promiscuous. While you're at it, pick up a cheap, simple ring. You'll need a story to go with it – something about your husband coming to meet you in a day or two.

That should take care of much of the harassment, but count on some rude remarks, catcalls and pinches anyway. Do your best to ignore them and keep walking. Or, alternatively, react with clarity and confidence and tell them you don't like it. If you get followed, head into a nearby busy shop and tell the owner.

For information on hitchhiking safety, see p.136.

If you're alone and see a crowded or well-lit area in sight, consider running (note: make sure you have shoes that allow you to run). If the harasser chases or grabs you, scream for help. This is, in fact, how most women escape rape. Pleading and stalling are not very effective. Kick in the knees or privates and don't think twice about jabbing him in the eyes. Feel free to use any objects nearby to aid your fight: pen, car antenna, rock or camera.

How to avoid scams

The best trick, really, is just to learn some of the most common scams. Con artists are hatching new plans all the time, but they tend to be slightly mutated versions of the ones you'll read about here. Keep your guard up, but not too high. Not all foreigners are out to scam you. Many of their gestures, although odd, are genuine acts of hospitality that you wouldn't be likely to experience at home. You'll have to trust your instincts.

Credit card scam

A store owner takes your credit card to a back room to swipe it, then swipes it again for another price. You sign one, then he forges your signature on the other.

How to beat it: keep a close eye on your credit card and ask the person to run it through the machine in front of you. Take a business card from the shop when you make any purchase so you can better alert the credit card company in case you later learn you were robbed.

Fake police scam

A kid comes up and asks for change for a small banknote. Not long after (most likely in a city park or on a quiet road), a man approaches, flashes a badge quickly and tells you he's a police officer. He explains that the note you just received from the boy was counterfeit and that he needs to take it back to headquarters and you will be fined for your involvement. At this point, just as you are starting to wonder if it's real, a large muscular "colleague" arrives and pressures you to pay up.

How to beat it: take a good long look at their badge and tell them that, although he is certainly a genuine officer, there are many impersonators and that, according to their own tourist ministry, you're suppose to make all such spot payments at police headquarters, and you'll be happy to follow him there on foot. Under no circumstances should you get into their "unmarked police car".

Border crossing scam

You become an unknowing drug mule when a seemingly innocent person asks you for the small favour of helping deliver a package, carry a suitcase, or push a buggy across a border.

How to beat it: never, never, never carry anything over a border for anyone, even if it's just a postage stamp for a nun in a wheelchair.

"Drug buy" scam

You buy a small amount of drugs from a local dealer, then he tips off his buddy, the police officer, who comes knocking at your door to demand a fee for not taking you to prison.

How to beat it: it's a dangerous game of chicken. You can pay the fine, try to bargain a little, or call their bluff and tell them you have no money, you were set up and that you're happy to go to police headquarters and explain it. Best just to avoid buying the drugs in the first place.

Taxi dash scam

You've paid your taxi and the driver leaves before you can get your bag out of the trunk.

How to beat it: leave your door open or don't pay up until you've got your bag.

"Fake travel agent" scam

You buy a ticket from a travel agency you found on the Web or on a direct mailing. The ticket never arrives and when you try to call you find out the place has gone out of business.

How to beat it: make sure you're signing up with an accredited agency. In Australia, check with the Australian Federation of Travel Agents (❀www.afta.com.au); in Canada, the Association of Canadian Travel Agencies (❀www.acta.net); in the UK, the Association of British Travel Agents (❀www.abta.com); and in the US, the American Society of Travel Agents (❀www.astanet.com). And pay with a credit card so you can stop payment if necessary.

Distraction scam

Someone "accidentally" spills something on you, offers to help you clean it off and robs you in the process. Variation: small children thrust cardboard or newspapers in front of you while their mates pick your pockets.

How to beat it: keep a firm grasp on your belongings and walk off immediately.

Exchange scam

You get a good price on moneychanging from an unofficial street dealer. He counts out the money with painstaking slowness and finds – in a show of false honesty – that it comes up a few notes short. So he adds a few new notes on top. However, while he's adding the new notes, he's discreetly pulling off even more from the bottom. Before you have a chance to double-check (not that you would, as you've just watched the world's slowest count), he's off.

How to beat it: avoid unofficial moneychangers, have the person put the money in your hand as they count it and always re-count (even at official booths where employees have been known to try to skim a little off the top from time to time).

Pay it later scam

Your taxi driver tells you not to worry about the price, or the meter, that you'll work it out later. Then, upon reaching your destination, they sting you for many times the actual fare.

How to beat it: always agree on a price before getting in the taxi, or make sure the meter is on. If it's too late, do your best to bargain, try to attract the attention of a nearby policeman and take down the driver's ID number and name so you can report him. Tour guides have been known to practise this technique as well.

Gem scam

A merchant gives you a "great deal" on some uncut gems that he tells you you can resell back home for several times the price. He even offers to throw in the postage and help you mail them. You watch him mail the parcel at the post office but the gems never make it to you back home, or they arrive but turn out to be worthless glass.

How to beat it: there are great gem deals, but knowing how to find them takes a professional eye and knowledge of world markets. Don't get involved unless you know exactly what you're doing. If you decide to mail gems, do it yourself, and don't be surprised if customs officials extract a fee on the way into your country before allowing you to claim them.

Free transport scam

You're met at the train or bus station by a tout who is offering free transport back to his hostel. You follow him onto a city tram and notice that it's not free – he just didn't pay the fare.

How to beat it: ask how you'll be getting to the hotel. If it's by public transport, make sure the tout is willing to cover your fare.

Help from your embassy or consulate

If you think of your government's embassies, consulates and high commissions as a safety net, you're liable to slip through one of the holes. They can't do much if you've been arrested for violating local laws, and they won't help send you home or give you a place to sleep if you run out of money. But they can, however, help you in the event of a lost or stolen passport. They can also provide contact information during emergencies; give you the latest travel advice; allow you to register your travel plans if you're heading into some treacherous areas (don't forget to check back in); and assist with overseas marriage and birth documents. And most of them make excellent cocktails, should you manage to attend one of their functions, so consider swinging by if you're in the neighbourhood during a national holiday.

16

Health

There's no need to place your health under a microscope when you travel. The things you should concern yourself with are actually quite basic: get your pre-trip health details in order before you leave (including all the necessary immunizations); take some fundamental precautions while you're on the road; keep an eye out for some specific symptoms, and get yourself to a doctor if you encounter any of them. Despite the tales you may have heard, many of the common illnesses are avoidable or easily curable with some of the basic information you'll find in this chapter. If you want more details, there's always *The Rough Guide to Travel Health*.

Pre-departure checkup

Far too many travellers neglect basic pre-trip medical arrangements and suffer needlessly as a consequence. Your first order of business is a checkup. Don't make the common mistake of putting this off till the last minute. A month or two before departure is a more sensible time to schedule an appointment. If the doctor finds something during the checkup and wants you to come back for a second consultation, your next-day flight is buggered. Besides, you'll want to get your checkup before you start the vaccinations. Some vaccinations should not be given if you have so much as a cold, or

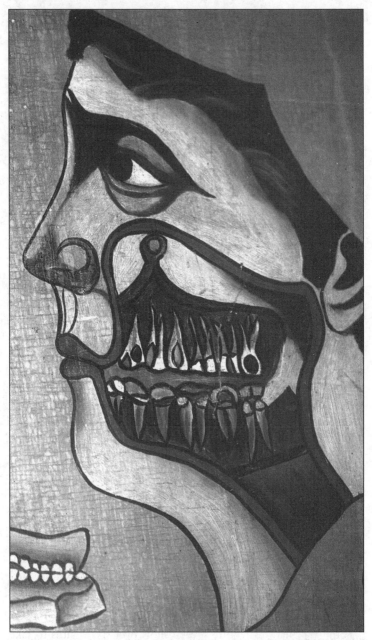

△ Brush regularly, twice a day!

if you're taking other medications. Make sure to ask for a copy of your clean bill of health to take along (this may require an additional fee if an official certificate is required), so you don't have to pay for one again if you end up working on a kibbutz or volunteering for an organization that requires one.

Schedule a visit to the dentist as well. It would be a serious setback to get a gnawing tooth problem while you're in a country not known for dentistry. Needless to say, getting this taken care of beforehand is a lot cheaper than flying home to do it.

If you wear glasses or contacts, you'll want to go to the optician. Make sure you have enough contacts and fluid to keep you going (you can always send some lenses ahead as well). Glasses are important backups even if you never wear them at home: you may find yourself in dusty environments where contacts don't function well. If you're trying to decide between two frames for your glasses, take the most durable, even if they're not the most flattering. Make sure you bring along a copy of your prescription and your optician's telephone number in case you need emergency replacements on the road or ordered from home.

Vaccinations

This part is surprisingly easy. Simply visit the Center for Disease Control's website (❀www.cdc.org) and select the places you're visiting. The website has the latest information and will tell you exactly which immunizations to get. Then call around to make sure you get a good price. A full course of shots might set you back $250/£160. If your country has a national health plan, a number of the shots (e.g. hepatitis A and polio) may fall under that policy and can be received free from your GP.

Confirm the information you get from the CDC with the doctor or clinic administering the shots, and be sure to inform them of any medical conditions (including allergies) and medications (including the pill) you're taking. Also, explain where you'll be staying and how long you'll be there. Even in a malarial region, for example, if you're staying in the main cities where mosquitoes are rare, there's often little risk. These risk-free oases are not usually mentioned on the CDC website, so be sure to ask.

Some vaccinations require several shots over six months to take effect, so don't leave it until the last minute, or even the last month. If you're getting several jabs, bear in mind that you may not be able to get them all on the same day. They may conflict with one another, require more than one course, or take time to become effective. However, if you're not entirely sure where you're headed, you don't need to get every needle in the cabinet. Vaccinations are all available on the road. Just make sure the clinic looks clean and professionally run and uses sterile needles. If you have the option, try to get this taken care of in more developed countries.

Get a vaccination record card and keep it with your passport while travelling. You may need to demonstrate that you've received certain immunizations to enter a country or obtain a visa. And, let's face it, with all these mega-syllabic names, it's hard to remember what you got, what you didn't want to get but got anyway, and what you were going to get but decided not to get at the last moment.

Cholera

Cholera is a serious diarrheal disease caused by consumption of contaminated water or shellfish. When there's an outbreak (it seems to follow natural disasters and wars), avoid the area if possible and be very careful what you eat (no ice, only bottled water, no raw food unless peeled). Until recently, there was no good vaccination for cholera. The old injectable vaccine was ineffective since it didn't provide resistance against the majority of cholera strains. Two new oral vaccines (Dukoral and Mutacol) have proven more effective (85–90% immunity within six months of taking the vaccination, decreasing to 62% immunity after three years) and should be considered if you're heading to areas where the disease is prevalent. Because the vaccine is new, it may not be available everywhere. At the time of printing, for example, it's not available in the US.

Diphtheria

Check your booster records, because you definitely want to make sure you're vaccinated against this bacterial illness. It's passed person to person quicker than an email chain letter and typical unpleasantness includes fever, chills and a sore throat. Eventually it can cause heart failure and paralysis. Be aware that if someone you know has it, they're highly infectious for ten days. Seek medical help if you suspect it: a quick throat swab can determine if you've been exposed.

Hepatitis A

Contaminated food, water and people pass this bowel blaster along. Good news: there's a vaccination. One poke with a Havrix vaccine will last a year. Follow it up with a second injection 6–12 months later and you're good to go for a decade. Downside is it takes nearly a month after the first dose to take effect. The more traditional gamma globulin shot works right away, and provides protection for three to six months. In the UK a combination Hep A and Hep B that will also give you ten years of immunity is available free from GPs. But you'll need half a year to get all three shots taken care of. Or ask your doctor about Hepatyrix, fifteen-year protection against Hep A and typhoid in one stab.

> ## Getting Hep A
>
> On one of my trips to Saigon for a Hong Kong art magazine job I landed, a large group of Vietnamese artists organized a large dinner in honour of my visit. They asked me if I liked seafood … which of course I do. They ordered, among other things an enormous platter of oysters. I had never seen oysters so big – they were larger than my hand – and this purplish colour I didn't even know existed on the colour spectrum. And they were delicious. However, the next day when I travelled to Hanoi, I felt like I was going to die. I mean I literally thought I was going to die in Hanoi. I was freezing cold, running a fever, puking and expulsing out the other end as well. I tried a few local concoctions, but they didn't do much. Then two Swedish expats recommended a doctor at their embassy. I managed to get over to the Swedish Embassy in a haze, shivering on my cycle. Once I took the prescribed antibiotics, I was fine in half a day.
>
> Amy Schrier
> Editor, Blue Magazine

Hepatitis B

This is Hep A's sinister, sometimes fatal cousin. It's transmitted like AIDS (most commonly via unprotected sex, foreign medical treatment and tattooing) but it's about a hundred times more infectious. The vaccination is a bit of a drag – three jabs over six months – but well worth it on a long trip. For those who have put it off to the last second, it's possible to get three jabs in three weeks with an additional booster, but it's slightly less effective. As previously noted, in the UK there's a combination Hep A and Hep B jab that will also give you ten years of immunity, available free from GPs.

Japanese encephalitis

Don't be fooled by the name. Mosquitoes carry this brain-attacking virus around parts of Southeast Asia, the Far East and the Pacific. It's both life-threatening and neurologically damaging. Once again, there's a vaccination. You'll need three shots over a month, plus ten days for it to become effective. The jabs should last you three years, but you may need an additional booster before then. This isn't found everywhere, and if you're not headed to affected regions, you don't need it. Prominent symptoms include a stiff neck and intolerance to light.

Meningococcal meningitis

Coughing and sneezing spread this much-feared disease, which is most recognizable by a rash that starts as pinprick blood spots on ankles and armpits, buttocks or groin and matures into purplish bruises that do not fade or disappear when pressed. Forget about trying to treat it yourself: just get to a doctor quick. Every second counts. However, you could simply get the vaccination before you go, especially if you're headed to Asia, Africa, Central America, or the Middle East. One shot gives you three to five years of protection and takes two weeks before it's effective.

Polio

If your parents were against the vaccination or your government was, now is the time to get your shots: a full three-dose course administered at monthly intervals. Otherwise, make sure your booster is up to date (within 10 years) if you're travelling anywhere outside of northwestern Europe, New Zealand, Australia and the USA. Of those who do contract polio, 95 percent will show no symptoms and, despite the reputation, paralysis occurs in only 0.1 percent of cases.

Rabies

Steer clear of packs of wild dogs in big cities and always enquire about a dog's biting habits before petting. That's cheaper than getting the vaccine (three shots over a month, plus another two if bitten, scratched, or even licked by a rabid animal), but possibly not as effective. Without the vaccine you're looking at nearly twice as many shots – although no longer the nasty ones in the stomach. If you have an encounter with an animal that puts you at risk, get tested immediately.

Tetanus

You've probably been vaccinated against this already. However, you may be up for your ten-year update. Check your health records to be sure the booster is taken care of. Spores enter the body through open wounds as small as a pinprick, and can be picked up through contact with dirt, manure and – the classic – rusty nails. You won't get the symptoms for five to twenty days, but the one that should get your attention (and any doctor's attention) are spasms of the jaw muscle. Those will spread across your face and into your torso, and that's when things get really nasty. It is potentially fatal. If you recognize these symptoms, get to a hospital immediately.

Typhoid

Areas with poor sanitation and poor health standards attract the most typhoid. This bacterial illness is picked up by ingesting contaminated food and water or by coming in contact with the feces of an infected person. A typhoid vaccine is available and recommended, but not overwhelmingly effective (eighty percent). The more contamination (that is the more typhoid-tainted food and water you ingest) the less the vaccine will protect you. After a fortnight's incubation period you'll experience high fever, increasing daily for the first week and accompanied by weakness, stomach ache, coughing and deafness. It's cured by antibiotics, but you can still infect others as a carrier long after it's gone, so follow up with tests.

Yellow fever

Ticks, flies and mosquitoes carry this fatal viral infection primarily just north and south of the equator in Africa and South America. It can be prevented by a common vaccination – in fact, many countries require this before allowing you to enter. If you do con-

Vaccination round-up

BCG (tuberculosis)
Full course 1 dose

Booster No booster required

Comments Not routinely recommended for travellers; to be considered for infants and health workers, as infection usually requires prolonged exposure to infected individuals in closed environment

Time before effective immunity N/A

Cholera
Full course 2 oral doses

Booster 1 week apart (killed vaccine) or 1 single oral dose (live vaccine)

Comments 85–90 percent protection for 6 months after 2 doses of killed vaccine; 62 percent after 3 years Considered for people going to endemic areas; not yet available in the US. Should be taken at least 3 weeks (1 week for live vaccine) before departure. Avoid antibiotics and malaria prophylaxis with proguanil 1 week before and 1 week after cholera vaccine

Time before effective immunity 1 week after the last dose

Hepatitis A
Full course Single dose

Booster After 6–12 months

Comments Gives good protection for at least 12 months; booster protection lasts more than 10 years

Time before effective immunity One month

Hepatitis A immunoglobin
Full course Single injection

Booster Only gives protection for 2–6 months, depending on dose

Comments Needs to be given close to departure

Time before effective immunity Immediately

Hepatitis B
Full course 2 doses 1 month apart plus a third dose 6 months later

Booster Provides protection for at least 10 years; booster dose is not recommended for adults with intact immune system

Comments More rapid 3-week courses are available if you're close to departure, but this gives lower immunity and requires a booster after 12 months

Time before effective immunity 1 month after the third dose

Japanese Encephalitis
Full course 2–3 doses over a month

Booster After 1–3 years

Comments More rapid courses available

Time before effective immunity 10 days after last dose

tract yellow fever though, you'll experience high fever, vomiting and abdominal pain, which will abate on its own after a week. For fifteen percent of those infected, there will be a lull of a day or two

Meningococcal meningitis

Full course 1 dose

Booster Every 3 years

Time before effective immunity
2 weeks

Polio

Full course Three doses: 4–8 weeks between first and second doses; third dose 6–12 months after second dose

Booster Ten years after the full course; no need for more than one lifetime booster

Comments Full course usually given in childhood; if pressed for time before departure it is still worthwhile to get the first and second dose

Time before effective immunity Two weeks after the second injection

Rabies

Full course
(Pre-exposure) 3 doses over one month

Booster After 2–3 years

Comments Pre-exposure immunization gives greater protection but does not eliminate the need for prompt treatment if you're bitten by a rabid animal

Time before effective immunity 2 weeks after completed course

Tetanus/diphtheria

Full course Three doses: 4–8 weeks between first and second doses; third dose 6-12 months after second dose. Usually given with diphtheria

Booster Every 10 years

Comments Full course usually given in childhood; if pressed for time before departure only first and second dose can be given. It's not useful to only take the first dose

Time before effective immunity A few days

Typhoid

Full course Single injection, or 3–4 oral doses at 2-day intervals

Booster Injection every 2 years; oral every 5 years

Comments The old injectable vaccine was notorious for unpleasant side effects, but the new one causes few side effects

Time before effective immunity
2 weeks

Yellow fever

Full course 1 dose

Booster After 10 years

Comments Should be avoided if you have severe egg allergy or compromised immunity; requires special consideration if you also wish to take Hep A immunoglobin

Time before effective immunity
10 days

after this first wave before it kicks in again with more severity, with symptoms including jaundice.

What you can't get vaccinated against

These are the ones you'll have to watch out for, and may just get anyway. Some maladies are more common than others and some more severe, so read through the descriptions to get acquainted with the symptoms and dangers you may face.

AIDS

You've probably heard an earful about this already. What you may not know is that in some areas of the world it affects over seventy percent of the sexually active population, and it's continuing to spread at a staggering rate. Among prostitutes and drug users, you may find even higher proportions with HIV. It's a pandemic poised to wipe out enormous portions of Asia and Africa and you as well if you don't take precautions. Consider this before you have unprotected sex or share a needle. For more on travelling with HIV/AIDS, see opposite.

Allergies

If you experience allergies at home, you'll probably encounter them on the road. Watery eyes, runny nose, sneezing, you know how it goes. Pack an antihistamine (chlorpheniramine or loratadine) to relieve the symptoms. If these don't help, visit a doctor.

Altitude sickness

This is more dangerous than most people believe, especially when others who don't have it are egging you on to keep going up. If your head feels like it's about to implode or you're dizzier than a wino trapped on a Ferris wheel, that's your cue to head down the mountain. It doesn't mean making a beeline for the base camp (unless it has reached a critical stage). Usually, the symptoms will abate after just a little descent, and you may even be able to continue once your body has adjusted at its own pace.

> Where **medications** are listed in this section, you'll only find the generic medical name. These are known by various commercial names in different countries. Simply check the label or consult your pharmacist or doctor.

If you have special health considerations that render you immuno-compromised, keep in mind that the bacteria and bugs that affect all travellers may have a more profound effect on you. Developing countries in particular pose significant risks for exposure to opportunistic pathogens. Your consulate or the International Association of Medical Assistance to Travellers (www.iamat.org) can provide English-speaking physicians trained in Europe or North America.

Vaccinations

The Center for Disease Control currently recommends that live-virus vaccines (except the measles vaccine) be avoided by people with immunodeficiency. "Killed vaccines" such as diphtheria-tetanus, hepatitis A, rabies and Japanese encephalitis are okay, and recommended for "healthy" HIV-infected travellers. However, the immune response to these vaccines might be reduced and is largely dependent on the degree of immunodeficiency. For more information, visit ⓦwww.cdc.com.

Medications

Discussing an emergency plan with your doctor prior to departure is an excellent idea. The CDC advises all HIV-infected travellers heading to developing countries to bring an antimicrobial such as ciprofloxacin (500mg twice a day for 3–7 days) for empirical therapy for diarrhea, although alternatives (such as TMP-SMX) should be discussed with a doctor. If the diarrhea does not respond to this treatment, there is blood in the stools, fever and shaking chills, or dehydration, get to a doctor.

Going through customs

If you are carrying a full array of HIV drugs, or just the virus, be aware that some countries have vague restrictions preventing those with "communicable diseases" from entering. So, faced with an inquisitive customs officer holding your medications, you might offer other half-truths about the things you're suffering from first (such as liver/heart/kidney problems), and delay mentioning HIV. If you're staying for an extended period to work or study, you may face a serological screen in many countries. Check out the unofficial list compiled by the US State Department: ⓦwww.travel.state.gov/HIVtestingreqs.html.

Fitness is only one factor: you could be a competitive triathlete and still get altitude sickness. Other factors are your rate of ascent, elevation, and how well your body happens to cope with it. At higher elevations, do what climbers do: don't go up more than 300m per day once over 3000m and hike up past the camping spot to acclimatize, then return and sleep. Follow a careful acclimatization plan and, most important, listen to your body. If you want to try a short cut, the drugs Acetazolamide and Nifedipine have been known to help combat the sickness. As have coca leaves (chewed or in tea), which are readily available in parts of South America.

Bed bugs

These are not merely bedtime story myths. They're out there, typically in the cheapest hotels, and they do bite. The bites aren't serious, but they seriously itch. And you'd have a better chance spotting Elvis than some of these critters. Your best defence is a good sleep sheet: make sure it's big enough to cover the pillow as well. A tight weave should keep most of them out. The bites look like two or three little red dots in a row. Treat with hydrocortisone or antihistamine cream and refrain from scratching.

Bilharzia

Truly exceptional spellers may know it as schistosomiasis. These micro-worms live in freshwater lakes, canals and still sections of rivers: the larvae penetrate your skin, head to your liver and lay eggs. You could get the disease by drinking the affected water or eating food washed in it. Without going into the full graphic detail of what these critters do in your body for one to ten weeks before you notice the symptoms (such as blood in the urine), you should know it is also called the disease of the "menstruating males." It mainly affects the urinary tract and gut and can be treated quickly once diagnosed. It's best prevented by avoiding stagnant water, especially in Africa (perhaps most commonly in the Nile, Lake Malawi and Madagascar). It can also be found in Southeast Asia, South America and the Middle East. If you suddenly realize you may have exposed yourself, hop out of the water and rub yourself thoroughly and abrasively with your towel in case your skin hasn't been fully penetrated yet.

Cold sores

Don't kiss people with lip sores or blisters. Don't share water bottles with them either. There's really nothing cold about these sores, which are actually herpes picked up by oral contact (fellatio and cunnilingus included), and are most likely triggered by too much direct sunlight. Once you've got the virus, you've got it for life. To keep the sores at bay, keep your lips well glossed while exposed to the sun and apply aciclovir cream (may require prescription) as soon as you feel the tingling sensation coming on (apply five times a day for five days; it may require prescription). Once the sore breaks open, the medicine won't help.

Constipation

Because people are so worried about travellers' diarrhea, they usually forget about this one, which can be nearly as uncomfortable and troublesome. Travellers who are new to the trail are especially susceptible. They take one look at a squat toilet (or one of its unsanitary hybrid cousins) and suddenly they don't have to go any more. A few days later the metal block has become an intestinal block. This can be solved by simply carrying some laxatives (senna) and not waiting too long to use them. Better yet, force yourself to go when you have the urge, no matter what the loo looks like. And a little diet altering won't hurt: more fruit, bran and fluids.

Dehydration

The trick here is to drink before you get thirsty. For a full day of walking in a hot climate, you should be drinking about four litres of water. In dry or high-altitude terrain, you'll need even more, and wind masks the amount you're sweating away. Once you're dehydrated, you'll experience a dry mouth, dark urine, headache and, in extreme cases, fainting. Find some shade, take it easy and mix your water with a rehydration solution so you get your salt balance back, and if fluid can't be taken orally, get to a hospital for an IV.

Dengue fever

Here's another great reason to use mosquito repellent. This viral infection is not typically fatal, but it hurts like hell for about a week and there's little you can do to treat it. It's most commonly found

For a list of basic medical supplies you should take with you, see p.118.

in sub-tropical Asia, the Caribbean, Central America, South America, Australia and Pacific Islands. These white-and-black mozzies tend to bite during mornings and late afternoons in shaded areas of the body. Once bitten, the incubation period is about a week. Then you're looking at high fever, joint pain and backache. As if that's not enough, you'll probably see an itchy rash develop on your torso and experience bleeding from your nose, mouth and rectum. You want to be in a hospital for this one, preferably in your own country, as weeks of depression may set in after the severe symptoms are gone.

Diarrhea

It has plenty of colourful monikers, from Delhi Belly to Montezuma's Revenge. Whatever you call it, you'll probably get it at some point, no matter what precautions you take. The good news is that it's most often extremely treatable and the troublesome symptoms can be cured in less than a day. This may be the single most valuable thing you get out of this book, and if it saves you a week of traumatic toilet dashes, the book will have paid for itself a few times over. You'll meet numerous travellers suffering from dysentery for days or weeks. The typical reason is that they're trying to ride it out. You want to do exactly the opposite.

The moment you start to "go liquid," drink a bottle of water mixed with a packet of rehydration mix that you should be carrying in your first-aid kit. And keep drinking. The biggest danger with dysentery is dehydration. Then, the next time you have to go, bring a little plastic film canister with you and put a stool sample in it. Either take the sample to a nearby clinic yourself or have a trusted fellow traveller do it for you. With a quick look under the microscope, a doctor will most often be able to identify the cause. If so, they'll write a prescription on the spot, which will likely include the pharmaceutical equivalent of a cork. Less than a day after you start taking the medicine, you may feel back to normal, or at least better. While recovering, stick to simple, unspiced foods like rice for a day or two just in case. Little tip: carry an anti-diarrhea pill (loperamide) in your passport pouch. If you're on a long bus ride or walking around town, it will come in handy more than you can imagine. Women travellers should be aware that diarrhea can reduce the effectiveness of the pill.

Hepatitis C

Less common than Hep A and Hep B (but with no vaccination) this one requires contact with contaminated blood. Which means stay alert where any needles are concerned. Always make sure they're opened from new sterile packages while you watch. If you get taken to a hospital in an emergency, ask for screened blood.

Hiking blisters

Nepal's Annapurna circuit is not the ideal place to try out a new pair of hiking boots. If you buy or rent some, give yourself at least a day or two for your feet to adjust (especially with new boots). For serious treks, make sure you bring Compeed (a skin-like blister cover), sport tape, Vaseline or a silicon spray and a needle (with antiseptic to sterilize) to drain blisters. Always make sure to puncture the blister in the centre, not on the sides where the skin is more sensitive. Also, give them as much time to dry out as possible before taping them up again. Some have success with a needle and thread, leaving the thread in the opening for better drainage. Tape can be applied in advance to trouble spots, then sprayed with silicon. Two pairs of socks are advisable, neither of them cotton. Polypropylene or silk (next to the skin) and wool make an excellent combination.

Hookworm

This one doesn't sound like much fun. And it's not. These tiny worms live in the soil, so avoiding them is simply a matter of wearing shoes. Otherwise, they enter the foot, make their way to the lungs and lymph glands and eventually end up in your gut, where they will probably cause you to be nauseous and generate loose stools and you'll experience general abdominal discomfort while they go about laying eggs. A simple stool sample can identify the worms. Once identified, it's easily treatable and there are a number of drugs suitable for the task, including mebendazole. Iron tablets should also be used if anemia is detected.

Hypothermia

A lot of people say they're freezing, but hypothermia is the real thing. The medical definition of loss of core body temperature starts at 35°C. The condition begins with uncontrolled shivering and is followed by slurred speech and mental confusion and, eventually, stiff muscles, abnormal heart rhythms, coma and death. Sufferers should be gradually warmed (not rubbed, as that can cause the skin to come off) and given sugary drinks (not a St Bernard-style shot of whisky). Alcohol, exhaustion and illness all weaken the body's ability to keep warm.

Infected cuts and scrapes

In tropical environments, cuts don't tend to heal like they do back home. They're easily infected and can actually grow in size. Use antiseptic ointment or powder and try to expose the cut to direct sunlight so it has a chance to dry out. Visit a doctor if you're unable to stop the growth of the wound on your own.

Jetlag

An alarming number of travellers don't take simple steps to combat jet lag, and are then plagued by fatigue for days (typically, one day per time zone), starting off their trip on the wrong foot. If you can sleep on the plane and sleep well your first night in the new time zone, you're not going to experience much jetlag, if any. Sleeping on the plane, if you're not naturally gifted at the art, can be achieved with an over-the-counter or prescribed sleeping pill.

According to all studies, drinking alcohol is exactly the wrong approach. The next worst thing you can do is stay up late watching a movie and eating. There's no reason to eat dinner at 11pm, then watch a movie at midnight simply because you're at 30,000 feet. Eat a meal in the airport, pop the sleeping pill when the plane leaves the ground and drink plenty of water when you wake up. Then refrain from naps until bedtime and take another sleeping pill if you wake up during that first night or pop a Melatonin tablet (only available over the counter in the US) before bed to ensure you sleep a little longer.

Malaria

The reason this mosquito-carried disease gets so much press is that there's no simple fire-and-forget jab in your arm that will prevent it.

You have to take pills regularly. And which pills you take (or don't) depends on where you're headed, how long you'll be there and how your body reacts to them. Lariam (mefloquine) is the most common, and gets the most complaints for side effects (typically panic attacks and nightmares), though your chances of getting these are minimal. Chloroquine, once the all-purpose prophylaxis, is now only used in places where mosquitoes haven't become resistant to it. And doxycycline is typically used just in places where chloroquine and mefloquine no longer work. Therefore, it's vital that your information is up to the minute. For long-term care, the chloroquine/proguanil combo can be used up to five years provided you get frequent eye checks. Otherwise, Larium is prescribed for up to a year.

None of the prophylaxes are a hundred percent effective. And because of the side effects, some travellers (especially ones living or travelling in a malaria region for a long time) opt not to take them.

Symptoms typically take one or two weeks to develop and involve three stages: cold shivering and shaking; high fever with rapid heartbeat; then sweating and a drop in temperature. You can also expect coughs, joint pains, vomiting and general unpleasantness. If you suspect it after one day (even if you're feeling okay the next day) get to a clinic, even if you're already back in your home country. You can come down with malaria up to two years after your trip. A simple blood test will reveal if you have the disease, and the treatment is best administered under medical supervision. In an emergency, if you're unable to

Getting malaria

I was a ball of twine and the malaria was a great big frisky cat. It started batting me around about a month after I got home from a protracted stay in the swamps of Indonesia. One hot summer day, I started shivering intensely, shaking so badly that my teeth rattled. Later, I found that the convulsive first stage of an attack usually lasted about two hours. It was exhausting. After shaking myself asleep, or at least half conscious, I'd doze while a fever soared. White-hot dreams bloomed and detonated somewhere in the back of my mind. The final two-hour segment of my typical malarial attack involved sweating. I could go through two or more thick terry cloth robes and leave them sopping. At first the disease hit me every week. Gradually, it subsided to once a month, then once a year. I haven't had an attack in over three years, and while it is very exotic to be treated for malaria, in Montana, where I live, the price of celebrity, in this case, is intolerable, and I don't miss it, not even a little bit.

Tim Cahill,
Author, *Hold the Enlightenment: More Travel, Less Bliss*

get to a doctor for days, you strongly suspect malaria and you have mefloquine, take 20–25 mg per kilo of body weight as a single dose.

Anti-malarials aren't enough when the bugs are out in force. Use DEET mosquito spray or lotion at all times. At night or when you're relaxing in your room, burn mosquito coils (easy to find anywhere there's a risk of malaria). And use mosquito nets when provided, or buy your own if you arrive and find they are not regularly provided in that area.

In the end, how you prevent malaria is up to you. What's important is that you make an informed decision. If you do decide to take prophylaxes, make sure you also use mosquito repellent and take other precautions. And remember, the drugs take time to become effective (1 week for cholorquine/proguanil, 2 weeks for mefloquine, 2 days for doxycycline), so you will need to start taking them before you arrive in an at-risk area.

Motion sickness

It's not serious, but it's bad enough to ruin a day or two of your trip. On a winding bus ride, try to sit near the front (although not at the front, where you'd be the first one through the windscreen) and next to a window or air vent. Make sure you get out to stretch your legs whenever the bus stops. On a boat, stay above deck and try looking at the horizon. Take deep, relaxing breaths or simply try to stay busy. And, in any event, have a motion sickness pill or a skin patch (hyoscine or scopolamin) ready just in case. It takes at least an hour before the effects of these pills are noticeable, so you may need to take them in advance of boarding.

Rashes

You'll be encountering plants, fruits and bugs that your skin has never been exposed to before. It's common for travellers to experience a host of new body art. Try applying topical antihistamine, calamine lotion or steroid creams (hydrocortisone) to the area. If it persists, visit a local doctor.

Snake, spider and scorpion bites

If you're not a professional snake handler, don't approach snakes. Follow this essential strategy and they'll almost certainly leave you alone: if you are walking in tall grass in a known snake area, wear high, protective boots and carry a leafy branch to keep any you meet at bay. If the snake is dead, bring it along for identification so the proper antivenin can be administered if necessary. Otherwise, try to get a good description without getting bitten again. Do not suck on the bite, apply ice or make an incision. Place a firm bandage (not tight) on the torso side of the bite, just a few inches above the wound. Wash and apply cold compresses if possible. Otherwise, just keep the limb immobilized while you get to a medical facility. Antivenin is the only direct treatment, and it should only be administered by a medical professional.

Spiders are less likely to be dangerous, but apply the same guidelines for bites from unknown and poisonous ones (black widow, redback and brown recluse). Scorpions are found in arid regions; the treatment is the same as with spider and snake bites. To help with the severe pain, administer painkillers and antihistamines liberally while en route to a medical facility. And get in the habit of shaking out shoes and sleeping bags before using.

STDs

Just because you're choosy about who you have sex with doesn't mean they were. And once is all it takes to wake up with syphilis, gonorrhea, chlamydia, chancroid, trichomoniasis or herpes. Symptoms include: unusual vaginal or penile discharge, pain when passing urine, itching, abnormal vaginal bleeding and genital ulceration. There's only one thing to do if you get any of these: go to a doctor. With chlamydia it's a little more tricky. Most women don't notice they have it. Some never find out. Some only learn of it at an infertility clinic while trying to find out why they can't get pregnant.

Sunburn

Sunscreen keeps you from burning, but it also keeps people out in the sun longer with more UV exposure, and the long-term effects of this are yet to be determined. Still, burning is bad. So get in the habit of using SFP 25 sunblock and reapplying it frequently. For those on medications, note that some reduce your skin's ability to fend off the sun's powerful rays: ciproloxacin, tetracycline group antibiotics, sulphonylurea (for diabetes) and thiazide (for high blood pressure).

Eating the "wrong" food

There's a travel health mantra that if you can't peel it, boil it or cook it – forget it. Only one problem with this approach: in practice, over the long haul, it's basically worthless. You can't travel around the world in a hermetically sealed suit, and you're going to be taking some culinary chances at some point whether you want to or not. There's simply too much interesting food out there to painstakingly investigate its biological properties three to five times a day. Rely instead on your own good judgment. Are the locals drinking the water? Are there bugs visibly swimming in it? Does the meat look like it has been cooked long enough? Is it dead? Are flies laying eggs in the fruit? Is the street vendor jamming his hand down his pants between servings? On a long trip, you're almost certain to entertain an occasional spell of traveller's diarrhea. Accept it and don't worry about it. The cure is usually quick and painless (see p.192) and your stomach will most likely get stronger as you travel.

Vaginal thrush

Warm climates, tight nylon underwear and increased sexual activity are among the factors that lead to higher incidence of yeast infections on the travel circuit. Men who carry the fungus do not usually show any signs of it. For women, soreness, discomfort during sex, pain while urinating and passing a white or yellowish discharge are among the symptoms. It's easily treated by an antifungal preparation that should be easy to find in most countries, but you may want to carry one just in case. In a jam, try applying regular plain yoghurt and altering your diet briefly: no sugars, breads, beer, wine, mushrooms, Vegemite and other yeast-containing or yeast-encouraging foods.

If you do get sick

Here's the basic approach: with high fever, loose stools or vomiting – anything very painful or unusual – get to a doctor and have blood and/or stool tests conducted. It's generally quick and cheap and far better than trying to wait it out. With a quick diagnosis and the right medicine, you may be feeling fine within a day or so.

This is also a great time to check into a decent hotel with a private toilet and phone. You owe it to yourself and your fellow travellers. Hostel dormitories are not meant as recovering wards (beyond temporary alcohol-related afflictions). When you check in, tell the desk clerk that you're not feeling well and see if they have a doctor who can pay you a visit. You can always ring for an ambulance or taxi if things take a turn for the worse.

If things seem serious, don't take chances. Get yourself to a hospital and contact your family and travel insurance company. If you're in a remote area, get to a major city immediately.

17

Special
considerations

For many, conquering street food, crowded bus rides, aggressive market touts and squat toilets without lighting are challenge enough. But there are some groups who must also cope with a number of issues, from a medical condition to sexual-preference discrimination. This chapter focuses on the concerns these travellers face and offers a few tips that will hopefully smooth out their journeys.

Senior travellers

Retirement can be a perfect time in your life to travel, and you don't need to be in outstanding physical condition, as long as you plan your trip well and stay prepared. There are a number of specialty items available these days, from lightweight canes that can be collapsed and stored in a hand luggae to inflatable back support rests, that can make a mild trip comfortable and rough ride tolerable. Browse senior travel websites such as ⓦwww.seniorssuper stores.com for ideas.

Health

When planning your itinerary, consider the medical facilities of the country you're visiting. The Netherlands, for example, will have a more modern health-care system than Pakistan. But also keep in mind that many developing countries have at least one world-class, English-speaking hospital, which often support the large number of expatriates working there. Guidebooks list such facilities where available.

Consider the temperature of the places you're headed. Even if you've experienced such sweltering heat before, it can be another thing entirely if you're out walking in it most of the day or staying in places without air-conditioning.

If you're concerned about pre-existing ailments, discuss them with your doctor before leaving and keep an eye out for symptoms. Depending on your case, it may not be a bad idea to bring a copy of your medical file along, or at least the relevant pages. Check your medical insurance for travel coverage and supplement it with any special travel insurance you may need (see p.92).

Medications

Bring your prescriptions if you want to get refills, but ask your doctor to include the generic name since some brand-name prescriptions are not available abroad. Keep medicines in their original labelled container to avoid problems at customs and have the prescriptions handy. (The label on the plastic bottle is not always enough, especially if you're transporting stronger pain medications which may require a special permit obtained at the pharmacy.) If you need medication refilled in an emergency, a good travel-insurance plan will assist. And keep the phone number of your doctor and pharmacist with you for backup.

Security

Sadly, seniors are especially vulnerable to theft. It is perceived that your guard is down more often, you're more likely to be carrying valuables, and are less likely to give chase or fight back. To combat this, take special notice of the tips in the security section. As always, you can best avoid putting yourself at risk by carrying very little, and disguising what you do have. Then take special care when and where you wander. Get good information from the reception clerk on which areas are dangerous and which to avoid after dark.

Discounts

There's enough material to write an entire book on senior discounts. In fact, someone has. Actually, several have. One of the things that seems to get better with age is the amount of rebates available. Seniors might get anything up to fifty percent off museums and other sites, and local transport. Look for notices at ticket windows, check your guidebook, and get into the habit of asking.

Flights

On airlines, the magic discount age is usually 60 or 62. Rates vary, but you can typically get ten percent off "the lowest published fare". And that's exactly how you should phrase it when you ring a travel agent. Not only that, but you're often allowed to bring someone of any age along at the same rate. Some airlines offer flight coupons for seniors. These are a block of one-way tickets valid in certain zones (eg North America) with an individual airline for a bargain rate. Four such tickets cost around $700 on American Airlines and can be used whenever, without regard to typical restrictions like weekend stopovers.

Accommodation

Typically, hotels offer seniors ten to fifty percent off normal rates at major hotels (and some minor ones) worldwide. Always enquire when you book. International Youth Hostel cards for seniors cost just $15/£10. There are also special organizations, such as non-profit-making Elderhostel (ⓦwww.elderhostel.org), which run trips around the world for those 55 and older. For roughly $50/£30 a day, you get a room, food, educational classes on a variety of subjects and the chance to meet plenty of like-minded interesting people.

Disabilities

Don't let anyone tell you that you can't travel around the world. There's going to be more planning than an able-bodied person may face, more hassles, and you may have to give up more independence than you'd prefer at times, but if you're prepared to accept this, the rewards are immeasurable.

No matter how much planning you manage, you'll still need to prepare yourself for the unexpected: unstable or missing handrails, faulty ramps, narrow passages, and assigned assistants with little training and even less enthusiasm. Greet them with good humour and look for ways to solve the problems on the spot.

What you can do to prepare

Much depends on your degree of disability, and no one has a better grasp of that than you. Stay in control of your options. An activity that may not be a possibility for someone else could be fine for you. But if a travel agent or tour operator hears that you're disabled first, they may decide which things are appropriate for you and present you with an inappropriately limited selection. In other words, look into things you'd like to do, then ask questions to find out if you can be accommodated. Don't simply look for "disabled activities".

Before you begin your trip, whether you're joining a tour or doing it alone, think about ways to enhance the experience of travel and remove potential obstacles. For example, a deaf person may wish to purchase a rail pass in advance to avoid the hassle of buying individual tickets at a station counter, and a sight-impaired traveller might pick up souvenir replicas of the famous monuments once they arrive to help get a better understanding of the structures they're standing in front of. Consider activities that can be done on an equal level. For those in a wheelchair, a cultural show, garden and recommended restaurant should take minimal preparation beyond confirming that they can accommodate you where stairs and doorways are concerned.

What you'll face

In most wealthy countries you'll find a mix of excellent accessibility and complete lack of it. However, there should be a fundamental infrastructure in place and your requests for assistance will often find an experienced ear. In less developed countries, expect to find little infrastructure, if any at all. What you may experience, however, is a refreshing abundance of helpers with an enlightened indifference towards disability. On the other hand, you may feel like a novelty act at times. If so, keep in mind that you may be one of the first independent disabled people that locals have seen.

Several of the world's great attractions are still inaccessible, or at least extremely difficult for manoeuvring, such as the tombs in Egypt's Valley of the Kings, the ruins of Machu Picchu, or the trail down the Grand Canyon. At such times, you'll either have to content yourself with a view from afar, have a travelling companion videotape it and replay it on the spot, or find alternative activities.

It's not impossible to find accessible toilets, but it may not be easy. Make sure there's one at your hotel. Access-Able (⊛www .access-able.com) has a database of hotels that accommodate those with disabilities, plus listings of places to rent special medical equipment and get it repaired.

Getting around

Whether you're travelling around the world or around a vast country, flying may just be the best of a sorry selection of choices. The toilets may be impossibly narrow and the seats painfully uncomfortable, but at least it's generally the quickest option. Always call the airline well in advance if you need any special assistance. If you have a wheelchair, let them know which kind and be prepared for a transfer to a special aisle-sized chair. At ⊛www.everybody.co.uk, there's a list of airlines that cater to those with disabilities with detailed information on what they do. Another option is to travel by sea: a ship with special assistance and accessibility can make transport a breeze.

On the ground, taxis are usually the most convenient, most comfortable option, but also the most expensive. In some enlightened cities (Vancouver and Wellington for example), there are local discounts for the disabled. Few buses and trains are well equipped for wheelchairs, but taking the time to find out where they're available will be a big budget saver. With assistance, the transport possibilities are as limitless as your imagination. Take a ride on a dhow, rickshaw, hydrofoil or elephant.

If it still seems a bit overwhelming, or you'd like some help just getting started, there are a number of organizations set up for this very purpose:

Can Be Done Travel Agency ⓦwww.canbedone.co.uk
Disability Travel ⓦwww.disabilitytravel.com
Flying Wheels Travel ⓦwww.flyingwheelstravel.com
Moss Rehab Hospital ⓦwww.mossresourcenet.org
The Society for Accessible Travel and Hospitality
 ⓦwww.sath.org
Trips Special Adventures ⓦwww.tripsinc.com

Gay travellers

It's certainly much easier for gay people to travel openly than it was twenty years ago, with scores of guidebooks, travel publications and websites devoted to gay travel. Parts of the world are far less enlightened than others. In Pakistan, for example, where it's normal for straight men to walk hand in hand down the street, homosexuality is still illegal and punishable by flogging and imprisonment. In India, it carries life imprisonment (though not for women). Obviously, you want to check this out before arriving.

See p.189 for issues affecting travellers with HIV/AIDS.

Public affection

Unless you're trying to make an active protest against an intolerant government, learn the social and legal conditions before you display any behaviour that may land you in a foreign jail. If you're not sure, simply avoid public affection, which is often frowned upon no matter who's doing it. Take special care in Muslim countries, where "inappropriate" or revealing clothing may cause problems. A good place to start is the International Lesbian and Gay Association's database on treatment of gays and the legal status around the world (ⓦwww.outandabout.com).

Vegetarian travellers

It's one thing to organize your diet at home, and quite another to maintain your eating habits in places where being vegetarian is a little-known concept. But it can be done. And it doesn't even have to be stressful. Naturally, your chosen destinations are a major factor. Knowing where to look is another. A number of supermarkets, restaurants, resorts and B&Bs around the world cater specifically to vegetarians.

In terms of where to go, India is a vegetarian's paradise. So is Thailand. Delicious non-meat Italian pastas and pizzas can be easily found. Japan's food is lovely, especially if fish is an accepted part of your diet. Argentina, Scandinavia and New Zealand, on the other hand, don't offer quite the selection. In general, the ethnic vegetarian food you eat at home will be offered in wider variety in the country it comes from. There are a few excellent online resources that will lead you to a vegetarian restaurant anywhere in the world: ⍟www.vegetarianguides.co.uk, ⍟www.VegEats.com, ⍟www.VegDining.com and ⍟www.happycow.net.

The International Vegetarian Union (⍟www.ivu.org) lists foreign phrases to help you explain, or at least state your dietary requirements. Most good guidebooks provide vegetarian alternatives when available.

Eating veggie as you travel

Start by booking a vegetarian meal when you arrange your flight, then confirm it when you check your luggage. It's that easy. If you forgot, you can usually request the meal up to 48 hours before departure. Some veggie meals receive better reviews than their carnivore counterparts, while others are dire. Check ⍟www .vegparadise.com/airline.html for airline contact information, and to check out the different vegetarian menus.

Trains, ferries and buses have captive audiences, and that doesn't just apply to the music they're often fond of pumping at you. Your best shot at feeding yourself a decent vegetarian meal during the trip is if you buy one at a supermarket before boarding. Doing this is also a great money saver, so you're helping your wallet as much as your digestive tract.

18

Documenting your trip

J ust because you're travelling with your best friend, or an
entire overland group, doesn't mean you're going to collec-
tively remember everything. When you're going solo, it's even
harder. A journal, camera, tape recorder, video camera,
colour pencils, paints and watercolours are the most common
tools for recording your journey and its impact on you. Taking
along all these is overkill, but keeping some record of your trip is
an excellent idea.

Keeping a journal

Many travellers say this is the single best thing they brought on
their trip. Or buy it when you arrive: hand-pressed paper from
France, India or elsewhere gets you off to a good start. If you've
kept a journal before, you'll be bringing one anyway. If not, this is
the perfect time to start. It's not easy to process, or even remember all the places and people and stories. And simply putting your
thoughts down on paper can have a soothing, therapeutic effect. It
can be a friend when you're alone or provide structure for your
day. If you have some artistic skill, spend a little more and get paper
that will soak up your watercolours or hold ink better.

Taking photographs

Bringing along a camera is pretty obvious. Which kind, how to use it, and what to do with your film isn't. The temptation for many is to get a "good camera" – that is, one above their level of expertise. If you're a professional or exceptional amateur, bring what you need. Just be aware of the security risk of carrying valuable gear. Remove the brand names from the bags, try to select a case that doesn't look like a camera case, and minimize your lenses and accessories. If you're not a pro, go for an inexpensive pocket camera (APS or regular film). An SLR will have more features than you need and won't make up for poor photo composition. Plus, they're bulky, expensive and more likely to get stolen.

Because you can keep a pocket camera handy in a day bag (if it's really small, even a pocket) and pull it out quickly without attracting much attention, you're much more likely to use it. And – here's one of the oldest photography tricks in the book – the more photos you take the

When not to take photos

There's a reason it's called taking a picture: rarely is permission requested. It may be your camera, but it's their image or holy site and either of those trumps whatever you've got in your hand, even if you're holding a Nikon with a Swiss lens. The path to pictorial enlightenment involves respecting local bans on photography and asking all subjects for the right to snap their photo. Everything else – including the zoom-lens sniper approach – is nicking pictures. That sounds a bit dramatic, but for many, photography is their only interaction with locals, and it's a relationship largely based on selfishness and insensitivity (the author has been guilty of this as well at times). For some cultures, our swinging lenses can feel as intrusive as if someone walked up and took your picture while you were lying on the beach half-naked or stuffing your face at a restaurant. To get those great portraits you see on guidebook covers and in magazines, simply ask permission. Or go one better and try to initiate conversation. Make a few friends or even a small connection and it will add another dimension to the picture. Then, if you can, get an address and send them a copy. Giving photos has a much nicer ring than taking them.

more likely you'll get a great photo. The real decision here is between digital and film.

A regular pocket camera may be your best bet. These days the quality of a basic point-and-shoot is remarkable. Skip the zoom, though. It jacks up the price, runs down the battery, brings down the quality, and is not very powerful. If you take one to three steps forward, you'll get the same effect for free. Plus, if the moving zoom parts get so much as a grain of sand in them, kiss the camera good-bye for a month or two while it gets sent back to the manufacturer.

Digital cameras lack the bulk of SLRs, but the decent ones are nearly as expensive and therefore as likely to get stolen. They eat up batteries like a starving sumo wrestler (unless you pack along bulky recharging gear) and you may run out of memory before you can download your images. However, you can see the results immediately, attach them to your emails and save loads on developing.

Essential tips for pocket-camera users

Don't worry so much about the postcard shots. Just buy the postcard. Those photographers used the best equipment, found the

Carrying your gear

.The biggest challenge with carrying camera equipment in any situation is to be constantly aware without being suspicious. The gear is valuable, but you have to remember that it's just gear and it's replaceable. For example, I'm often in remote places and find myself in the middle of a group of kids who want to see my camera – look through the lens, take a few pictures. Some photographers freak about that. My feeling is that some kid has never seen a camera, really wants to, and I'm not going to deprive them of that. I'll keep a hand on the strap, but let them play with it.

That doesn't mean I make it easy for professional thieves whose full-time job is trying to figure out what people have and how to get it. First, I try to be inconspicuous. Camera bags attract too much attention. I currently use a regular bike messenger bag. I wear dark clothes and my camera is dark, so that works as camouflage while it's half tucked under my arm. Then I think about the picture before I take it. I don't compose my shots through the viewfinder, so I'm not keeping my camera visible for long.

This doesn't always work though. I was in the Central African Republic going through a crowded market. I was carrying my gear in this utility belt around my waist. I call it my batman belt. It's so close to the body, I can feel if anyone touches it. And it's not easy to cut through or open. Plus my shirt flops over it so it's not easy to see. Anyway, I thought I felt something. So I turned around and there was this guy holding my light meter. The reporter with me said that it looked like there was some kind of silent agreement between us. I just fixed his gaze. Then calmly removed the light meter from his hand.

Chris Anderson, a photojournalist who travels the world for publications such as *New York Times Magazine* and *National Geographic Adventure*

best vantage point, and waited until the lighting was perfect. Nothing will put your friends and family back home asleep quicker than endless landscape shots.

Photograph things that show your life on the road. It takes some effort to remember to photograph them (doorways, weird meals, freaky buses, scary toilets, charismatic taxi drivers and so on). And besides, it feels odd taking out your camera in the middle of the restaurant and snapping a picture of the meal. Also, resist the urge to photograph your travel companions posing. Catch them off guard and you'll get a more honest, interesting photo.

With scenery, and often even with people, try to compose the photo so there's something very close, something mid-range, and something in the distance. If you want to photograph someone standing in front of a waterfall, for example, try positioning yourself just behind a texture-rich tree branch and allow it to appear in a third of the picture.

Despite the fact that things seem brighter, daylight actually flattens images and provides unappealing photos. For people, animals and objects, you

△ capturing the wildlife

want overcast skies or indirect light. A cloudy day is the perfect time to get great pictures. If you must shoot people in the middle of a sunny day, use your flash to eliminate unattractive shadows or have your subjects step into a shaded area.

For pocket cameras, 100–400 ASA film is pretty versatile for action, both indoor and outdoor, and it's available everywhere. Special professional films, conversely, are extremely difficult to come by in remote places, so make sure you pack enough.

Airport X-ray machines

Never pack your film in a check-in bag. The strong X-ray machines used for checked luggage can fog your film with a single pass. With carry-on luggage X-rays, even if the machine is covered with signs stating that it will not harm film, that's not entirely true. One or two passes through may do nothing, but repeated exposure can fog unprocessed film, especially high-speed film. Ask nicely to have your camera and film hand-checked. Even if this isn't allowed everywhere, it may save your film a few extra zaps from the machine. Keeping all your film handy in a clear zip-lock bag should speed up inspection. Otherwise, you may wish to try a portable lead pouch for protection.

Developing film while you're travelling

Figuring out what to do with your pictures gets a little tricky, no matter how you do it. With film there are three basic options:

- **Get the film developed locally, send the prints home, and keep the negatives.** You run the risk of having the photos butchered by a local developer, but if it looks like a solid operation and you've had a recommendation from a traveller or local, you shouldn't have to worry much.
- **Send the film to an online photo company**. They'll develop your film, send the negs home and post all the photos on the Web so you can caption them and send them around. Then just print the photos you really want: ⊛www.ofoto.com, ⊛www.snapfish.com and many others offer such services. Before you put any film in the mail (see p.161), you'll need to protect it against X-ray machines.
- **Wait until you get to a big city, and search for a professional developer.** Then, before dropping your prints and negs in the mail, you might want to scan your favourites and email them at an Internet café for backup. This is going to be the most expensive option, especially if you're sending them with priority mail or with a private courier.

Recording sound

If the sounds of a place conjure stronger memories for you than photos, or if you'd prefer to dictate your journal, mini-cassettes and mini-discs are both good options. If it's a digitized format, you may be able to upload sound clips and attach them to emails at Internet cafés. Consider what you'll be using it for when you select a microphone. For voices, go for a unidirectional mic. For ambient sounds, you'll want a wider spread. Some of the better microphones are equipped with both.

Making videos

Many of today's smallest digital video cameras can slip into a jacket pocket. Plus they record sounds and make still video images. The downside is that they cost $1000–2000/£635–1270, take low-resolution digital stills, and don't record sound that well without an additional microphone.

Like photography, video has spawned stacks of books on method and technique. If you're going to shoot, here are two simple tips. The first is to hold the camera very steady even if it's equipped with an electronic stabilizer. That may mean leaning against a tree or lamppost. Better, however, is to bring a tripod. Nothing induces headaches like watching shaky footage. The second tip is to resist letting the camera follow your natural head or eye movement all the time. For example, allow someone to walk across the field of vision – entering on one side and disappearing on the other. This will make editing much easier once you return home.

Drawing and painting

Watercolours, colour pencils and sketching charcoal are relatively cheap and extremely easy to transport. Even if you don't have much artistic skill, or much that you're aware of, this is an ideal time to give it a shot. It's a nice alternative to reading or writing when you're stuck somewhere for a long time. Which, invariably, you will be at some point.

What to do with souvenirs

Send them home. Few travellers need any help selecting souvenirs, but most seem to need some help carrying them. No matter how small, lightweight and space-saving the items may seem individually, the best thing you can do – unless you're at the tail end of your trip – is a big round of shopping when you get to a market you like, then ship everything home the same day (see p.160). Your glass turtle earrings, Dutch windmill decanter and fake Ray-Bans from Vietnam will have a much better chance getting broken, stolen, or lost under your care than that of a postal service. Naturally, there are several levels of security available (as well as private couriers) at a range of prices. Consider the reliability of the postal service (are you in Denmark or India?), the weight of the package and the value of what you're sending, before you ship. There's no magic formula, but it's not uncommon to pay more for postage than the actual item enclosed. Keep that in mind when you're about to buy that set of traditional fire-walking rocks in Fiji.

Mementoes of your trip

Memories fade, surprisingly quickly. After a few days back home on the sofa in your old pair of jeans, the entire experience can feel like it never actually occurred. Best to jot things down while they're still fresh in your mind.

You can create an online scrapbook – it will basically happen on its own if you use one of the online photo developers. Just make sure you don't forget to label the photos with names and places as you go. It may seem obvious at the time, but several months down the road when you finally return and get around to assembling the photos, it's not going to be quite as clear. (If you're getting film processed along the way, remember to write names and places on the back of the prints.)

Until we know how long digital memory lasts (and how well) you'll eventually want to convert your photos to prints. And make sure you've got a friend or parent saving and printing out the e-dispatches you're sending back. Those can provide the backbone of the memorabilia you may wish to piece together later. Towards this end, one of the best things you can do aside from taking photos or painting is to collect small, flat items that catch your eye and evoke a memory: concert and train tickets, a beer label, fortune-cookie prediction, even a sample of the abrasive toilet paper that once gave you some trouble. Send it home with your film or wedge it into your journal for safe transport.

Another thing to remember is the legality of exporting antiques. Just because a vendor in a market is willing to part with it doesn't mean you're allowed to bring it out of the country, so the authentic fifteenth-century porcelain spittoon you bargained for may not be getting off the plane with you when you land back home. Nor is it likely to arrive in the mail. If it looks old and valuable, consult your guidebook. You may need to get a certificate of authenticity from a museum. Shopping caution also applies to plants, seeds and items made from wild animals, which may be removed by customs officials. You won't be reimbursed for any of this, but you may get fined.

19

Returning home

I t probably feels a bit premature to be thinking about coming back home already, but this information may affect your planning, so best that it's addressed now. Let's assume you've circumnavigated the planet. You've fended off wild animals in Africa, hitchhiked across Asia and walked barefoot across scorching Fijian rocks. You've learned to eat rice with chopsticks and dhal with your fingers. You can intimidate a thief and bungee-jump off a bridge, yet meditate with monks. You have new friends on every landmass, a new global outlook and even a few new parasites. All you have left is to return home.

But here's where things can get problematic. With a comfortable bed and fresh set of clothes in sight, it's tempting to lower your guard. Instead, you're going to need to brace yourself for a potentially rough re-entry.

Re-entry shock

Many people coming home from a long trip experience a bigger shock on their return than when they first went abroad, and at a time when they're least prepared for it. The good news is there are a few simple things you can do to turn the experience into a smooth landing, and the most important of these is just knowing what to expect.

The stages of re-entry mirror those of culture shock: honeymoon, crisis, recovery, and readjustment. The honeymoon is the initial exhilaration of returning home, and precisely what most are expecting. The surprise left hook is the "reverse culture shock", which lasts until you acclimatize to your home surroundings and eventually return to your old self (with a bit more wisdom and experience).

The degree of the reverse culture shock you experience largely depends upon how integrated you became into foreign cultures during your journey, and how different they are from your own. Upon returning, you may miss the regular and close social interaction you had with your foreign community and other travellers. You may find yourself revolted by the aggressive marketing campaigns you had previously learned to ignore. More likely, you may feel a distance has come between you and your friends and family because they can no longer relate to your "new" well-travelled persona – one that has grown and been shaped by your range of different experiences. Instead, they're treating you the same way and don't have the patience to hear the thirty hours of stories required to bring them up to speed. And if you're returning to a job, you may notice reduced responsibilities and little acknowledgement for your overseas accomplishments.

This is compounded by The Questions. If you've ever broken your leg and had to explain what happened to everyone you met for a month, you already have a good understanding of what it's like to be a human recording. But when you're trying to sum up a few months or a few years of life-changing experiences in one or two cute lines, it's even more frustrating. The Questions tend to be the same worldwide. They'll start with "How was the trip?" go on to "What was your favourite?" and quickly get to, "So what are you going to do now?"

Coping strategies

Scuba diving and cultural immersion are similar in at least this one respect: a little decompression is a good idea. Before you return home, try to build in a little stop for mental refuelling. It needn't be a month of silence at a monastery: a beach will do fine. You just need a place with minimal stimulus. It can take a while to process the lifetime of experiences that you've just crammed into a ridiculously short period. And more important still, you need to begin to engage with the concept of returning home. You're going to have enough to worry about when you get back, so try to work out a game plan in advance: where you're going to stay, who you plan to visit and so on.

Bracing others for your arrival

The best single thing you can do in this respect is keep your friends and family up to speed during your trip with short, regular dispatches from the road. The easiest way to do this is with a group email. Let them know where you are and what you're up to. In general, people will have more patience to read about your experiences in bite-size chunks than to listen to them all in one go.

Writing that last dispatch from the road

When you're just about to head home, take some time to sum up your trip in your last email or letter. Answer the questions they're likely to ask. Tell them what your favourite places are, if in fact you have any. Tell them what your plans are. Those around you will want to get that extra dose of info when they see you in person. Help them out. Give them something they can ask about. You might say "For a beer, I'll be happy to fill in the details on the time I ... But the time I ... is worth at least two." Or: "I'll be carrying around a very small selection of photos in case you're curious to see some of the things I've been writing about. If there aren't clean sheets on the bed, I'll be forced to show you the giant photo collection."

Staying in touch with people you met

Stay in touch with the friends you made on your trip. It improves the chance you'll see them again, have a free place to stay (and a cultural guide) when you head abroad next time, and gives you a free support network.

Keeping involved with the places

Join an organization that supports a place or cause you found on the road. Study that language you were dying to speak at the time but couldn't. Read fiction or nonfiction books on the subject. If you do eventually head back to any of these places, you'll be able to appreciate them on another level.

Seeking out travellers in your area

There's probably a hostel in your area, or certainly an international group. Spending time with travellers, visiting students, or an immigrant crowd can be just enough of a dose to remind you that you're sane after all.

Having patience

It's common to feel superior to those around you who haven't had such international experiences. Suddenly, their views may seem pedestrian and insular and you feel the continued need to "set them straight". Just remember: your own views may not be that popular, either. Time outside your own country tends to highlight its faults, and you may come off sounding like a born-again critic. Take heart. You will have enlightened perspectives, but don't expect others to come around easily.

Getting busy

If you have the possibility to arrange your work/study schedule before returning, keep this in mind: a little down time at home is wonderful, but too much can be self-defeating. Finding that right balance is up to you, but in general the less the better. One or two weeks is usually sufficient.

Reviving the memories

If you need a quick fix, you might try escaping back into your travels for a brief tour. This is where a good scrapbook and well-kept journal come in handy (see p.207). Using your notes and images, it can often be helpful to write about your experiences more fully. Who knows? This may be the chance to release that budding travel writer within.

Start travelling again

If all else fails (except your finances), hit the road again. It doesn't have to be a long trip, or even an international one. Just taking some trains and buses, packing up your rucksack, sleeping in a few ratty hotels and meeting some other travellers can be enough.

First-Time Around the World

Regional profiles

Africa

Africa is much less daunting than most travellers tend to think, and there are a myriad sights, sounds and experiences to draw you to the continent. The Arab hospitality in the north can be overwhelming, the wildlife and landscapes of sub-Saharan Africa are unmissable, the music of West Africa is infectious and inspiring and you'll be stunned by the continent's dramatic southern coast. In other words, there's a lot more to Africa than a bunch of wild animals stomping around outside your tent, although that can certainly be arranged.

Main attractions

● **Maasai Mara** Kenya. The northern sister park of Tanzania's Serengeti, the Maasai Mara in Kenya stretches for 3000 square kilometres and serves as the living room, kitchen and playground for elephants, lions, zebras, giraffes and other photogenic species. It's also the home of the Maasai, a tall and striking warrior people who still hunt on the grassy plains, though more recently they've been pushed into selling handicrafts and performing for video cameras.

● **The Great Pyramids** Egypt. They're more than just the world's largest tombstones. The precision of their construction represents the highest level of science and craftsmanship and a remarkable understanding of astronomy. And, what's more, they're really just a sample of what the ancient pharaohs left behind, a wealth of archeological treasures that stretch far down the banks of the Nile.

● **Victoria Falls** Zimbabwe. These days, Vic Falls has come to represent more than just a spectacular 1.7-kilometre-wide, 100-metre drop into the Zambezi River. It's an entire action-adventure park, with bungee-jumping, whitewater rafting, ultralite flying and horseback safaris. Not surprisingly, it's the largest crossroads on the African backpacker circuit. Keep in mind that from March to May the floodwaters kick up so much spray you can hardly see the falls.

● **Zanzibar** Tanzania. A former trading centre, once populated with Phoenicians, Sumerians, Persians, Indians, Arabs, Portuguese and English. Stone Town, the main port, is an intricate web of streets that are a delight to get lost in. And, if you time your visit to avoid the crush of tourists, you just might. The beaches around the island are a big draw.

● **Cape Town** South Africa. You might expect something grand to happen where two oceans converge, and the tip of Africa does not disappoint. Cape Town is one of the most naturally stunning cities on the planet, with clouds regularly spilling over the kilometre-high Table Mountain like a candyfloss waterfall, white beaches strung along the rocky coast and world-class vineyards maturing just a short bus ride away.

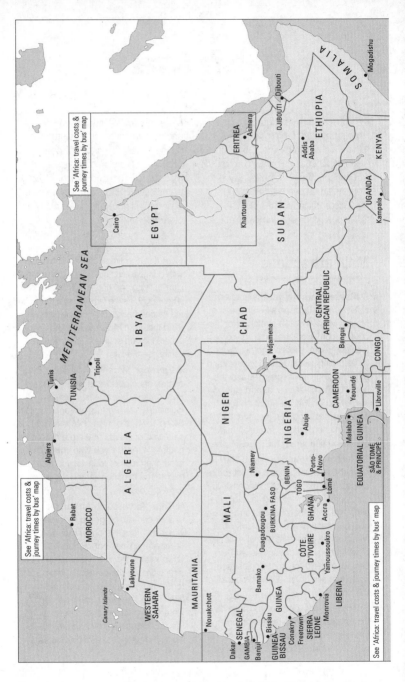

See 'Africa: travel costs & journey times by bus' map

See 'Africa: travel costs & journey times by bus' map

See 'Africa: travel costs & journey times by bus' map

MEDITERRANEAN SEA

Canary Islands

MOROCCO

Rabat

Algiers

Tunis

TUNISIA

Tripoli

LIBYA

EGYPT

Cairo

Khartoum

SUDAN

ERITREA

Asmara

DJIBOUTI

Djibouti

Mogadishu

ETHIOPIA

Addis
Ababa

SOMALIA

KENYA

UGANDA

Kampala

CENTRAL
AFRICAN REPUBLIC

Bangui

CONGO

Libreville

CAMEROON

Yaoundé

EQUATORIAL GUINEA

Malabo

SÃO TOMÉ
& PRÍNCIPE

CHAD

Ndjamena

NIGER

Niamey

NIGERIA

Abuja

Porto-
Novo

BENIN

TOGO

Lomé

GHANA

Accra

BURKINA FASO

Ouagadougou

CÔTE
D'IVOIRE

Yamoussoukro

MALI

Bamako

ALGERIA

Laâyoune

WESTERN
SAHARA

MAURITANIA

Nouakchott

SENEGAL

Dakar

GAMBIA

Banjul

GUINEA-
BISSAU

Bissau

GUINEA

Conakry

SIERRA
LEONE

Freetown

LIBERIA

Monrovia

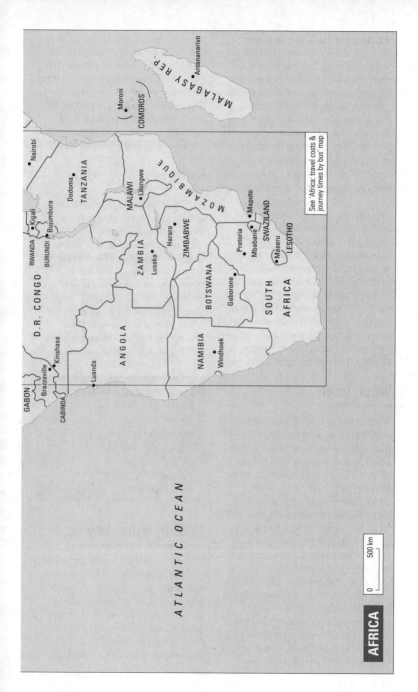

AFRICA

0 [____500 km____]

See 'Africa: travel costs & journey times by bus' map

ATLANTIC OCEAN

GABON
CABINDA
Brazzaville
Kinshasa
D.R. CONGO
RWANDA
Kigali
BURUNDI
Bujumbura
Nairobi
Luanda
ANGOLA
ZAMBIA
Lusaka
TANZANIA
Dodoma
MALAWI
Lilongwe
MOZAMBIQUE
Harare
ZIMBABWE
NAMIBIA
Windhoek
BOTSWANA
Gaborone
SOUTH
AFRICA
Pretoria
Mbabane
SWAZILAND
Maseru
LESOTHO
Maputo
Moroni
COMOROS
MALAGASY REP.
Antananarivo

- **Bazaars of Fès and Marrakesh** Morocco. You don't need 10,000 alleys and streets to get lost, but it certainly helps. The spice and handicraft vendors add to the confusion, in streetscapes as surreal as an Escher painting. Open spaces brim with acrobats, snake charmers, storytellers and, at every turn, there are more interesting characters parading by than a Hollywood studio could cast with a limitless budget.

- **Mount Kilimanjaro** Tanzania. Kili, as it's often called, is the storybook mountain silhouette you first learn to draw in primary school: the perfect heaven-scraping cone shape with a jagged snowline near the top. Whether you're climbing the 5895-metre high "mountain that glitters" (as the name means in Swahili) or simply having a picnic in its shade, the peak is mesmerizing. It's typically hiked in five or six days: good hiking gear, strong legs and pristine lungs make the task much easier. Not to mention $700/£450 for permits, guiding and food.

When to go

The temperature in Africa doesn't vary more than ten degrees throughout the year (although it's not uncommon for it to drop twenty degrees each night). Your bigger concern is rainfall. In eastern Africa, there are "short" and "long" rains. The short ones (Oct–Nov) might mean an afternoon thunderstorm that muddies the roads and keeps the roof hatch closed on the safari van. The long rains (March–May) may make the roads impassable. Most people prefer travel to this eastern region in June to October, often trying to coincide with the Great Migration of over one million wilde-beest, 300,000 gazelles and 150,000 zebras around July/August. Madagascar cyclones typically occur in November to March, and an eye should be kept on the weather reports if you do travel during that

period. In Western Africa, those put off by heat should aim for Nov/Dec. Otherwise, keep a lens cover ready for the dusty har-mattan winds (Dec–March) that roll in from the Sahara. In the North, along the Mediterranean coast, the winter (Dec–Feb) can be wet and mildly unpleasant. For ideal weather conditions at various African game parks, go to Ⓦwww.onsafari.com.

Costs

There is certainly luxury accommodation catering to the extremely rich, but, with some exceptions – notably West Africa – Africa is a budget-travel zone. Those exceptions include Libya, which only grants visas to groups and likes to ensure they are shepherded to nice resorts; Botswana and Zambia, which are trying to go after the upmarket, low-impact tourists; and Namibia. South African cities can get a little expensive but, overall, prices are still reasonable.

Lowest daily budget
Expensive ($40/£26+): Botswana
Mid-range ($25–$40/£16–£26): Cape Town, Libya, Namibia, Zambia
Budget ($8–$25/£5–£16): Everywhere else

Getting around by air

It's not the cheapest way to get around, but then flying rarely is. It can, however, help bridge gaps so you spend more time covering the ground you want to cover. The basic guidelines for air travel take on more importance in Africa, par-ticularly when you're not using major international carriers. This means you really ought to:

● Confirm your flight a couple of times (including the day of the flight).

● Arrive early. You may end up winning a seat on an overbooked flight, even if you had a ticket and didn't think the seat would require any winning. Plus, many flights have open seating, so you might even get a seat with some legroom.

● Some baggage inspectors may take their time rifling through your things, either out of curiosity or hopes of financial payoff. If a bribe or "gift" is requested, and your belongings are in order, politely stand your ground. At a pinch, try handing over something that isn't hugely important to you.

Air passes

British Airways and partners issue a Visit Africa pass which allows access to a total of fifteen cities in Namibia, South Africa, Zimbabwe, Zambia, Kenya, Djibouti, Eritrea, Sudan and Somalia. Prices range from $62/£40 to $160/£103, depending on the connection, which are about 35 percent cheaper than standard fares. There's a minimum purchase of two flights (in different zones), which means the cheapest possible package would cost $152/£98.

Sample fares

Cairo to:
Cape Town $1000/£643
Marrakech $700/450
Nairobi $450/£289

Johannesburg to:
Dar es Salaam $350/£225
Marrakech $1000/£643
Windhoek $175/£113

Overland routes

The continent may stretch 7000km from north to south, but the limited infrastructure has created surprisingly well-trodden overland routes. The most common is from Cape Town to Nairobi, which passes through Namibia, Botswana, Zimbabwe, Zambia, Malawi, Tanzania (often with a side trip to Zanzibar), then into Kenya. Most travellers now fly between Nairobi and Egypt due to the fighting in Sudan and near the Ethiopian/Eritrean border, but depending on political conditions, you may be able to make it all the way overland or catch a flight in Addis Ababa instead. Check with nearby embassies and other travellers for the most recent information.

The other primary route passes down the west coast between Tangier, Morocco and Yaounde in Cameroon. From the north, it makes the tricky crossing of the western Sahara, heads onto Mauritania and Senegal, then turns inland and traverses Mali. In Burkina Faso, the route either goes south to Accra on the coast or passes through Niger and Benin. The trails meet again in Nigeria and press on to Cameroon. From there, it's common to fly to Nairobi or Windhoek and continue south overland.

You can get nearly everywhere in Africa without your own transport. A combination of buses, trains, and boats is going to be your best option. Your thumb may come in handy as well. You may not get there exactly when you want to, but of course that's all part of the adventure. Because some of the routes are so poorly maintained, you'll probably have quite an adventure in your own vehicle as well. So long as you're armed with plenty of patience, you'll be fine.

Buses

Top-end buses, typically in South Africa and Namibia, are comfortable and will generally leave on schedule and adhere to the one-person-per-seat rule, but

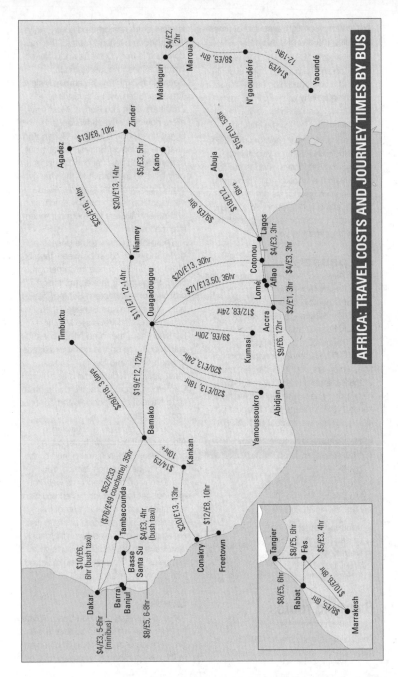

AFRICA: TRAVEL COSTS AND JOURNEY TIMES BY BUS

Maroua — $4/£2, 2hr
Maiduguri
N'gaoundéré — $8/£5, 8hr
Yaoundé — $14/£9, 12-19hr

Zinder — $13/£8, 10hr
Agadez
Kano — $5/£3, 5hr
Abuja
$15/£10, 53hr
$8/£5, 22hr
Lagos — 8hr+
$9/£6, 8hr
$20/£13, 14hr
$25/£16, 14hr
Niamey
$11/£7, 12-14hr
Ouagadougou
Cotonou — $4/£3, 3hr
Aflao — $4/£3, 3hr
$20/£13, 30hr
Lomé
$21/£13.50, 36hr
$2/£1, 3hr
$12/£8, 24hr
Accra
$9/£6, 20hr
Kumasi — $9/£6, 12hr
$20/£13, 24hr
Timbuktu
$20/£13, 18hr
Yamoussoukro
$19/£12, 12hr
Abidjan
$28/£18, 3 days
Bamako
Kankan
$14/£9, 10hr+
$76/£49 couchette), 35hr
$52/£33
Tambacounda — $4/£3, 4hr (bush taxi)
$10/£6, 6hr (bush taxi)
$20/£13, 13hr
Basse Santa Su
$12/£8, 10hr
Conakry
Barra
Banjul
Freetown
Dakar
$4/£3, 5-6hr (minibus)
$8/£5, 6-8hr

Tangier
$8/£5, 6hr
Fès — $5/£3, 4hr
$10/£6, 8hr
$8/£5, 6hr
Rabat
$8/£5, 6hr
Marrakesh

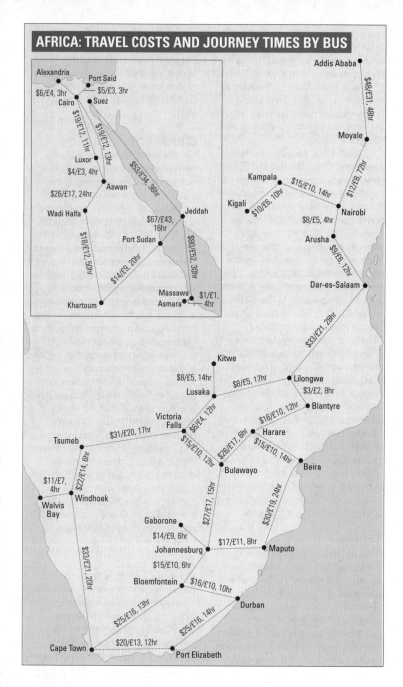

AFRICA: TRAVEL COSTS AND JOURNEY TIMES BY BUS

Addis Ababa

$48/£31, 48hr

Moyale

$12/£8, 72hr

Alexandria

$6/£4, 3hr
Port Said
$5/£3, 3hr
Cairo
Suez

$19/£12, 11hr
$19/£12, 13hr

$53/£34, 36hr

Luxor
$4/£3, 4hr
Aswan

$26/£17, 24hr

Wadi Halfa

Jeddah

$67/£43, 16hr
Port Sudan
$80/£52, 30hr

$18/£12, 50hr

$14/£3, 20hr

Massawa
$1/£1, 4hr
Asmara

Khartoum

Kampala
$15/£10, 14hr
Kigali
$10/£6, 10hr
Nairobi

$8/£5, 4hr

Arusha

$9/£6, 12hr

Dar-es-Salaam

$33/£21, 28hr

Kitwe

$8/£5, 14hr
$8/£5, 17hr
Lilongwe
Lusaka
$3/£2, 8hr
Blantyre

$16/£10, 12hr

Victoria Falls
$6/£4, 12hr
Harare

$31/£20, 17hr
Tsumeb

$15/£10, 12hr
$26/£17, 6hr
$15/£10, 14hr
Beira

$22/£?, ?
$11/£7, 4hr
Bulawayo

Windhoek

Walvis Bay

$27/£17, 15hr
$30/£19, 24hr

Gaborone
$14/£9, 6hr

$33/£21, 20hr

Johannesburg
$17/£11, 8hr
Maputo

$15/£10, 6hr

Bloemfontein
$16/£10, 10hr
Durban

$25/£16, 13hr

$25/£16, 14hr

Cape Town
$20/£13, 12hr
Port Elizabeth

some drivers are a little overzealous with the air-con and, with a high-tech stereo system under their command, may simply bad-music you into a coma. Otherwise, buses depart when full or at the driver's whim, stop constantly, are driven wildly and cram up to five times the maximum allowable number of passengers on board.

In South Africa, there are a number of alternatives. There's the Baz Bus (Ⓦwww.bazbus.com), a hop-on hop-off minivan for travellers that moves along the main travel circuit. A one-way trip from Johannesburg to Cape Town on Baz will cost $160/£103. Intercape (Ⓦwww.intercape.co.za), Greyhound (Ⓦwww.greyhound.co.za) and Translux (Ⓦwww.translux.co.za) all run luxury bus services along the main routes. A direct trip from Johannesburg to Cape Town is around $25/£16, not including a fifteen-percent student discount. So far Greyhound offers the only bus passes – 7 days ($130/£84), 15 days ($250/£161) and 30 days ($425/£273) of unlimited travel, which isn't much of a bargain, but Translux is planning to introduce a pass soon and Interscape offers an international service to Namibia and Botswana. Between Johannesburg and Bulawayo in Zimbabwe, Zimbabwe Travel (Ⓦwww.gozimbabwe.co.za organizes an air-conditioned bus ride. From there, you can connect to a train and arrive in Vic Falls 24 hours after leaving Jo'burg, assuming you don't get held up at the border.

Trains

There will be ample opportunities to ride a train, but there's not enough track around Africa to make rail travel your sole mode of transport. Aside from South Africa's plush and outrageously priced Blue Train, spanning the scenic gap between Johannesburg and Cape Town (less expensive trains on this route can be booked weeks in advance in

June–July and Dec–Jan), there's the Mombassa–Niarobi line, Cairo–Aswan line and the Dakan–Barnako line. These all offer reasonably priced second-class service, some fitted with sleeper cars, and uber-cheap third-class compartments.

Cars

For years travellers have been driving themselves around Africa, setting their own schedules and venturing off the main routes at the change of a breeze. For drivers, the overland route between Nairobi and Egypt is completely cut off due to the fighting in Sudan and near the Ethiopian/Eritrean border. Check current conditions before heading that way. And Congo has a current chokehold on overland passage as well. But there's still plenty of driving to be had. There are four basic options: renting a car, renting a car and a driver, buying a car locally or shipping/driving a car from home. If you're travelling in countries that require an international driving permit (Ⓦwww.theaa.co.uk), pick one up before you leave. The Carnet de Passage (p.42) is a must for most countries except Algeria, Lesotho, Malawi, Morocco, Namibia, South Africa, Tunisia, Zambia and Zimbabwe, which issue temporary import permits for free upon entry or don't require one. But to pull off anything more than a rental, you'll need to do some homework. Try these books for starters: *Sahara Overland* by Chris Scott and *Africa by Road* by Bob Swain & Paula Snyder.

Rental

Of the four options, the least practical and economical for a cross-continent road trip is likely to be renting a car. The rental companies (such as Ⓦwww.aroundaboutcars.com and Ⓦwww.kaeferhire.net) know the conditions of the roads and the toll they take on vehicles and will charge you accordingly. Many will not even allow you to drive across borders, or limit you to Botswana, Lesotho, Namibia, Swaziland and Zimbabwe. However, in these countries you'll find quite decent roads – long highways that are actually easy to navigate – and you may find a two-wheel drive rental is the best way to go. They're reasonably priced and start at around $20/£13 per day for economy car. For $60/£39, you can get a VW minivan with built-in camping top or a 4WD. Be sure to get recent carjacking information so you know where to take precautions.

Rental with chauffeur

This is an informal arrangement with a taxi driver or, preferably, the owner of a four-wheel-drive vehicle. And it will probably cost you less than a rental ($10/£6–$50/£32 per day), depending on the car, length of journey and your bargaining skills. Just make sure you negotiate a day or week rate for the driver's services and pay the petrol separately. If the driver is paying for the petrol, they may do what they can to save it, even if it means driving very slowly, turning off the air-con and headlights (if they exist), and trying to refuse suggested detours. If there are any car problems, they're the driver's responsibility. Give yourself the option to bail out if the delays look serious and, in the first instance, try to sign up with a driver whose car looks roadworthy.

Buying a car

Here's the classic decision: Land Cruiser or Range Rover. As more than one African overland aficionado will explain, Land Cruisers are reliable, but the spare parts aren't that easy to come by, while with a Range Rover, you can find the spare parts more easily, but you're going to need them. It's not going to be cheap, but you should get your money back when you sell the car, if it's in reasonable shape. South Africa is a good place to pick up a vehicle. If you're buying secondhand, take the car to a mechanic for an independent inspection. If you're just driving on the well-surfaced roads around South Africa, Namibia and Botswana you can skirt the 4x4 issue and pick up a cheaper travel-friendly VW minibus or sport wagon instead. Have your documents well organized and ready for presentation at each border. Keep your cool with the border guards and act like you're not in a hurry. In fact, just don't be in a hurry. That makes it even easier. For more tips see p.40.

Bringing your own car

Typically, travellers take cars on the short ferry journey from Spain to Morocco. The costs for shipping a vehicle from Europe to sub-saharan Africa is $1000–2500/£640–1600, depending on the destination. Just be sure to lock down or remove anything than can be taken off with a screwdriver or it may not be there when your vehicle arrives. Again, you'll need a Carnet de Passage (see p.42), and all the necessary permits and documents. If you plan to sell the vehicle in Africa, that should be pre-arranged when you get your Carnet, so your deposit can be easily refunded. But you'll still have to pay the import duties in the country you're selling it in, so find out what that figure is beforehand. (For recommended vehicles, see the paragraph above on buying a car.)

Bikes

Pedalling is a fine way to see Africa. Rental cycles are available in most places you would want to ride a bike. And when they aren't, don't be afraid to ask ordinary people about renting their bikes, or go to a bike repair shop and make the same request. You'll find people quite flexible in this regard. For serious touring, bring a bike from home and make sure it can handle potholes and gravel with ease. Even if you stick to the main routes, you'll undoubtedly be stopping in places that most travellers speed by and leave choking in a cloud of dust. Of course, on a bike, you'll be eating a good deal of dust yourself, and you may want to bring a face mask. Also remember to plan your food and water carefully over long stretch-

Visa and vaccination requirements for Africa

Algeria Visa (30 days) required, free to $38/£24, no entrance if passport stamped by Israel, Malawi or Taiwan

Angola Visa required, $80/£51. Two-week processing time, separate visa for air or overland entrance

Benin Visa required ($40/£26). Proof of sufficient funds and onward travel

Botswana No visa (90 days) except for citizens of Canada, New Zealand, Australia, Spain and Portugal

Burkina Faso Visa required

Burundi Visa required (30 days), $40/£26

Cameroon Visa required (90 days), $50/£32

Central African Republic Visa required, $150/£96, onward travel

Chad Visa required (30 days), $75/£48

Congo Visa required (14 days), except for French visitors

Congo (former Zaire) Visa required (30 days), $75/£48

Côte d'Ivoire Visa required except for citizens of Germany, France, Ireland, Italy, Norway, Sweden, Denmark and Finland

Djibouti Visa required, $29 except for citizens of France

Egypt 1-month visas may be bought at airport on arrival ($22/£14) or in Nuweiba from Jordan overland route.

No visa available at border with Israel or Libya (get beforehand or at embassy in Tel Aviv, Eilat or Tripoli); no visa required if you are only staying in Sinai between Sharm el-Sheikh and Taba (free 14-day stamp at border.)

Guinea Visa required, $45/£25

Eritrea Visa required, requirements vary ($25) onward travel, sufficient funds

Ethiopia Visa required, $68/£44

Gabon Visa required (90–120 days), $20–60/£13–39, week or more to process

Gambia Visa required (one year), $25/£16, except for citizens of Belgium, Denmark, Finland, Germany, the Netherlands, Norway, Spain, Sweden

Ghana Visa required (30 days), $20/£13, onward travel funds, 3–4 days processing time

Guinea Visa required (30 days), $25–50/£16–32), onward travel funds, cholera vaccine

Guinea-Bissau Visa required (30 days), onward travel funds

Kenya Visa required (90 days), $50/£32, except for citizens of Denmark, Germany, Ireland, Italy, Norway, Spain, Sweden

Lesotho Visa required, onward travel, sufficient funds

es; cycle early in the morning and in the late afternoon and rest in the shade during the heat of midday; try to coordinate your trip with the coolest months; get permission from villagers when camping near their settlements; and don't be afraid to use public transport. You can almost always toss your bike on a bus at a pinch. One more thing: you don't have the right of way on a bike . . . ever. Practise your emergency swerve.

Liberia Visa required (90 days), $45/£29, apply for additional visitors' permit on entry

Libya For nations allowed entrance, visa required (90 days), $30–50/£19–32). Passport must be translated into Arabic, no entrance if Israeli stamp in passport. HIV test

Malawi Visa required, $40/£26. No visa required (30 days) for citizens of France

Mali Visa required, $20/£13 except for citizens of France

Mauritania Visas required for all citizens except France and Italy, letter of introduction, onward travel, valid for 3 months ($15/£10). In Senegal, they can cost over $100/£64

Mozambique Visa required (30 days), $10–20/£6–13 (same-day service in South Africa, Tanzania), cholera vaccine

Namibia No visa for up to 90 days' stay but onward travel required

Niger Visa required (30 days), $35–50/£23–32, onward travel, sufficient funds

Nigeria Visas are required. Difficult to obtain unless you get them from the embassy in your home country. One-month visa typically $30, but $200 for UK citizens. Valid 3 months from date of issue.

Rwanda Visa required (90 days), $50/£32 except for citizens of Germany

Sao Tome, Principe Visa available at airport (30 days), $60/£39

Senegal Visa required (90 days) except for citizens of Belgium, Denmark, France, Germany, Ireland, Italy, Luxembourg and the Netherlands

Sierra Leone Visa required (90 days), $45/£29, onward travel, sufficient funds

Somalia Visas required

Sudan Visa required, $35–80/£23–51, unreliable embassies, no visa for passports showing Israeli stamp

Swaziland No visa required (up to 60 days

Tanzania Visa (90 days) available at border, free–$50/£32

Togo Visa (7 days) granted on arrival

Tunisia No visa required (up to 90 days) with onward travel

Uganda Visa (90 days) available at major borders & airports, $30/£19

Zambia Visa (90 days) $25/£19, plus sufficient funds, onward travel. No visa required for citizens of Norway, Sweden, Yugoslavia, Ireland. Visa fee for UK citizens $50/£32

Zimbabwe Visa required, $30/£19, except for citizens of Sweden and Ireland

Hitching

Hitching is part of the African way of life. In some towns you can actually hitch rides downtown. With an array of several modes of transport to choose from, it may still be your best choice. Other times, it may be your only choice. As a foreigner, you're a bit of an oddity on the side of the road and have a good chance of catching a quick ride, but you will invariably be expected to pay something. However, don't stand too close to large groups of hitchers, as the person who stops for you may not want to try to squeeze an entire group into the vehicle. See the section on hitching safety on p.136.

Boats

You may decide to float down the Nile on a felucca, starting in Aswan and ending just short of Luxor; cross Lake Victoria by ferry; or sail among the islands off the coast of Lamu. If you don't mind crocs, hippos and elephants within a paddle's length of your canoe, you might consider a trip down the Zambezi well below Victoria Falls or along Botswana's Okavango Delta. Few of these boats get you somewhere you couldn't otherwise access, but they do greatly enhance the "getting there".

Reading list

- Chinua Achebe *Things Fall Apart*
- Karen Blixen *Out of Africa*
- Shirley Deane *Talking Drums*
- Dian Fossey *Gorillas in the Mist*
- Kuki Gallman *I Dreamed of Africa*
- Barbara Kingsolver *The Poisonwood Bible*
- Ben Okri *The Famished Road*
- Nelson Mandela *Long Road to Freedom*
- V.S. Naipaul *A Bend in the River*
- Ngugi wa Thiong'o *A Grain of Wheat*
- *The Traveller's Literary Companion – Africa* Edited by Oona Strathern

Visas

Many African countries require yellow fever and cholera immunizations, though these aren't the only immunizations you should have (Chapter 00 on Health), or even the most important. But without them, you could be turned away, even with a visa. Enforcement of this varies from rigid to nonexistent, and often only applies to people coming from an infected area. Check with an embassy or the country's website for up-to-the-minute info.

"Onward travel" means officials want to see that you've got a ticket back home or on to someplace else and, thus, do not have aspirations to stay permanently. Again, this is rarely enforced, especially if you can demonstrate sufficient funds ($500/£320 per month or major credit card) and show your intended overland route.(see box on pp.230–231 for more).

Asia

To some travellers, Asia is the home of the most exhilarating natural landscapes on the planet: the soaring Himalayas. To others, it's a collection of frenzied cities and remote cultures connected by rough local transport through countless terraced rice paddies. Many see Asia as the epicentre of spiritual enlightenment. Some think of the geisha tea houses of Japan or the surfable breaks of Indonesia. And some travellers simply think: it's cheap.

The truth is that Asia has something for everyone. It's really just a matter of deciding what you're after. The low prices (outside Japan, Bhutan, Hong Kong and Singapore anyway) make most activities and journeys financially feasible to travellers on the lowest budgets. Surprisingly though, much of Asia is still relatively untouched by the travel circuit, and if you're willing to forego the comforts of the backpacker infrastructure, it's yours to discover.

Main attractions

● **Nepal** Here's an activity that people come from around the world to try, yet it's almost never practised by locals. Nepalese simply don't head out on trekking tours. Many walk on the same trails, but only when they need to get somewhere. The hair-raising vistas, sense of adventure and cheap guesthouses along the trails lure tens of thousands of travellers each year.

● **Varanasi** India. The religious centre of India is practically carved into the banks of the Ganges River in north central India just as it has been for over 2000 years. Those looking for eternal enlightenment are cremated on the ghats, and those seeking a less permanent fix bathe not far away. Be especially respectful of religious customs regarding photography and conservative dress.

● **Angkor Wat** Cambodia. This remarkable collection of 100 temples and palaces (stretching over 60 square kilometres) was built by Khmer kings between the ninth and fourteenth centuries. It's only part of a much larger holy site that has since been swallowed by the surrounding jungle over the last 500 years.

● **Taj Mahal** India. Bring your sunglasses. This white marble mausoleum has glacier-like reflective properties that your retinas won't forget in a hurry. Built in 1632–1653 by Emperor Shah Jahan in loving memory of his second wife, Mumtaz Mahal, who died prematurely from childbirth complications, the Taj is an architectural marvel that has been crafted down to the most minute detail.

● **The Great Wall** China. The unusual thing about this attraction is that you can't see it. You can, of course, see a tiny portion of it no matter where you stand – perhaps 20–40km in either direction – but precisely what makes it so incredible is the other 5960km out of

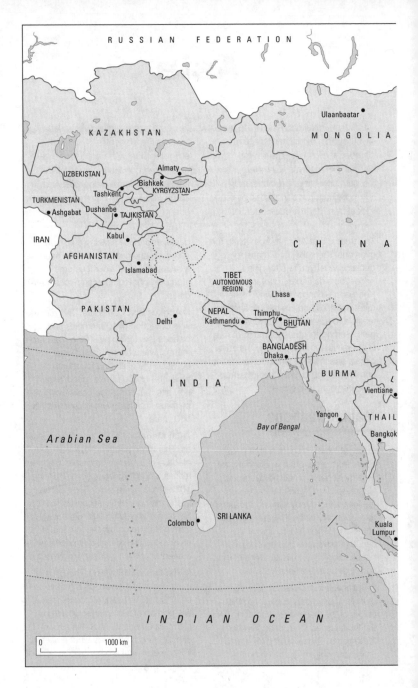

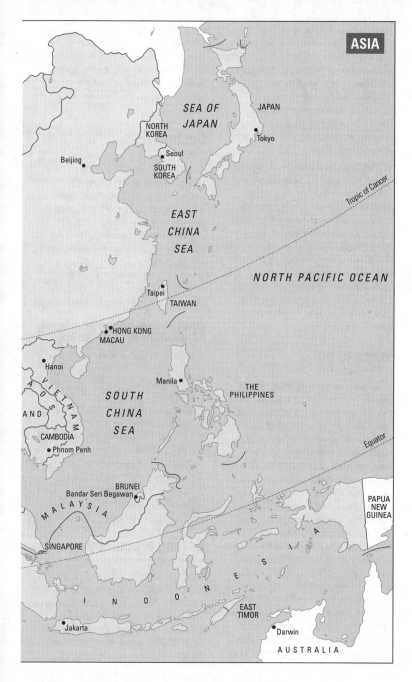

view. Its appeal certainly isn't its defensive record – it was never effective at keeping invaders out. Most people just rode up, bribed the guards at one of the checkpoints, and went on through. The Wall was, however, an example of China's forward thinking. Who else could have imagined the publicity payoff of giving astronauts something to look at from outer space?

● **Thailand's beaches** Thailand doesn't have a monopoly on Southeast Asia's great beaches, but travellers simply can't seem to return home without an obligatory white-sand sizzle (both sides, extra crispy) on Ko Pha Ngan, Ko Samui, Krabi, Phuket or Ko Phi Phi. There are still undeveloped stretches to be found, but as the word gets out, little palm-tufted islands and inlets are transformed from cheap backpacker hangouts into fully fledged resorts right before your eyes.

When to go

In northern Asia, spring (March–May) and autumn (Sept–Nov) are ideal, summer can get stifling, but the harsh winters (Dec–Feb) make travelling the most uncomfortable. Which is fine, because that's a great time to be in southern Asia, the Indian subcontinent in particular. The trickiest thing, perhaps, is planning a good time to trek, if that's your cup of chai. In Nepal, September to December is widely regarded as the best trekking season, but October to November is so popular that the crowds can easily disrupt the enjoyment and make it feel more like a weekend queue for the Louvre. Consider mid-September and early- to mid-December, the brief shoulder seasons without the human traffic jams. The famous monsoon of India could keep you hot and drenched from June to September (though not in the northern hills), but it's not as severe in Cambodia, Laos, Thailand or Vietnam. In southern Thailand, Malaysia and parts of Indonesia, finding better weather can simply be a matter of heading to the opposite coast, a few hours away.

Costs

Asia has the cheapest and the most expensive countries in the world. Outside of the most expensive cities, where you can probably find dormitories, you'll be able to save funds by sharing a double room with someone. In the cheapest countries, the saving often isn't significant, but it can help when you're trying to get by on pocket change. Be sure to head for the markets for food if you're looking to save money.

Lowest daily budget
Expensive ($40/£26+): Bhutan, Brunei, the east coast of China, Japan, Hong Kong and Singapore
Mid-range ($25–$40/£16–£26): Mainland China, Malaysia, Mongolia, Philippines, South Korea, Taiwan, Thailand
Budget ($8–$25/£5–£16): Bangladesh, Burma (Myanmar), India, Indonesia, Laos, Nepal, Pakistan, Vietnam

Getting around by air

Some domestic flights are surprisingly cheap, so before you head off to a bus station for another twelve-hour journey, consider taking a peek at some local fares. You may decide it's worth the extra $20/£13–$70/£45, or whatever the difference may be. From Bangkok, you can fly nearly anywhere in Asia for $50/£32–$150/£96. Domestic one-way tickets in China cost $100–$300/£65–£195 and in India about $200/£130.

Air passes

Most air passes must be purchased in advance, outside the country, and are probably best coordinated with your international ticket. If you've already arrived with an international carrier and you have a clever travel agent back home who has all the records from your trip, you may be able to work things out and have a ticket sent to you.

Asia

The ASEAN Air Pass covers travel to over 25 cities in Brunei, Indonesia, Laos, Malaysia, Myanmar, Philippines, Singapore, Thailand and Vietnam. For $360/£231, you get 3 flight coupons that you can use over 2 months. Each additional coupon (up to 6) costs $120/£97. However, the air pass is only available to people arriving in one of these countries on an international flight using one of the following airlines: Royal Brunei Airlines, Garuda Indonesia, Malaysia Airlines, Philippine Airlines, Singapore Airlines, SilkAir, Thai Airways International and Vietnam Airlines.

India

Indian Airlines has two passes: $500/£322 for 14 days and $750/£482 for 21 days. You are allowed unlimited flights as long as you don't backtrack.

Japan

Both JAL and ANA have a Japan air pass made up of a series of flight coupons (maximum 5): you can buy these for only $100/£64 each if you arrive in Japan on an international flight. They have to be used within 2 months and some date restrictions may apply.

Thailand

A Thai Airways pass costs $149/£96 and entitles you to fly to three cities during a 3-month period. The pass must be purchased outside of Thailand as part of an international flight.

Overland routes

Asia has several classic travel routes which can be avoided, adhered to or mixed and matched. One route connects Europe and Australia via the old hippie trail that cuts across Pakistan, India, Bangkok, Singapore, Malaysia and Indonesia, and includes either a short flight between Bangladesh and Burma and Burma and Thailand or a detour through Nepal and China (see p.84).

From Moscow, you can take the Trans-Mongolian or Trans-Manchurian railways (see p.38), to Beijing – or vice versa. From Beijing, you've got a few options: the most expensive (based on per-day travel costs) are to head down the coast to Hong Kong or across the strait by ferry to South Korea and then on to Japan.

The four cheaper options are to head inland, then either:

● Through Tibet and into Nepal (check current visa info on this border crossing) and on to India, where you can pick up the trail going on to Australia

● Along the old silk route, over the Khyber Pass to Pakistan, where it, again, picks up the route to Australia via India, Thailand, Malaysia, Singapore and Indonesia.

● To Hanoi, then Laos and Bangkok

● From Hanoi, going to Ho Chi Minh City to Phnom Penh and (possibly with a short flight here) on to Bangkok.

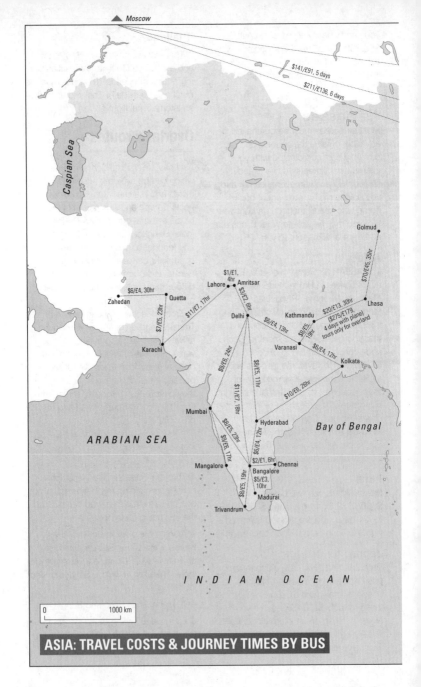

Moscow

$141/£91, 5 days
$211/£136, 6 days

Caspian Sea

Golmud

$70/£45, 35hr

$6/£4, 30hr   Quetta   Lahore   Amritsar   Kathmandu $20/£13, 30hr   Lhasa
Zahedan   ($275/£179,
                    $1/£1,   4 days with plane)
                    4hr   tours only for overland
                         $3/£2, 6hr
$7/£5, 23hr $11/£7, 17hr   Delhi $6/£4, 13hr $9/£5,
                                                        19hr
                                        Varanasi $6/£4, 12hr   Kolkata
Karachi
                    $9/£6, 24hr $9/£5, 11hr

                    $11/£7, 18hr $10/£6, 26hr

            Mumbai
                                        Hyderabad   Bay of Bengal
        $8/£5, 23hr $6/£4, 12hr

ARABIAN SEA $9/£6, 17hr
                                        $2/£1, 6hr   Chennai
    Mangalore   Bangalore
                                    $5/£3,
                                    10hr
                        $8/£5, 19hr   Madurai
                    Trivandrum

INDIAN   OCEAN

0   1000 km

ASIA: TRAVEL COSTS & JOURNEY TIMES BY BUS

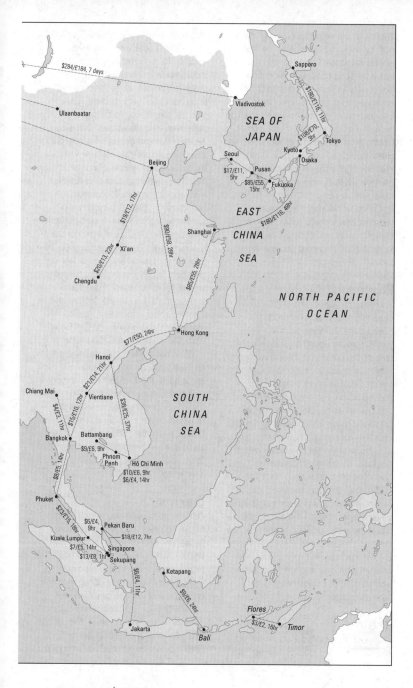

$284/£184, 7 days

Sapporo

$180/£116, 11hr

Vladivostok

SEA OF
JAPAN

Ulaanbaatar

$109/£70, 3hr

Kyoto   Osaka   Tokyo

Beijing   Seoul

$17/£11, 5hr   Pusan

$85/£55, 15hr   Fukuoka

$19/£12, 7hr

EAST
CHINA
SEA

$180/£116, 48hr

Shanghai

$90/£58, 28hr

$20/£13, 22hr   Xi'an

$86/£55, 28hr

Chengdu

NORTH PACIFIC
OCEAN

$77/£50, 24hr   Hong Kong

Hanoi

$21/£14, 21hr

Chiang Mai

$15/£10, 12hr   Vientiane

$38/£25, 37hr

SOUTH
CHINA
SEA

$4/£3, 11hr

Bangkok   Battambang

$9/£6, 9hr

Phnom
Penh

Hồ Chi Minh

$9/£5, 14hr

$10/£6, 9hr
$6/£4, 14hr

Phuket

$23/£15, 18hr

$6/£4, 9hr   Pekan Baru

Kuala Lumpur

$18/£12, 7hr

$7/£5, 14hr   Singapore

$13/£8, 1hr   Sekupang

Ketapang

$6/£4, 11hr

$9/£6, 24hr

Flores

$3/£2, 16hr   Timor

Jakarta   Bali

There's an incredible selection of transport available, from some of the world's least comfortable buses to high-speed trains with champagne service, and from colourful hand-decorated bicycle rickshaws to dusty grey elephants. Between most points, however, you'll be choosing among buses, trains, planes, boats and (if you're in a group) a taxi. In cities, public transport can be daunting. With the right frame of mind (relaxed, perhaps mildly hungover) you will eventually get the hang of it, even if you get lost once or twice in the process. Whether or not that's easier than learning to bargain and getting a feel for the local taxi and rickshaw prices is a tough call.

Buses

There are modern buses in Asia. The ones that run in Japan or around Thailand are especially stunning. But you'll invariably spend a good deal of time on the other kind. Despite what you may have heard, it's rarely the bus that's the problem. It's more likely just the chain-smokers, jammed-shut windows, screaming babies, crater-like potholes, unpoliced roads and reckless drivers with an affinity for high-pitched synthesizer pop music played at conversation-halting decibels. Thus the mention of "bus" and "Asia" will often conjure up "bus ride from hell" stories, which is fine because – and here's what you need to remind yourself when hearing these – the person telling them obviously survived. Buses may not be the safest methods of transport (see p.117 for advice on bringing your own seatbelt), but they're often the cheapest, and sometimes the only way to get where you want to go.

Trains

Japan, China and India boast the most extensive rail networks in Asia and are a nice alternative to the buses. That's not to say they'll offer the same level of escape. To even mention Japan's and India's trains in the same sentence requires a disclaimer: no two rail systems could be more different. The smooth, sterile, comfortable and climate-regulated high-speed trains in Japan arrive and depart on a schedule that many actually do set their watches by. Indian trains, provided you're not in first class, feature a cast of characters that ranges from hot-food sellers to relentlessly inquisitive businessmen looking for a joint-venture partner, to the sweeper who brushes out the constantly accumulating layer of garbage on the floor. China's trains are somewhere in between, largely dependent upon what type of cabin you're in: "hard seats" (more people than seats), "soft seats" (same number of people as seats), "hard beds" (hard beds) or "soft beds" (fairly soft beds in a four-bed suite).

While not cheap, Japan's rail passes (ⓦwww.japanrailpass.net/eng/en02.htm) are at least good value – really the only way to afford the trains. With the bullet trains, you could easily travel half the length of Japan in a day and spend $300/£193 in the process. The passes come in three basic flavours: 7-day pass $250/£161; 14-day pass $375/£241; 21-day pass $500/£322.

Cars

Get a taste of what you're getting into before you rent a car. Sit in the front passenger seat of a taxi as you move about town for a few days and see if the high-speed chaos feels like something you'd be able to handle. If not, you can often hire a driver and pay even less, especially if you can find one or two other travellers to help share the cost. In more developed countries the traffic laws may not be as much of a problem, but navigating can be. In Tokyo,for example, directions are so complex most companies have resorted to printing small maps on the backs of their business cards.

If you're planning to buy a car or motorcycle, head into it with your eyes open. That means a full understanding of the paperwork and visas you'll need to cross any borders – which could take months to organize – and figuring out which countries require separate permits for each province. If you are handy with engines, make sure you buy a model you feel comfortable fixing, plus the tools and parts you'll need. If you don't have the know-how, make sure you have a model that can be fixed locally (ask about this upon arrival). Better still, get a model that won't require fixing. But that's going to cost a lot more and it'll have a greater chance of getting stolen, scratched or broken into. If you want the flexibility and convenience of a car and you're not heading across the continent, the best bet may be to hire one with a driver included and make sure you both agree on the ground rules (in fact, put it on paper) before embarking on a long journey. For more on car travel, see p.40.

Bikes

Asia is the home of the bicycle. Having said that, you're unlikely to come across any models with dual suspension, titanium frames and French derailleurs. Renting or buying a bike to ride in cities is recommended where it's widely practised (such as Beijing) and inadvisable where it's not (Bangkok, for example).

Bike paths are almost nonexistent and there's very limited space on the shoulders of major roads so long-haul cyclists should seriously consider a mountain bike with adequate shock-absorbers, and sticking to secondary roads.

As a cyclist, you're at the bottom of the highway food chain and cars and trucks will expect you to move out of the way. But, just in case, consider bringing ample visibility enhancers (orange flags and Day-Glo strips) to help alert drivers who aren't accustomed to seeing cyclists and may be kind enough to swerve.

Bring all the spare parts you'll need for such a journey. Outside of Japan, Singapore and Taiwan, you'll have a hard time locating anything that will work with your bike, including inner tubes.

Boats

In parts of Asia, river travel is not just a nice way to break up a trip or save some money, it's the only way to access certain destinations. Whether or not you head up Cambodia's Tonlé Sap to Ankor Wat, float your way along the Yangzi for days, or skirt the traffic in Bangkok on the long-shaft-motor *khlong* boats, you'll have plenty of opportunities to ply inland waters.

Hitching

Hitching is not common in Asia, but it can be done. There's a larger chance of a communication gap; a raised thumb may be misunderstood as an offensive gesture. To stop a car, you'll have better luck waving your arm. A sign is very helpful for finding rides (have someone help you write it in the local language). Then, to be sure, use a map and point to the place you hope to go. It's polite to offer a token gift in exchange for your ride (a pack of cigarettes or little knick-knack from home). Asian drivers do have a habit of running errands on the way without much warning, so don't be too alarmed if the driver doesn't seem to be taking the most obvious route, but otherwise normal hitch precautions apply (see p.136).

Afghanistan At time of writing, no visas issued except for journalists and aid workers

Bangladesh Visas for all are valid for six months from the date of issue and are good for stays of one or three months ($40–60)

Bhutan All must sign up for pre-arranged itinerary with official tour and pay per-day fee based on season (high: March, April, May, September, October and November $200 per night; low: January, February, June, July, August and December $165 per night). Visa must be obtained before flight can be booked. Visitors pay $20 upon arrival when visa is stamped.

Brunei Visa (14 days, extendable) required, onward travel or sufficient funds

Burma (Myanmar) Visa required for all visitors (28-day; $20) typically issued same day in Bangkok, two 14-day extensions possible

Cambodia Visa (30 days) required, available at some border crossings, $20/£13

China Visa (30 days) required, $30/£19, special permits required for Tibet, Xinjiang, onward travel

East Timor 90-day entry permit issued upon arrival. Onward travel

Hong Kong No visa required (90 days), onward travel

Indonesia No visa required (60 days), onward travel

India Visa required for all visitors (6 months standard, but valid from date of issue, not entry), $60/£30

Japan No visa required (90 days)

Kazakhstan Visa (7–21 days) required, letter of invitation, 3 weeks processing, $90/£58

Kyrgyzstan Visa (30 days) required, $50, letter of support, restrictions loosening at time of writing

Reading list

- Jung Chang *Wild Swans*
- James Clavell *Shogun*
- Larry Collins & Dominique Lapierre *Freedom at Midnight*
- Pico Iyer *Video Night in Kathmandu*
- Clive Leatherdale *To Dream of Pigs*
- Zhisui Li *The Private Life of Chairman Mao*
- François Ponchaud *Cambodia Year Zero*
- Salman Rushdie *Midnight's Children*
- Mark Salzman *Iron and Silk*
- Paul Theroux *Riding the Iron Rooster*

Laos Visa (15 days) required, available at main airports & Vientiane Friendship Bridge or in advance, $30/£19

Macau No visa required (20 days)

Malaysia No visa required (60 days)

Mongolia Visa (30 days) required, $50/£32, may be available at border

Nepal Visa (60 days) required, available at border, $30/£19

North Korea Visa required, lots of paperwork, no journalists get tourist visas, denials on whim, $10/£6. No tourist visa for US unless family reunion

Pakistan Visa (90 days) required, $20/£13–$50/£32

Philippines Visa (21 days) required – available on entry, onward travel

Singapore No visa required (14 days, extendable), sufficient funds, onward travel

South Korea No visa required (30 days)

Sri Lanka 30-day visa issued upon arrival

Tajikistan Visa (14 days) required, $50/£32, much red tape, few embassies

Taiwan No visa required for 14 days for citizens of Australia, Austria, Belgium, Canada, Costa Rica, Czech Republic, France, Germany, Greece, Hungary, Luxembourg, Italy, Japan, Netherlands, New Zealand, Poland, Portugal, Singapore, Spain, Sweden, Switzerland, USA, UK. Those not listed must pay $40 for 30-day visa.

Thailand Visa (60 days) required, $15/£10

Turkmenistan Visa required, exact itinerary needed in advance, visa support letter, 2-week processing, $35/£23

Uzbekistan Visa (15 days) required, $50/£32.

Vietnam Visa (30 days) required, $50/£32–$100/£64, 6–8 days processing

Visas

Laos, Philippines and Vietnam are the countries requiring most travellers to get a visa for a one-month stay or longer, but double-check with embassies. Sometimes this differs when arriving by air or overland. Nearly all countries require that your passport be valid for at least six months from your date of entry, and have proof of onward travel (plane ticket) and/or sufficient funds to finance your stay and your trip home. Usually, a major credit card will help demonstrate this. See box for more.

Australia, New Zealand and the South Pacific

Australia is as diverse as it is overwhelmingly vast. With just over 18 million people in a space bigger than all of Europe, most of the country is as sparsely populated as an Icelandic beach in December. The reason is that the outback, however stunning, renders most of the country largely uninhabitable (by Western standards), and with world-famous diving, surfing and fishing, it's easy to understand why the vast majority of Aussies have decided to settle within 20km of the coast. New Zealand, while far smaller, seems to pack more diversity (not to mention sheep and rugby players) per square kilometre than just about any place on the planet: from fjords to volcanoes to some of the most gentle rolling green hills you've ever laid eyes on.

With developed infrastructures and politically stable climates, the concern is less on being able to get around in a scheduled or safe fashion, and more on how to cover the butt-flattening distances, try all the hair-raising activities and cope with the increased lager intake. Aussies and Kiwis are among the best travelled humans on the planet. So, not only do they sympathize with the budget traveller, they cater to us so well that some people claim it has taken a good deal of the adventure out of the journey. Just the same, it would be a pity to miss the experience. People don't get much more welcoming – a slap on the back and a shared beer and you're practically related. Which means cultural immersion is within easy grasp.

Whether you're sailing or flying your way around the planet, you may have an excellent opportunity to visit one or more of the 3300 South Pacific Islands spread over 11 million square miles of ocean – home to some 6 million unfathomably friendly people (the Fijians were voted the "world's friendliest people" in *Condé Nast Traveler* magazine). Most arrive by yacht or plane (several RTW tickets offer stops) and Tonga, Vanuatu, Fiji, New Caledonia, Samoa, Tahiti, the Cook Islands and the Solomon Islands are among the most popular. Nearly all offer excellent diving, fishing and beaching and, for most, it's just a question of making time for more than a stopover (and saving some money) so the islands can be thoroughly explored.

Main attractions

● **Sydney Opera House** Australia. Tickets are readily available to many

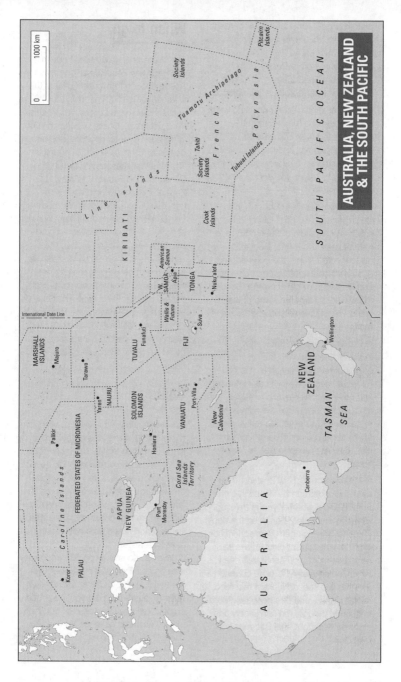

performances, although this Australian icon is best known for the view from the outside. The beautiful shell-inspired design came from a Dane – Jorn Utzon – who abandoned the project before completion due to political interference.

● **Uluru** Australia. Commonly known as Ayer's Rock, this mammoth rust-coloured landmark is sacred to Aboriginal peoples and the most-visited site in Australia. Familiarize yourself the local debate before you decide whether or not to climb it.

● **Great Barrier Reef** South Pacific. Beginning at Lady Elliot Island in the south and extending 2300km north to New Guinea, the Barrier Reef follows, in disconnected strips, the outer edge of Australia's continental plate, between 50 and 300km from the shoreline. Beneath the waves, it harbours some of the world's most diverse and spectacular marine life.

● **Queenstown activities** New Zealand. Credited with the commercial origins of the bungee-jump, this picturesque mountain town has expanded into other eyeball-ejecting ventures, from jet-boating down a narrow canyon river to parasailing to skydiving to flying gliders to . . . if you can think of something else, they're probably open to suggestions.

● **Milford Sound** New Zealand. This natural wonder can be visited in a multitude of ways: whether you're trekking, kayaking or sipping a drink on the deck of a ship, this southern hemisphere fjord is not likely to disappoint. Unless it's raining so much you can barely see it, which, unfortunately, is quite common as it has the second highest recorded rainfall in the world (7m per year). More frequently, though, the rain simply adds stunning waterfalls, majestic mist and rainbows.

When to go

There's never a wrong time to be in Australia/New Zealand, as long as you're flexible enough to migrate towards the weather you prefer. The main tourist season is the summer holiday, which runs from just before Christmas until the end of January. Expect resorts, buses and domestic flights to fill up during this time. The shoulder seasons are October to Christmas and February to May. New Zealand gets a little cold and drizzly between June and September, but the far north is still balmy. Australia's outback season is October to November and March to May. Outside of that, you'll either sizzle during the day or freeze at night. If Melbourne gets too cold and wet in the winter, just head north until the temperature feels right. The South Pacific is fine so long as you miss the cyclone season around November to March, which can be escaped as close by as the Marshall Islands, just to the north.

Costs

Ask any Australian or Kiwi travelling, and they'll tell you the name of their currency is the Devalued Dollar. The recent fluctuations in the market have made travel down under cheaper in recent years, and a burden for Aussies overseas. If you're coming from Southeast Asia, it won't seem that cheap, but it's a little better than Europe and most North American prices.

You can scrape by on $25/£16 a day with some effort (a bit more easily in Australia), but $35/£23 a day is more realistic, and $80/£51 if you like a little comfort, drink a lot of beer or enjoy a weekly gastronomic treat. With scuba diving, bungee-jumping, crocodile tours and such, it's not difficult to top $100/£64 per day. The South Pacific islands are similarly priced, or slightly more expensive, mostly catering to high-end tourism, and just a few with budget accommodation. Tahiti may cost even the most budget-conscious traveller more than $60/£39 a day, so watch out that the week-long stopover on the way home doesn't burn a hole in your passport pouch. Fiji and the Cook Islands are more popular budget stopovers.

Hostels cost $15/£10–$20/£13 per person for a dorm or $30/£19–$40/£26 for a double. If you're staying at such places, consider picking up one of three cards (in addition to the ISIC): an International YHA card (around $25/£16; ⓦwww.hiayh.org); a VIP card ($16/£10; ⓦwww.viprez.com); or a Nomads Dreamtime card ($16/£10; ⓦwww.nomadsworld.com). The VIP- and Nomad-accepting hostels tend to be more centrally located than the International Youth Hostels, and both cards give about ten percent off room rates and a wide range of discounts on other goodies, from museums to telephone calls.

Getting around by air

In Australia, a plane is a decent way to connect some overland segments. The shorter distances in New Zealand make it less appealing, but flights are cheap enough to prevent any unwanted backtracking. In the South Pacific, flying is the best way to visit the islands, and there are seemingly more air passes in this region than coconuts; see below, or check ⓦwww.pacificislands.com /air_passes.

Air passes

● **Boomerang Pass** This pass divides the region into "zones": Western Australia, Central Australia, Eastern Australia, New Zealand, and South Pacific Islands (stops at Samoa, Vanuatu, Fiji, Tonga, New Caledonia, Solomon Islands). If you fly within the zones, it's $150/£96 per flight. If you fly between them it's $200/£129 per flight. You just have to purchase a minimum of two flights and a maximum of ten. ⓦwww.goway.com/passpages/du_air_ passes.html

● **Circle South West Pacific Pass** You buy a minimum of two coupons ($160/£103–$320/£206 per coupon) to travel from Australia to Papua New Guinea, Samoa, Vanuatu, New Caledonia, the Solomon Islands, Kiribati, Tonga, Guam, Nauru, Tuvalu and the Wallis Islands, provided your entire trip does not exceed 28 days. ⓦwww.hideawayholidays.com.au /circle_SW_Pacific.htm

● **Explore New Zealand Pass** Air New Zealand and Mount Cook Airlines offer a minimum of three coupons for a total of $250/£161 that will help you connect your overlanding. Or do the whole thing by air (max: 8 coupons) with additional flights at $75/£48 a pop. Valid for one year.

● **Explorer Pacific Pass** You get three flights for $450/£289, with additional flights at $75/£48 each (eight-flight max). The pass expires in 30 days, so doesn't give much opportunity for extensive exploration on the islands, but connects Australia or the Philippines with Nauru, Guam, Kiribati, Fiji, Micronesia and the Solomon Islands. ⓦwww.pacificislands.com/air_passes/pacific.html.

● **G'Day Pass** This works like the Boomerang pass, and is priced accordingly, only there's no South Pacific coverage and Australia is divided up into two zones instead of three. Which means if you don't plan to use the pass to access the South Pacific, it's a slightly better deal. ⓦwww.pacificislandtravel .com/australia/passes/air_ansett.html

● **PolyPass** This allows 45 days of travel to Western Samoa, Fiji, Tonga, American Samoa, Sydney, Brisbane, Melbourne, Adelaide, Canberra, Wellington, Christchurch and Auckland ($1099/£707). Honolulu, Los Angeles and Tahiti cost extra. ⓦwww .polynesianairlines.com.

Overland routes

Getting around down under is about as easy as it gets. And with no political conflicts to avoid and a reliable infrastructure, it's easy to design your own route. Both Australia and New Zealand offer excellent, outdoorsy packaged and unpackaged adventures.

In Australia, the popular overland path forms a circle, starting in Melbourne or Sydney and going up the east coast, hitting the SPF 25 hangouts (Byron Bay, Airlie Beach, Whitsundays, Magnetic Island), then cutting inland and south to

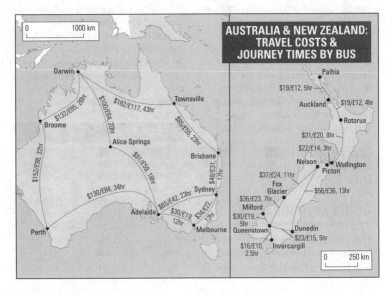

AUSTRALIA & NEW ZEALAND: TRAVEL COSTS & JOURNEY TIMES BY BUS

Uluru and finally looping back around to Melbourne and Sydney by way of the Great Ocean Road. If it's the same price on your RTW ticket to stop in Perth on the way in or out (even if it's a little more), a glimpse of Australia's barren west coast can be well worth the effort. Crossing the country can be done by bus, train and car. A less-travelled route will take you up the rugged north coast (unfortunately, you can't see the coast from the road for much of the journey) through Broome and on to Darwin, where you can see the nearby saltwater crocs first hand.

From Auckland, you can catch a ride south to Wellington, then take one of the frequent ferries across the channel to the South Island. You can make an overland circuit of South Island: go east and swim with dolphins on your way to Queenstown or make for the west-coast glaciers. Whatever you miss on the way down you can catch on the way back up.

Buses

Traditional bussing is, after hitchhiking and cycling, the cheapest way to move about. The main routes are followed by McCafferty's (❂www.mccaffertys.com .au) and Greyhound- Pioneer (❂www .greyhound.com.au) in Australia, and Intercity (❂www.intercitycoach.co.nz) and Newmans Coachlines (❂www .newmanscoach.co.nz) in New Zealand. All but Newmans offer a range of passes with unlimited stops that are well worth looking into. Be warned, though:

the two big catches with these tickets are that they are typically nonrefundable and don't allow backtracking.

There are a number of bus companies such as the Kiwi Experience (❂www .kiwiexperience.com) and sister tour Oz Experience (❂www.ozexperience.com) that will shuttle you, at a very reasonable rate, from one pre-selected hostel to the next, stopping for all the important places (read: ones that give the company kickbacks) along the way so there's very little decision-making left for the traveller. It can be something of a party on wheels if you're looking for that sort of thing. Plus, the guides may be knowledgeable and they do take you to attractions that aren't easily accessed on other bus routes. The classic "boomerang" pass lasts six months with unlimited stops and forms a loop from Sydney, taking in the east coast and then swinging through the centre of the landmass for a visit to Uluru ($520/£334). You can save about $25/£16 if you buy the pass before arriving in Australia, and save another $25/£16 if you have a discount card. With over thirty different itineraries to choose from (not including the flight combo passes), it's hard to find something you want to do that doesn't match up with one of their routes. The Kiwi Experience has nine bus passes to choose from and trips average about $500/£322, though you can pay twice that for the "Fully Monty" pass.

The New Zealand Travel Pass

The **New Zealand Travel Pass** (aka Best of New Zealand Pass; ❂www.travelpass .co.nz) also offers several interesting combinations that let you ride on buses, trains and ferries – even one domestic flight, so you don't have to backtrack. If you want to mix up your transport a little, don't feel like taking one of the backpacker buses and prefer to carry just one ticket, this is probably the best way to go. The passes are available for six months and allow for between 5 and 22 days of travel. They range from $150/£96 for a five-day bus- and ferry-pass in low season to $620/£399 for a 22-day pass in high season with bus, ferry, train and a flight.

Trains

The rail lines aren't nearly as extensive as the bus routes (or quite as cheap), but for longer hauls they tend to be more comfortable and more scenic. Australia's Indian-Pacific line, between Sydney and Perth, is the world's second-longest (three full days of travel), with 478 continuous kilometres of completely unbending track (⊛www.gsr.com.au/indian/index.htm). For other rail info, try the Country Link (⊛www.countrylink.nsw.gov.au. New Zealand's TranzAlpine line (⊛www.tranzscenic.co.nz) between Christchurch and Greymouth is particularly stunning, as is the Overlander line (Auckland to Wellington). In both countries, trains offer a nice respite from bus travel and are certainly worth at least one leg of the journey.

Cars

Driving is not a bad idea, especially if you have some specific off-road locations in mind or are hooked on back-road travel. You can rent (if you're 21), but at about $25/£16 a day for local rentals and $65/£42 for longer distances, it's a painfully quick way to lighten your moneybelt. If you plan to spend at least a month in the country, buying is a better way to go. You can pick up a used rust-bucket for about $1000/£645 and hopefully you'll be able to off-load it at the end of your trip.

A safer bet, and one that might keep you out of the repair shop, is to spend $2000–$3500/£1286–£2250 on a Holden Kingswood or Ford Falcon, the reliable (or at least fixable) road warrior of the traveller. For serious bushwhacking, check out a Toyota Land Cruiser. A road-weary model may set you back around $8000/£5145, but these things almost never give up. Depending on how much you fix up the vehicle and how clever you are at the buying and selling, you could get anywhere from 65 to 110 percent back on your investment. If you're hopeless with car mechanics get the car checked out by a pro (⊛www.nrma.com.au; $90/£58) before you buy it, especially if you're buying from a fellow traveller – and don't take a clapped-out old car into the outback, unless you're very well supplied with food and water. A buy-back plan is not a bad idea if you're arriving and leaving from the same place. You can find a dealer who's willing to offer you a price if you bring the car back in reasonable condition. If you're shopping for used motorcycles, consider the popular Yamaha XT600 Tenere (around $3000/£1930).

Whatever you get, you'll have to get it registered (⊛www.rta.nsw.gov.au). But before you do, check with REVS, the Register of Encumbered Vehicles (⊛www.revs.nsw.gov.au), to make sure you're not buying a stolen vehicle. You'll also need to check to make sure there's no outstanding loan on the car, or you'll end up paying it or having the vehicle repossessed (for just $6/£4, REVS will issue a Search Certificate that will prevent repossession by a financier if the seller still owes money on the vehicle.

If it's unregistered (also called "interstate" or "as is") you get to cough up a couple of hundred dollars for the process. Try to pick up a car with the registration of the state where you hope to sell it. The registration includes third-party insurance, but for an extra $50/£32 you can get theft protection. If you realize you got stuck with a real rust-bucket, joining an auto club (with free roadside assistance) is well worth the $30/£19 or so.

Just so you're familiar with the terms (in Sydney, anyway – each state has its own rules) a Blue Slip is the registration, which you'll need to prove transferred ownership, and keep updated. The Pink Slip is a safety check report, stating in rather vague terms that your car works, and also must be updated. The Green Slip is the obligatory third-party insurance.

Bikes

Cycles can be rented just about everywhere you go, and are a great way to navigate the cities and venture a little further afield. If you don't have powerful tree-stump thighs and want to head between cities, the distances are a little more manageable in New Zealand. In northern Australia pay particular attention to your water intake and sun exposure.

Boats

Ferries run from the North Island of New Zealand to the South Island (●www .interislandline.co.nz) and around several of the island groups in the SouthPacific (Fiji ●www.pacificnavigator.com, Tahiti ●ww.aranui.com) plus between Australia and Tasmania (●www.tt-line .com.au). They range from high-speed catamarans to rusting freighters to oversized dinghies.

Hitching

Hitching can be a good way to get around, although it's not officially endorsed anywhere (this book included). The 1992 "backpacker murders" in Australia targeted women, men and couples, and changed the way people looked at hitching. In New Zealand, you'll often find there are so many people hitching in the prime spots, it'll feel more like you're standing in a queue.

With so many travellers owning vehicles, it's not difficult to post notices in the backpackers' hostels and catch a lift without wagging your thumb. You chip in for petrol (it's about 70c a litre/$2.80/£1.80 gallon), cram into the backseat, and hope the driver didn't get stuck with a lemon.

In the South Pacific islands, the locals are so friendly it's not unheard of for taxi drivers to pick up hitchhikers and give them a lift for free. More likely, though, a shared taxi or minivan will pull over and pick you up for a small fee.

Reading list

- John Birmingham *The Tasmanian Babes Fiasco*
- Bill Bryson *In a Sunburned Country*
- John Muk Muk Burke *Bridge of Triangles*
- Peter Carey *The True History of the Kelly Gang*
- Bruce Chatwin *Songlines*
- Sean Condon *Sean and David's Long Drive*
- Alan Duff *Once Were Warriors*
- Keri Hulme *The Bone People*
- Mark McCrum *No Worries*
- Nevil Shute *A Town Like Alice*

Visas

Having a visa (●www.immi.gov.au) is not an absolute guarantee that you'll be allowed into Australia – immigration officials may well check again that you have enough money to cover you during your stay ($500/£320 per month), and that you have a return or onward ticket. In extreme cases they may refuse entry, or more likely restrict your visit to a shorter period.

Twelve-month working holiday visas are easily available to British, Irish, Canadian, Dutch, Japanese and Korean single people aged 18–25, though exceptions are made for people from other countries up to 30 years of age, and young, married couples without children. It is not normally a chance to

Visa requirements for Australia and New Zealand

EU Visa required prior to arrival, but issued free for 3-month stay. Can be done through a travel agent, usually for a small fee. A 6-month visa costs around $35/£23 and must be obtained through an embassy/consulate.

USA/Canada Visa required prior to arrival, but issued free for 3-month stay. Can be done through a travel agent, usually for a small fee. A 6-month visa costs around $35/£23 and must be obtained through an embassy/consulate.

further your career since the stress is on casual employment: you are meant to work for no more than three months at any one job. Unfortunately, you must arrange the visa before you arrive in Australia, and several months in advance to avoid disappointment, as numbers are sometimes capped. Working visas cost £60 in the UK and CAN$150 in Canada; some travel agents such as Trailfinders in the UK can arrange them for you.

In New Zealand (ⓦwww.immigration .govt.nz), the granting of a visitor permit or tourist visa is dependent upon your having evidence of sufficient funds to support yourself without working (about $500/£320 a month, or $200/£130 a month if your accommodation is pre-

paid), in the form of a bank draft, cash, travellers' cheques, a statement from a New Zealand bank account, one of the major credit cards, or a friend or relative who is prepared to guarantee your accommodation and maintenance. You must also have a confirmed onward ticket and right of entry to your proposed destination.

Nearly all the South Pacific islands have the same visa requirements: an onward ticket and sufficient funds. Upon arrival, you get an automatic visa if needed, and permission to stay about a month. The island of Kiribati is one of the few exceptions, requiring visas from US and Australian passport holders.

Central America and the Caribbean

The Mayans never realized they were laying the framework for a future travellers' trail. Much of Central America – the Ruta Maya (the Mayan route) – has become just that. Alongside spectacular ruins set against jungle backdrops are coasts that please divers and surfers alike, desertscapes, mountains, gorges, welcoming indigenous peoples and prices that are gentle on your pocket. Keep moving west (better get on a boat for good measure) and you arrive at the Caribbean, a string of island nations that stretch across vodka-clear waters from Florida to South America. Though many are rich with culture, the all-inclusive, tradition-free holiday is the major revenue source. Few people take the time to venture past the duty-free shops, meaning that travellers are left with plenty to explore.

Main attractions

● **Caribbean diving** The crystalline waters of the Caribbean make most people want to do one thing: jump in. With a snorkel or a basic scuba course, you can peek through the looking glass at the coral reefs, wrecks and phospho-rescent fish on the other side.

● **Tikal** Guatemala. Guatemala's ancient Mayan ceremonial centre of temples, pyramids and plazas lies in the north of the country where it battles the ever-encroaching rainforest. Howler monkeys provide the soundtrack as you wander between the trees and ruins, feeling like you're lost in your own Tintin adventure.

● **Bay Islands** Honduras. Located 50km off the north coast of Honduras, these are the budget travellers' Caribbean islands. Western Roatán and all of Utila are, anyway. Guanaja and eastern Roatán have gone upmarket. This paradise has one little drawback, though: insatiable sandflies.

● **Panama Canal** Panama. The 87-kilo-metre splitting of continents was com-pleted in 1914 by the United States just before World War I. The engineering feats of this man-made wonder include a series of three sets of locks that raise and lower ships 26m, a dammed river creating Gatun Lake, and the Culebra Cut, a fourteen-kilometre-long, 150-metre-wide channel through a moun-

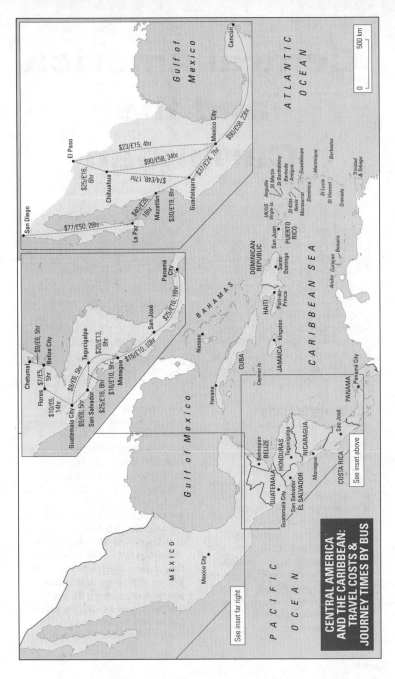

CENTRAL AMERICA
AND THE CARIBBEAN:
TRAVEL COSTS &
JOURNEY TIMES BY BUS

See inset far right

See inset above

Mexico inset:

Cancún

Mexico City $90/£58, 23hr

El Paso $23/£15, 4hr

$90/£53, 34hr

$25/£16, 6hr

Chihuahua

$37/£24, 7hr Guadalajara

$74/£48, 17hr

$40/£26, 8hr

Mazatlán $30/£19, 8hr

San Diego

$77/£50, 26hr

La Paz

Central America inset:

Panamá City

San José $26/£16, 16hr

$9/£6, 5hr Belize City

Chetumal $7/£5, 5hr

Tegucigalpa $20/£13, 8hr

$15/£10, 10hr

Flores $10/£6, 14hr

$9/£6, 5hr

Managua $16/£10, 9hr

Guatemala City $25/£16, 8hr

$9/£6, 5hr San Salvador

Main map labels:

P A C I F I C   O C E A N

ATLANTIC OCEAN

Gulf of Mexico

CARIBBEAN SEA

B A H A M A S

MEXICO

Mexico City

GUATEMALA
Guatemala City

BELIZE
Belmopan

HONDURAS
Tegucigalpa

EL SALVADOR
San Salvador

NICARAGUA
Managua

COSTA RICA
San José

PANAMA
Panamá City

CUBA
Havana

Cayman Is.

JAMAICA
Kingston

HAITI
Port-au-Prince

DOMINICAN REPUBLIC
Santo Domingo

PUERTO RICO
San Juan

Nassau

Aruba Curaçao Bonaire

UK/US Virgin Is.
Anguilla
St Martin
St Barthélemy
Barbuda
Antigua
St Kitts
Nevis
Montserrat
Guadeloupe
Dominica
Martinique
St Lucia
St Vincent
Barbados
Grenada
Trinidad & Tobago

0   500 km

tain. It takes the 12,000 ships that use the canal annually about nine hours to cross.

● **Acapulco** Mexico. This *grand dame* of beach resorts has been pulling in sun worshippers by the busload for well over half a century and lining them up under umbrellas on white sands. The pre-bungee cliff divers of La Quebrada are world renowned for their 45-metre plunges. Just inland, you'll encounter the often ignored darker side: garbage, poverty and traffic, though this real-life city is certainly worth a look.

When to go

The chances of getting blasted by a Caribbean hurricane are slim at best, but it only takes one to toss your journey through a window or wrap it around a palm tree. With a close eye on the weather, these June to November storms can be avoided (most hit Aug–Oct), but it might mean an expensive last-minute flight. Also, because North American and European winter-sun worshippers get their tropical fix in the region, accommodation tends to fill up just after Christmas. Otherwise, with some minor highland-to-coast migration in certain spots to avoid rains or uncomfortably warm temperatures, it's good all year around.

Costs

Nicaragua, Honduras and El Salvador are the cheapest countries in the region, but even here, prices can go up along the nice coastlines. The all-inclusive resort areas, particularly in Mexico and around the Caribbean, are laughably expensive, especially considering how cheaply the locals live. You can find inexpensive eats, but there aren't always hostels, and camping is sometimes forbidden, so you may end up paying for the occasional $60/£39 room, which can be a budget-crippler. The only way to tackle some of these top-end destinations on a limited budget, therefore, is going to be staying at informal family guesthouses and yachts in the marina with bunks for rent. Such arrangements are not guaranteed, but can be found for $10/£6–$25/£16 when available, and you may also be able to negotiate cheap meals as part of the stay. International Youth Hostel cards and ISIC cards, outside of Costa Rica, anyway, will not be that useful. And with fewer dorm-style hostels, you're going to save money on accommodation if you travel with a partner or find a traveller on the way to help share costs.

Americans heading to Cuba will need to make sure they have ample US$ or travellers' cheques, as many places will not accept US credit cards. Or the US could confiscate the credit card charge, which you'd need to repay. Credit cards, even Visa and Mastercard, that are not tied to US banks are fine.

Lowest daily budget

Expensive ($40/£26+):
Aruba, Barbados, Bahamas, Bonaire, Martinique, Puerto Rico, St Vincent & the Grenadines, St Kitts & Nevis, St Lucia, St Martin, Turks and Caicos, Virgin Islands

Mid-range ($25–$40/£16–£26):
Antigua & Barbuda, Belize, Cuba, Jamaica, coastal resorts of Mexico

Budget ($8–$25/£5–£16):
Costa Rica, El Salvador, Guatemala, Honduras, Haiti, Mexico (except the coastal resorts), Nicaragua, Panama

Getting around by air

International flight prices in Central America send a clear message to the budget traveller: take ground transport. Most of the Caribbean islands are within three hours of the southern US, but many flights stop a few times on the way to the more southerly destinations. However, if you can put a group together, a chartered flight among the islands shouldn't cost you any more than a standard fare, and it'll leave at your convenience. Caribbean air passes supply the most convenient way to see the islands; the only other options are hitching on yachts, using some of the limited ferry services, or doing expensive one-way hops.

Air passes

Central America

The best option is probably the Latin AirFlex pass by the TACA consortium. You need to pick up a minimum of four coupons, and it's about $150/£96 per flight within Central America. Ask your travel agent or try ⓦwww.exitotravel.com for more details. There's a Mayapass available through Mexicana (ⓦwww.mexicana.com): you buy three coupons, which cost $60–$150/£40–£95 for domestic flights and

$120/£77–$260/£167 for international flights: they include limited stops in Central America and flights from destinations in the US.

Caribbean

Liat Airways has three air passes: the Explorer is valid for three stops over 21 days ($280/£180 – not available for purchase in Venezuela or the Caribbean); the Super Explorer has unlimited travel for 30 days ($475/£305 – not available for purchase in Venezuela); and the Eastern Caribbean allows 3–6 flights ($85/£55 per flight, only available in Europe).

BWIA West Indies Airways air pass costs $399/£257, allows for 4 stops in 30 days, and the schedule must be fixed at the time of booking. Changes cost $20/£13 each.

Air Jamaica's CaribHopper Pass allows you to visit up to 14 islands (one stop per island except Barbados and Montego Bay) in 30 days for £299/£192 plus departure taxes.

Overland routes

The major overland route runs from the US to South America, with a boat ride or flight to avoid the Darién Gap (see p.289), a lawless, roadless, guerrilla-infested region between Panama and Colombia. The route runs through either Honduras or El Salvador and is most commonly done by bus. Driving private vehicles down from the US is also an option, but one that may prove more frustrating and come with more delays than the local transport. See also Ferries (p.138) and Yachts (p.30).

Buses

In Central America, you've got everything from the chicken bus to the luxury bus, but mostly it's just chicken buses. When

---

Sample fares
Mexico City to:
Cancún $160/£103
Guatemala City $320/£206
Panama City $530/£341
San Salvador $390/£251
Miami to:
Martinique $350/£225
Puerto Rico $160/£103
St Thomas $270/£174

planning overland routes, consider that any more than two or three hours in a day on one of these, particularly if you wouldn't describe yourself as "petite", is going to be punishing. There are direct buses from the US into Mexico and from Mexico to Belize and Guatemala. From Guatemala City, relatively modern Tica buses (Ⓦwww.ticabus.com) connect the major cities all the way to Panama City (in 60hr by the most direct route). In the Caribbean, most foreigners go by taxi or rental car, so the local buses are almost exclusively ridden by locals. The timing can be hard to calculate since many originate at the far end of an island, which can mean plenty of delays by the time they arrive in the main city.

Trains

The Central American railway system is virtually nonexistent, either due to jungle, lack of planning or recent government privatization. Mexico has kept a few scenic tourist lines alive, such as the Copper Canyon run from Chihuahua to Los Mochis (14hr; $115/£74; Ⓦwww.railsnw.com).

Ferries

Island-hopping ferry services in the Caribbean are simple in places and challenging in others. Between Martinique, Guadeloupe, Dominica and St Lucia there's a high-speed catamaran service called Express des Isles which runs five days a week (Ⓦwww.whitchurch.com /express.htm) and costs $55/£35–$95 /£61 for each hop. Ferries in the Virgin Islands run regularly and cost $3/£2–$40/£26 (Ⓦhttp://st-thomas.com /week/ferries.html or Ⓦwww.bviwelcome .com/ferries.html). After that, it's just the odd connection here and there. French St Martin and Anguilla are connected by a link called, aptly enough, The Link (Ⓦwww.link.ai), which leaves three times daily and costs $10/£6. Albury's Ferries

service the Bahamas between Great Guana and Scotland Cay, Man-O-War Cay, Hope Town and Elbow Cay. There are ferries linking Baja to mainland Mexico as well as the Caribbean islands of Isla Mujeres and Cozumel.

Cars

Rentals in the Caribbean and Central America can cost as much or more than in the US or Europe and, on top of that, some Caribbean countries like to make you buy a temporary visitors' licence. In Central America, an international driving permit will be useful if you plan to spend some time behind the wheel. You may want to take a few taxi rides first to get a firsthand look at the driving conduct (or lack thereof).

Buying a car or motorcycle in the US and driving overland is probably the best option for a long-term trip. To get a vehicle into Mexico, you don't need a Carnet des Passages, but you'll need a temporary import permit ($11/£7, paid only with major credit cards), available at the customs office near border crossings (you might also pick up some Mexican auto insurance while you're there). The vehicle's certificate of ownership must be in your name, and you'll need a valid registration card and driving licence. Then you can't leave the country without the vehicle. If it's wrecked, or you have an emergency, you must seek permission at the Federal Registry of Vehicles in Mexico City or a treasury (hacienda) office elsewhere. Petrol prices in Mexico are higher than in the US and there are very expensive toll roads ($70/£45 from Nuevo Laredo, on the Texas border, to San Miguel de Allende, north of Mexico City). You'll also be likely to encounter road blocks for drugs and weapons searches, so think twice (if it even requires that much thought) before you carry either in your car.

Bikes

Central American roads are notoriously narrow, so you're going to be swerving or balancing on what's left of the road's shoulder. In the large cities, it's even more dangerous. So, while you're riding you'll want your bike to be as visible as possible. And when you're not riding make sure your bike is discreet, hidden and locked. On smaller roads, however, cycling is gaining popularity. From June to September, the rains may make cycling an uncomfortable and muddy affair, but the rest of the year is fine weather-wise.

Hitch

Hitching is not a part of the Central American tradition, largely because the local buses are so cheap. In fact, you'll have a hard time to prevent the local buses from pulling over and offering a ride each time they pass. It can be done on less-frequented routes, though trucks (slow) and the back of pick-up trucks (unsafe) are going to be the most common options. Your best bet is going to be a posted note at a hostel or traveller café to share petrol costs with travellers who already have a vehicle.

Reading list

- Paula Burnett (ed) *The Penguin Book of Caribbean Poetry*
- Zee Edgell *Beka Lamb*
- Jamaica Kincaid *A Small Place*
- V.S. Naipaul *A House for Mr Biswas*
- E.A. Markham (ed) *The Penguin Book of Caribbean Stories*
- Salman Rushdie *The Jaguar Smile, a Nicaraguan Journey*
- Jean Rhys *Wide Sargasso Sea*
- Rosario Santos (ed) *And We Sold the Rain: Contemporary Fiction from Central America*
- Paul Theroux *The Mosquito Coast*
- Derek Walcott *Omeros*

Visa requirements for Central America

Belize No visa required for 30 days

Costa Rica Australia and New Zealand: no visa required for 30 days. EU, USA and Canada: no visa required for 90 days. Easier to leave the country for 72hr and re-enter than extend visa

El Salvador No visa required for 90 days

Guatemala 90-day stay without a visa except for EU citizens other than those of France, Germany, Ireland, Netherlands and UK who should obtain visa prior to arrival. 90-day renewals available in Guatemala City

Honduras No visa required for 30 days. 30-day extensions can be obtained for up to 6 months at local immigration office

Mexico No visas required for stays up to 6 months, but tourist card ($18/£23) needed for stays longer than 72hr: available on arrival

Nicaragua Australia and New Zealand: no visa required for 30 days. EU, USA and Canada: no visa required for 90 days. Stays can be extended for up to three months

Panama Can enter for 30 days on tourist card or visa obtained at airport at arrival or embassy prior to departure. Can be extended to 90 days while in the country; those entering overland should obtain visa beforehand since tourist cards can "run out"

Visas

US, Canada, EU passport holders can stay between a few weeks and several months in all the Caribbean islands (except Cuba) without a visa. New Zealand and Australian passport holders just need a visa for the following: Trinidad and Tobago and Cuba. And New Zealanders need a visa for the Dominican Republic. See box opposite for more.

Europe and Russia

All roads don't actually lead to Rome. Swedes aren't all blonds. And the French don't tongue kiss when they meet. However, none of these little disillusionments are reason enough to skip Europe on your trip. Europe offers the traveller more architecture, music, fashion, theatre and gastronomy per square kilometre than any other continent. Which means heading off the main routes will still land you waist-deep in cultural treasures. The introduction of the euro currency makes spending easier, and at least you're not giving away as much to the money-changers. What you do with this saving is quite limitless: climb an Austrian Alp, taste wine at an Italian palazzo, rent a surf-board in France, throw back a shot of Russian vodka, cool down with an icy Spanish gazpacho or soak your toes in the Adriatic from the Croatian coast.

Main attractions

● **Venice** Italy. The lovely canals and palaces of Venice are approached with more expectations than a George Lucas movie, yet never seem to disappoint. If you can see over the heads of all the tourists, the views are breathtaking at every step. Only after a visit can you finally understand the pains Marco Polo endured to return here.

● **The Louvre** France. This Paris museum could eat most sports stadiums for breakfast and still have plenty of room left over. It opened in 1793 and was immediately stuffed full of stolen goods pillaged by Napoleon's armies. Courtesy of architect I.M. Pei, it now sports a snazzy glass pyramid entryway with a calming reflective pool that helps tranquillize the waiting crowds.

● **The Sistine Chapel** Italy. Michelangelo, without the aid of a chiropractor, mind you, painted the world's most famous ceiling fresco here in Rome. Beyond that, there's a vast collection of statues, frescos, maps and illuminated texts that leave visitors stunned.

● **The Kremlin** Russia. It's not just a building, but an entire elevated citadel in the centre of Moscow. About sixty percent is off limits to all but government personnel, but you can access the cathedrals, Patriarch's Palace, and Armoury, which houses a fascinating collection of royal carriages, hand-made weapons and Fabergé eggs.

● **Versailles** France. Louis Quatorze certainly knew how to live. There's the grand entrance, enough rooms to properly house all your party guests, endless gardens that require an army of trimmers and pruners, and a hall with more mirrors than a Las Vegas magic act. It's good to be the king.

● **The British Museum** England. Whatever Napoleon didn't manage to abscond with was snapped up by His or Her Majesty's far-flung forces – Egyptian Mummies, Roman and Greek statues, Benin bronzes and exquisite Japanese prints are all amazingly under one roof. The current policy seems to be this: the rightful owners may not have their national treasures back, but, like you, they're free to come and look at them in the British Museum and leave a donation on the way out to help finance the security system, lest they be stolen by someone else.

● **Auschwitz Concentration Camp** Poland. A visit to Auschwitz (or Dachau, near Munich) may just be the most profound and enduring memory you take back from Europe. After a glimpse into the gas chambers, a view of the barracks and a walk around the compound, you begin to get a terrifying sense of what life here must have been like under Nazi control. It's impossible to leave unmoved.

When to go

There's no time when Europe should absolutely not be visited, but it can get rather cold and bleak in the winter (Nov–Feb), even in much of Turkey, and crowded in the summer (July–Aug). If you're not a beach person, this could actually work to your advantage, as you shouldn't have to queue for museums or reserve hostel beds. July and August are nice in northern Europe and the Alps, and a little too warm for comfort in the south. March to June and September to November are ideal for southern Europe, with perhaps a little overlap into the tourist season so you can appreciate what you're steering clear of.

Costs

Despite the high cost of living in many European countries and the large economic differences between some of them, budget travel accommodation and supermarket food prices – the entire budget travel infrastructure, really – are all fairly consistent. Once you start staying in nice hotels, eating in restaurants and hitting the bars, price differences become more pronounced (Norway, Sweden and Switzerland shoot up in the rankings, for example). There are a few budget factors to consider. In Sweden, for example, you have the right to camp for free in many places. In Norway, no matter what your budget is, the $7/£5 beers are painful. And you could live for two weeks in Peru on the amount you'd have to spend to cross Monte Carlo in a taxi. Not including transport (since train and bus passes are so popular), see the box for guidelines on what you might spend.

> ## Lowest daily budget (excluding transport)
>
> **Expensive** ($35–$45/£23–£29): Britain, France, Germany
>
> **Mid-range** ($25–$35/£16–£23): Austria, Belgium, Croatia, Denmark, Italy, Netherlands, Norway, Poland, Russia, Sweden, Switzerland
>
> **Budget** ($15–$25/£10–£16): Greece, Latvia, Lithuania, Spain

Getting around by air

With the proliferation of discount airlines, flying around the continent has never been cheaper. Getting out to the airports accessed by these lower-priced airlines might cost $20/£13, but the saving is well worth it. Air passes no longer

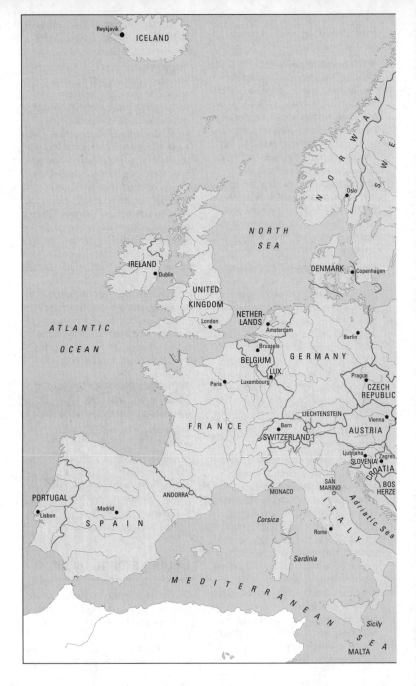

First-Time **Around the World** | WHERE TO GO

EUROPE AND RUSSIA

0   500 km

—DEN

FINLAND

Helsinki

Stockholm

Tallinn
ESTONIA

BALTIC SEA

RUSSIA

LATVIA
Riga

Moscow

LITHUANIA

Vilnius
KALININGRAD
(RUSSIA)

Minsk

BELARUS

Warsaw

POLAND

Kiev

UKRAINE

SLOVAKIA
Bratislava

Budapest

HUNGARY

MOLDOVA
Chisinau

ROMANIA

NIA-
GOVINA

YUGOSLAVIA

Belgrade

Bucharest

BLACK SEA

Sarajevo

BULGARIA
Sofia

ALBANIA
Tirana

Skopje
FYROM

Ankara

GREECE   Aegean

TURKEY

Sea

Athens

Crete

CYPRUS

seem like the same attractive deals they once were.

Air passes

● **Discover Europe** with the Star Alliance. Ten European airlines within the Star Alliance service this air pass of

3–10 distance-priced coupons ($60/£39–$220/£141). To qualify, your travels to and from Europe have to be on a Star Alliance carrier.

● **EuropebyAir FlightPass** (Ⓦ www.europebyair.com). Travellers heading to Europe can fly on 26 different

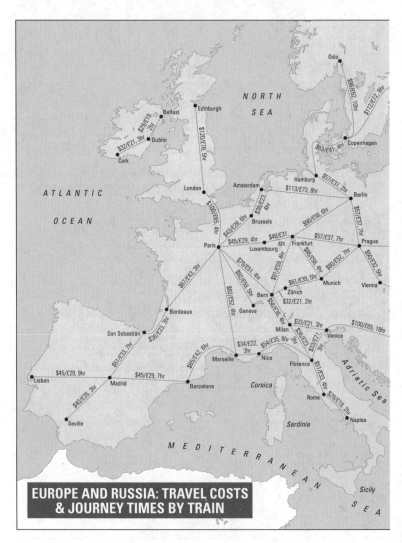

EUROPE AND RUSSIA: TRAVEL COSTS & JOURNEY TIMES BY TRAIN

airlines to more than 150 cities within Europe at the flat rate of $99/£64 per flight plus airport taxes. Each $99/£64 coupon is valid for 120 days on non-stop flights between any two cities within the system. Reservations can be made before or after you arrive in Europe.

Overland routes

Europe doesn't really have overland routes, it has an overland web. With open borders, an extensive infrastructure and travellers using bus and train

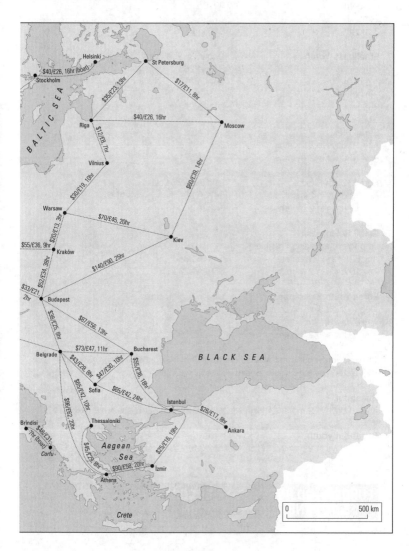

Europe travel passes

17 Eurail countries: Austria, Belgium, Denmark, Finland, France, Germany, Hungary, Italy, Luxembourg, Norway, Portugal, Ireland, Spain, Sweden, Switzerland, Greece, Netherlands

Eurailpass	1st class
1-month	$918/£590
2-month	$1298/£835
3-month	$1606/£1033

Eurailpass Youth	Under 26/2nd class
15-day	$401/£258
1-month	$644/£414
2-month	$910/£585
3-month	$1126/£724

Eurail Flexi	1st class
Any 10 days in 2 months	$647/£416
Any 15 days in 2 months	$888/£571

Eurail Youth Flexi	Under 26/2nd class
Any 10 days in 2 months	$473/£304
Any 15 days in 2 months	$622/£400

Eurail Selectpass (up to five adjoining countries)	1st class
Any 8 days in 2 months	$444/£285
Any 10 days in 2 months	$502/£323

Eurail Youth Selectpass (up to five adjoining countries)	Under 26/2nd class
Any 8 days in 2 months	$310/£199
Any 10 days in 2 months	$502/£323

11 Busabout countries: Austria, Belgium, Czech Republic, France, Germany, Italy, Netherlands, Portugal, Spain, Switzerland, Britain

Busabout
Any 10 days in 2 months   High season $399/£257   Low season $359/£231

Busabout youth
Any 10 days in 2 months   High season $349/£224   Low season $309/£199

Eurolines
2 months unlimited   High season $385/£248   Low season $305/£196
Eurolines youth
2 months unlimited   High season $295/£190   Low season $240/£154

passes like amusement-park tickets, there's more darting around on whims than specific A to B passage. The more socially inclined migrate like wildebeests to the three major backpacker-endorsed festivals: Pamplona's Running of the Bulls, Berlin's Love Parade, and Munich's Oktoberfest. A railpass (possibly in combination with a cheap one-way flight at the beginning or end) is your best bet (both for cultural reasons and leg room), although not quite as cheap as a bus pass. Biking and driving are viable options as well.

Buses

There are two bus passes worth looking into, and they both undercut the train fares: Eurolines (❿www.eurolines.com); and Busabout (❿www.busabout.com). Eurolines is cheaper while Busabout takes you right to a hostel (one they hope you'll stay at), and provides onboard movies and a guide. That gives you less reason to look out the window and less opportunity to meet locals, but it will save you time and the hassle of picking and finding a hostel.

Trains

Europe is train country. How else would you describe a rail network totalling 240,000 kilometres? (By comparison, there's 45,000km of rail in US and Canada, an area more than twice as large.) It's not necessarily the cheapest way to get around the continent, it's simply the preferred way. And not because the rail routes are often more scenic, but the facing seats provide an opportunity to meet locals, the aisles allow you to stretch your legs, some carriages allow full reclining at night and the train's chug-chug adds an authentic travel beat to any conversation. Prices change, but the chart below should give you an idea. There are several more

passes available at ❿www.raileurope .com: see p.57 to best take advantage of them.

In Turkey, the express trains and sleepers are worth looking into and provide a nice leg-stretching change from the bus rides, but the local (yolcu and posta) trains barely surpass the speed of rust.

Cars

Rental

For a longer road trip, rental is on the expensive side. To make it affordable, a travel companion or group of them will put the adventure within a reachable price range. If you're renting over 17 days, you can lease from a place like ❿www.kemwell.com, ❿www .europebycar.com or ❿www.renaultusa .com, agencies that take advantage of tax loopholes by leasing out new cars then selling the practically new vehicles on the used market. A comfortable car for four is going to run to about $350/£225 a week. A compact is $200/£129. And with petrol prices at over $1/£0.60 per litre ($4+/£3+ per gallon), plus tolls and parking fees, one month of travel – figuring on five hours' driving every other day – in a compact car for two is about $1000/£643 per person (that's $725/£466 per person if you drive every third day, $635/£408 if you drive every fourth day). With four people in a larger car, that's around $600/£386 per person driving five hours every other day, or $475/£305 driving every third day. Rental companies generally lease to those 18 and over, but some require drivers to be over 23. Rentals are best booked in advance, which can be done direct, via a travel agent or through the mainstream online flight booking sites.

Buying a car

Buying a car in Europe is a fun alternative, provided you don't run into mechanical trouble or get stuck trying to off-load it before your flight leaves. For language reasons, the UK is a good starting point, though you'll want a left-hand drive if you'll be spending most of your time on the continent. To see what's available, look at the newspaper classifieds, *Loot* magazine and *Exchange and Mart* magazine. At Ⓦwww.thegumtree and Ⓦwww .tntmagazine.com/uk/ you'll find other travellers' cars and camper vans, which, for high-mileage reasons, may not make the most sense (although, with the purchase they may be able to help you with all the paperwork details as well as some great tips). Some of the vehicles are registered on the continent, and as long as you're not keeping the car in the UK for more than 12 months, you can get around the UK registration. The AA (Ⓦwww.theaa.co.uk) and RAC (Ⓦwww.rac.co.uk) are the places to turn to for insurance; they have co-op arrangements throughout Europe for breakdowns. Once you cross into Asia or Africa, however, it's another story (one that begins on p.233 and p.221). Bring extra copies of your documents and leave others with a trusted friend, relative or in an online vault. They should include: road tax, insurance and owner-ship papers.

If you have a good driving record in your home country you may be able to get preferable rates with a European insurer. Get a letter from your insurance agent back home just in case.

In Germany, you might look into buying a Vorführwagen, a demo model which has been in the showroom and used for test drives, or a Jahreswagen, a typically low-mileage car in good condition that was bought at discount by a car-manufacturer employee and sold as soon as the law allows, which is one year.

EU driving licences are valid in all of Europe. Other foreign licences (US, Can, NZ and Aus) are accepted as well, but not in Italy, Austria, Spain and some East European countries, for which you should have an international driving permit, easily arranged in your home country (see p.127).

Bikes

This is a continent that deserves to be seen from a bike. The hamlets that tour-buses and cars roll past regularly are some of the greatest treasures. With the great bike races ripping by most places at some point or another (Giro d'Italia, Vuelta de España, Tour de France), you'll find an unrivalled respect for cyclists. There's always a small pub that's happy to refill your water bottle or a chateau happy to fill it with wine. On the other hand, Europe is crammed with narrow roads, high speed limits and no fewer than 20 million drivers who think they're Michael Shumacher. Denmark, the Netherlands, Belgium and Norway have some of the finest cycle-only touring trails for those who don't like to compete for space with motor vehicles or eat their exhaust.

Europe is also a great place to buy a bike, which will make a nice souvenir at the end of your trip. Or, if you can buy a popular international brand, you should have no trouble selling it in a hurry. All cities – and even many small towns – will have all the spare parts you'll need.

The larger cities all have bike rentals. In London, Paris and Rome, they may be more likely to get you a bed at a nearby hospital than where you're going, but in cities like Amsterdam and Copenhagen they make city exploration a joy and enable you to head well beyond postcard-and-souvenir streets.

Hitching

Thumbing it in Europe is a little hit and miss, and don't think about it without reading the section on hitching safety on p.136. In some countries, it's considered normal and drivers are sympathetic to your roadside plight (as many have done some hitching themselves). In others, such as parts of Scandinavia, you're something of a pariah. In places where it's not as accepted, take special care to dress well and get to service stations. Some countries have hitching organizations that will, for a fee, put you in touch with a driver heading in the same direction who wants to share the petrol costs. It takes away the thrill, but will likely get you where you want to go. Europe's best hitching spots and how to reach them are listed at ⓦwww.autostopguide.com.

Reading list

- Julian Barnes *Letters from London*
- Bill Bryson *Neither Here Nor There: Travels in Europe*
- Charles Dickens *A Tale of Two Cities*
- Fyodor Dostoyevsky *Crime and Punishment*
- Anne Frank *The Diary of a Young Girl*
- Adam Gopnik *Paris to the Moon*
- Ernest Hemingway *Death In the Afternoon*
- Homer *The Odyssey*
- Peter Høeg *Miss Smilla's Feeling for Snow*
- Peter Mayle *A Year in Provence*

Visas

In general, Brits, Americans, Canadians, Australians and New Zealanders don't need a visa to visit European countries, but there are some exceptions. Russia requires a visa, and you'll need a transit visa to get there overland through Ukraine and Belarus. Turkey requires visas, but typically allows you to pick them up upon arrival. Canadians, Australians and New Zealanders need visas for several Eastern European countries and should keep an eye on requirements when heading that direction. See overleaf for more.

Visa requirements for Europe

Austria No visa needed except after 3 months for citizens of Australia, New Zealand and Canada

Belgium No visa required

Bulgaria No visa required

Croatia No visa required

Czech Republic Visa required for citizens of Australia and Canada

Denmark & Greenland No visa required

Estonia No visa required

Finland No visa required

Macedonia No visa required

France No visa required

Germany No visa required

Greece No visa required

Hungary Visa required for citizens of Australia and Canada. US: no visa needed, onward ticket, proof of funds

Iceland No visa required

Ireland No visa required

Italy No visa required

Latvia Visa required for citizens of Australia, New Zealand and Canada

Liechtenstein No visa required

Lithuania No visa required

Luxembourg No visa required

Montenegro Visa required for US citizens, must go through Yugoslav embassy in Canada

Monaco No visa required

Netherlands No visa required

Norway No visa required

Poland Visa required for citizens of Australia, New Zealand and Canada. US: no visa needed, onward ticket, proof of funds

Portugal No visa required

Romania Visa required for citizens of Australia, New Zealand and Canada.

Russia Visa required

Serbia Visa required for US citizens, must go through Yugoslav embassy in Canada

Slovakia No visa required

Spain No visa required

Sweden No visa required

Switzerland No visa required

Turkey Visa required, get at border. EU: no visa required for 3 months except for citizens of Austria, Greece, Ireland, Italy, Portugal, Spain and the UK, who must purchase 3-month visa on arrival

United Kingdom No visa required

Middle East

Let's cut right to the chase: is it safe? About as safe as anywhere else. Violence does occur, and it's certainly horrifying, but the fact that there are so many news bureaus covering such a small plot of land means that the violence ricochets around the world. When the region is plagued with headline-grabbing incidents, the good news is that there's a chance you'll be visiting some of the world's greatest archeological sites in relative solitude. You'll also be able to enjoy the calming effect of walking barefoot over the hand-woven carpets of a mosque, tasting Jordan's fresh-squeezed fruit juices, experiencing the hospitality and hummus of the Syrians and taking a desert safari in the United Arab Emirates.

Main attractions

● **Petra** Jordan. This ancient Nabatean city, built into the rose-coloured canyon walls in the Jordanian desert, had been lost to the outside world for over 1000 years when it was rediscovered in 1812 by Johann Burckhardt. The ruins are approached on foot via the Siq, a 1.2-kilometre canyon not much wider than a queen-size mattress.

● **Jerusalem** Israel. If you can see past the skirmishes that continue to mar this city, you'll find an architectural beauty forged from thousands of years of chaos. There's the Dome of the Rock, where Mohammed is believed to have ascended to heaven; the Church of the Holy Sepulchre, the last stop on the Via Dolorosa, where Christ was believed to have been crucified (the nearby Garden Tomb is also a possible site); and the Western (or Wailing) Wall, the closest piece of Israeli real estate to the ancient site of the Second Temple (where the Dome of the Rock now stands), before it was destroyed by the Romans in 70 AD. As a traveller you're free to roam (after passing through metal detectors) to all three sites and pick up falafels, fresh dates and pistachio nuts along the way.

● **Palmyra** Syria. What remains today is the stone exoskeleton of a once magnificent city. The art and architecture of this oasis in the Syrian desert was a mixture of the Persian and Greco-Roman civilizations borrowed from traders heading from Baghdad and the Persian Gulf to Damascus and Jerusalem.

● **Red Sea diving and snorkelling** Israel and Jordan. One moment you're on the edge of a bleak desert, getting blasted by convection-oven-like winds. The next you're in an aquamarine paradise surrounded by schools of multi-hued fish. You pop your head up again to be sure the desert is still there. It is. The stark contrast simply adds to the experience of diving one of the world's great reefs.

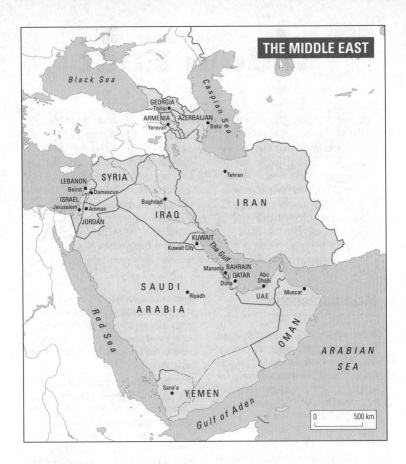

THE MIDDLE EAST

When to go

Winter is the most likely obstacle you'll
face, and that's only if you're trying to
avoid the snow, which has been known
to make many of the roads impassable.
You might also want to try to sidestep
the hot summer months if you're doing
more than diving the Red Sea and
swimming in the Med, but it's easily sur-
vivable. Throughout the region, spring
and autumn (April, May, Sept & Oct) are
the optimal times to visit.

Costs

Less than half of the countries in the
Middle East are easy on the money belt,
and by no coincidence, that's where
you'll find nearly all the budget travellers.
Israel, Jordan and Syria are the region's
backpacker havens. Student cards are
particularly useful, and can save you
well over 25 percent at some museums
and archeology sites. Keep a pocketful
of small change for baksheesh (tip) dis-
tribution; many of the irritating "services"

that are done for you (such as pointing you in a direction you're already going) do not deserve baksheesh, but slightly more helpful services should be rewarded. This is simply part of the culture. You might want to keep coins separate from your bills so you don't have to flash your money and potentially draw more attention than you'd like. Diving trips around the Red Sea and some private tours of the archeological sites (often well worth it) are the most likely to dent your budget.

Getting around by air

Flying is the most reliable and speedy way to get around the Middle East, but it's also the most expensive. If your kidneys are tired from the long bus rides, you might try one longer hop, but without air passes available it's a quick way to drain your finances. There are no flights available to Iraq, or between Israel and nearby countries, with the exceptions of Jordan and Egypt.

Sample fares

Amman to:
Cairo $215/£138
Muscat $500/£322
Dubai to:
Damascus $250/£161
Riyadh: $260/£167
Tel Aviv to:
Amman $100/£64
Istanbul $360/£231

Overland routes

There's really just one classic overland route. It goes from Istanbul to Cairo, via Syria, Jordan, Israel and the Sinai Peninsula (doing it in reverse makes things difficult if you allow the Israelis to stamp your passport, although they'll put it on a separate piece of paper if you ask). You could also pop over to Lebanon on the way, but the Lebanon/Israel border is still a little dodgy for crossings. Probably the best way to get around is on buses and trains, with hired taxis for harder-to-reach places outside of popular bus routes.

Buses

Outside of the rich, Sport Utility Vehicle-driving Gulf states, the bus is the most common mode of transport in the Middle East for locals and travellers alike. There are no bus package-deals for the region, but bus travel is so cheap that this isn't a problem. On some Arab buses, they like to collect passengers' ID cards. Hand over your least valuable photo ID. An old driving licence or ISIC card usually works fine. Some taxis function as buses as well. These shared taxis move a little more quickly, don't stop as long and cost a bit more. They don't have fixed times but run frequently on regular routes, and can often be flagged down from the side of the road if there's space available. (They usually leave from a regular departure spot when full, and places become available as they drop people off along the way.)

Trains

Trains are typically cheaper than buses, but they're also slower, less prevalent and less frequent. One train runs weekly between Istanbul and Aleppo (29hr;

$63/£41 including sleeper) and one between Damascus and Amman (11hr; $6/£4).

Cars

For more flexible travel, a long-term taxi or rental car is going to be the best

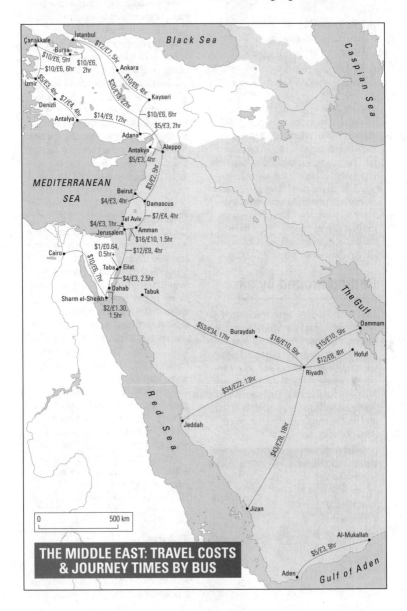

THE MIDDLE EAST: TRAVEL COSTS & JOURNEY TIMES BY BUS

Çanakkale
İstanbul
Bursa $10/£6, 5hr
$10/£6, 6hr
$10/£6, 2hr
$12/£7, 5hr
İzmir
$5/£3, 4hr
$7/£4, 4hr
Denizli
Antalya
$14/£9, 12hr
Ankara
$10/£6, 4hr
$20/£13, 12hr
Kayseri
$10/£6, 6hr
$5/£3, 2hr
Adana
Antakya
$5/£3, 4hr
Aleppo
$3/£2, 5hr

Black Sea
Caspian Sea

MEDITERRANEAN SEA
Beirut
$4/£3, 4hr
Damascus
$7/£4, 4hr
Tel Aviv
$4/£3, 1hr
Jerusalem
Amman
$16/£10, 1.5hr
$1/£0.64, 0.5hr+
$12/£8, 4hr
Cairo
$10/£6, 7hr
Taba
Eilat
$4/£3, 2.5hr
Dahab
Tabuk
Sharm el-Sheikh
$2/£1.30, 1.5hr

The Gulf
Dammam
$53/£34, 17hr
Buraydah
$16/£10, 5hr
$15/£10, 5hr
$12/£8, 4hr
Hofuf
Riyadh
$34/£22, 13hr

Red Sea
Jeddah
$43/£28, 18hr

Jizan

Al-Mukallah
$5/£3, 9hr
Aden
Gulf of Aden

0   500 km

option. Importing a car is unlikely to be worth the effort and expense, unless you plan to continue your trip across Africa or on to Australia.

Bikes

Bicycle touring is uncommon in the Middle East, but far from impossible. Syria provides perhaps the best conditions in terms of scenery, invites from locals to share a meal and, with some luck, a bus that will allow you to throw your cycle onboard if your legs run out of gas. The summer heat from June to August can literally melt you into the pavement. Keep a pair of lightweight trousers out and available to quickly slip on when you stop, as shorts are not likely to be a hit with the locals.

Boats

There are a number of boats that can bridge your overland travels in the region, including a three-hour ride between Aqaba and Nuweiba in the Sinai, and a 36-hour trip between Jeddah and Suez. Ferries are also useful to jump over to Europe (Turkey and Greece via Rhodes) from Haifa in Israel, and cost around $100/£64.

Hitching

Hitching, defined as getting a lift for free, doesn't really exist in the Middle East outside of Israel. You'll see many people standing along the road looking for a ride, but they're either waiting for a bus or a shared taxi or someone who will give them a ride for the price of a bus or shared taxi. In other words, you can hitch (no thumbing, just extend your arm palm down) but offer to pay for the ride. In Israel, hitching is common but not recommended, except for soldiers who hitch in uniform with their gun slung over their backs, and get rides immediately. Because of the tensions in the area,

Israelis are particularly wary of picking up non-soldiers, so you might try to befriend a soldier or two waiting for a ride and see if they'll ask the driver on your behalf for a ride. With an armed soldier in the car, they usually feel better about offering a lift.

Reading list

- ● T.E. Lawrence *The Seven Pillars of Wisdom*
- ● Thomas Friedman *From Beirut to Jerusalem*
- ● Larry Collins and Dominique Lapierre *O Jerusalem!*
- ● William Dalrymple *The Holy Mountain*
- ● Nawal El-Saadawi *The Hidden Face of Eve: Women in the Arab World*
- ● Tony Horwitz *Baghdad without a Map*
- ● Paul Theroux *Pillars of Hercules*
- ● Peter Mansfield *The Arabs*
- ● Naguib Mahfouz *Arabian Nights and Days*
- ● Edward Said *Orientalism*

Visas

For the Middle Eastern countries that require visas, it's not a bad idea to try to obtain them before leaving. Some visas are easier to get from home and some are easier to get on the road while in neighbouring countries. But even if you're turned down in your home country, there's nothing preventing you from trying again once you get in the area. Some visas may require a letter of recommendation from your embassy. Your embassy will have a standard letter for this purpose, but some embassies have been known to charge a small fee for issuing it. See overleaf for more.

Visa requirements for the Middle East

Iran Visas required prior to arrival (up to 1 month). Tricky to get, but easier to get extension while in Iran; visa refused with evidence of Israel visit in passport

Iraq Without press credentials, you might try at the embassy in Jordan, but heading in is probably not worth the risk

Israel Three-month visas are issued upon arrival. Without sufficient funds, you may be sent home or issued a one-month visa. If you're planning to visit Arab countries afterwards, try to get the Israeli stamp on a separate piece of paper or you may not be allowed in.

Jordan 2-week visa from border or airport. Can easily be extended for up to 3 months

Lebanon Visa (for up to 1 month) at airport on arrival. Multiple-entry 3-month visas easy to get at any Lebanese embassy if given letter from employer (proof of return); visa refused with evidence of Israel visit in passport

Oman Three-week visa required. Multiple entry valid for 6 months (3 weeks per visit). Onward travel

Saudi Arabia For a visitor visa, you need a Saudi sponsor. For a 24 or 48hr transit visa, you must show your plane tickets. A three-day transit visa may be issued for overland travel to Kuwait or Yemen, or a 7-day transit visa for overland passage to Jordan, Bahrain or UAE. To get an overland vehicle, it helps if you have a vehicle and carnet

Syria Try to get 15-day visa in home country prior to departure; letter of recommendation from your own embassy usually required. In theory, you can only apply for Syrian visa abroad if your own country does not have Syrian embassy/consulate. In practice, this is not true. In fact, it can be somewhat easier getting visas at the Syrian embassy in Cairo or Turkey. Extensions to be taken care of at end of stay in Syria.

Visa will be refused with evidence of Israel visit in passport

UAE 2-week transit visa or 2-month visit visa through sponsor (can be hotel, company or resident of UAE) prior to arrival. Hotels require up to 3-night stay to help arrange visa. Multiple-entry visas for up to two years available for US, British, Canadian and German citizens

Yemen Prior to arrival at embassy; usually valid 1 month. It's possible for EU citizens (except UK) to get visa at arrival at San'a airport, but it's lengthy procedure. Better to get visa prior to arrival at embassy

North America

Most people feel like they know America already, even if they've never set foot in the country. They know that American lifeguards can all afford plastic surgery; they know that American cars are often victims of high-speed police chases and have a tendency to blow up; and they know American bomb defusers have been trained to wait until the last possible second before picking the right wire to cut. But you really can't judge the country through a TV set. In fact, much of what you see isn't even America at all. It's Canada, the down-to-earth, bilingual ice-hockey power to the north where many of the hit programmes are filmed. Outdoor enthusiasts may find this land is especially worth a visit, with world-class hiking and skiing in the Canadian Rockies, pristine camping and paddling in the northern waterways, and the surging sixteen-metre-high tides in the Bay of Fundy.

What you may not learn about the US by watching Canada is that there's delicious Cajun cooking in New Orleans, some of the world's most dramatic rock formations in parks across Utah, Arizona and Colorado, a unique art community in New Mexico, and more warm hospitality than you can shake a pitcher of lemonade at.

Main attractions

● **Grand Canyon** USA. This unfathomably stunning hole in the ground is still getting bigger. Scientists estimate that the Colorado River is deepening the bottom at the rate of 15m per million years. Three million visitors come here every year, some of whom hike down to the bottom and others who stay up on the rim and watch the new IMAX film about hiking down to the bottom. The film, plus an array of postcards, may be your only chance to see the canyon if you arrive on a day when it is completely cloaked by smog pumped out by the Navajo Generating Station upriver.

● **Niagara Falls** USA/Canada. This natural wonder-cum-honeymoon retreat can be viewed from both the US and Canada. You don't have to ride over in a barrel to appreciate the force of the three cascades: Bridal Falls, American Falls and Horseshoe/Canadian Falls. A total of three million litres per second make the fifty-plus-metre drop over the 1.2-kilometre-wide rim.

● **New York City** USA. It was once, and arguably still is, the great gateway to the New World. These days, though, you have to take a special boat ride to float by the Statue of Liberty and land at Ellis Island (now a terrific museum of immigration). People-watching in Times Square will keep you busy for a good half-hour. And the city's 150 museums, 900 art galleries, 18,000 restaurants and 2000 bars and nightclubs will keep you occupied a lot longer.

● **Las Vegas** USA. Vegas offers a smorgasbord of sin, some fantastic shows and exuberantly over-the-top casinos based on New York, Venice, Cairo and so on, that take ostentation to new levels.

● **Banff** Canada. This national park is Canada's top year-round resort, the home of the country's first wildlife sanctuary and the aquamarine Moraine Lake. You'll find everything from hikes to hot springs, camping to caving and glaciers to . . . well, more glaciers. The nearby Columbia Icefield has around thirty of them.

When to go

There are two things to try to miss: the winter weather in central US and the north (Dec–Feb), unless you're skiing; and the crowded national parks in summer (July–Aug). In spring (March/April) the skiing is still good and the weather elsewhere is favourable. In the fall (Sept–Oct) the changing leaves paint the hills with wonderful Technicolor hues. If you're after the California surfin' safari beach scene, go from June until late August or September.

Costs

Grab a thick slice of pizza at a food stall, a bagel for breakfast or a burger at Mickey D's, and you shouldn't be spending more than $3/£2. If you're staying at hostels, you can get by on $35/£23 in the US and $30/£19 in Canada, not including inter-city transportation.

Getting around by air

American's love to drive, but they also like to get where they're going quickly, which explains why the enormous airport parking lots are usually full. Certain routes are cheaper than others, and there's a lot of competitive and seasonal price cuts. So as long as you don't attempt, as they do so often in the movies, to walk up to the counter and buy the next flight out, or book last minute during peak seasons, you can get some great deals. This can be helpful if you're looking for an occasional hop and a jump to help get you around. Crossing the continental US in the air takes five and a half hours, and from the West Coast to Hawaii is a little over five hours.

Sample air fares

New York to:
Chicago $120/£77
Las Vegas $105/£68
LA $130/£84
Miami $100/£64

San Francisco to:
Boston $200/£129
Hawaii $375/£241
New Orleans $200/£129
Seattle $75/£48

Vancouver to:
Anchorage $445/£286
Minneapolis $275/£177
Toronto $360/£231

The general deal available to those arriving from overseas by plane is to buy 3–10 coupons. Three coupons cost around $350/£225 and ten will set you back around $800/£514. Depending on the airline, special coupons must be purchased for the Caribbean, Hawaii and Alaska. Enquire with your travel agent, as coupons should be purchased when you buy your flight over.

Overland routes

North America's infrastructure allows for a range of routes. It's really more a matter of what type of transport you're using and connecting your favourite stops in some sort of mileage-friendly order. There's the New York to Key West drive; the route that leads down the eastern seaboard; and the classic from New York to LA via Chicago, picking up what's left of Route 66. Crossing Canada, you might head from Quebec to Vancouver via Montreal, Toronto and Lake Louise, then turn north and make your way to Anchorage along the Alaskan pipeline.

In terms of the best way to get around, it's a bit of a toss-up. Buying a car is a fine way to go – it's flexible, cheap and takes advantage of the zillions of miles of smooth highways (though you will, of course, be adding to the greenhouse gases the US is internationally frowned upon for producing). Trains are convenient where they exist, but don't provide much flexibility in terms of routes, and the buses leave a great deal to be desired.

Buses

Greyhound (Ⓦwww.greyhound.com) isn't exactly the pride of America but it works, linking all the major cities and some of the lesser ones. Often, in big cities, Greyhound stations are in the very

NORTH AMERICA: TRAVEL COSTS & JOURNEY TIMES BY BUS

seediest areas, so think twice about some of those late-night arrivals. Greyhound offers the Ameripass – $350/£225 for 30 days of travel and $525/£338 for 60 days – though you probably won't want to commit to that much time on a bus. The $120/£77 four-day pass seems more tolerable. The alternative is the Green Tortoise (🌐www.greentortoise.com), a bus bedecked with cushions, bunks, a fridge and a good sound-system. It runs primarily on the west coast between San Francisco and Seattle, but does make summer crossings to New York and Alaska with many activity-oriented stops en route.

Trains

North America's rail network is not extensive by European standards, nor high speed, but it does cover most of the major stops. Students get fifteen percent off normal ticket prices.

With presentation of a non-US passport you can pick up the USA Rail Pass at any Amtrak station (🌐www.amtrak.com). The one-month national pass is seasonally priced at $385/£248 (Sept–May) and $550/£354 (June-Aug). There are 15-day passes for $295/£190 and $440/£283 as well, and regional passes are about thirty percent cheaper (useful if you plan to just stay on one coast or the other).

Canada has a basic Canada Rail Pass package (❽www.viarail.ca). It's a flexipass, giving you 12 days' travel over a 30-day period. Adults pay $270/£174 (students $245/£158) for low season (mid-Oct to May), and $435/£280 (students $390/£251) during high season (June to mid-Oct). Extra travel days are $25/£16.

The North American Rail Pass (❽www.amtrak.com/savings/northeast/promo-passintro.html) is available to everyone. Allowing one month of unlimited travel, it costs $465/£299 for adults ($420/£270 for students) in the off-season (mid-Oct to May), and $660/£424 for adults (students $595/£383) in peak season (June to mid-Oct).

Cars

You needn't be jumping a convertible over washed-out bridges or driving full speed through police road blocks to enjoy an American road trip. The country is set up to be explored by car, and the low petrol prices make it economically feasible. Navigating city roads can be more than a little daunting, but the open highways, secondary roads and small towns are a breeze, and you'll have access to virtually any place you can find on a map.

Rental

To rent, you'll need to be over 25 and own a major credit card (or be prepared to leave a large cash deposit). At the cheaper end, you're looking at around $150/£96 per week, but check the websites of the major firms for regional or seasonal bargains. Insurance for other cars or people you may damage or injure is mandatory. For an extra $10/£6–$15/£10 per day you can get insurance for the car you're driving: some credit cards provide this if you use them to pay for the rental. If you're not covered, give it some serious thought, as otherwise you'll be liable for every scratch, scuff or dent the car returns with, whether you were in the car at the time or not.

If you're bringing the car back to the same place, you can often make a good leasing arrangement with local car dealerships, so call a few for price estimates. You might say you'll be doing some extensive touring in the region, probably going out of state at some point, but you may not want to mention that you're taking a cross-country road trip unless it's part of a legal document you're signing. However, it's generally best to go with the major rental firms (❽www.hertz.com ❽www.avis.com ❽www.thrifty.com or ❽www.budget.com), since they're better able to handle out-of-state breakdowns and other problems that may arise. Other cost-savers to consider: if you don't bring the car back to the same spot, rental companies will charge you a fortune in drop-off charges, possibly more than a week's rental fee. And if you don't mind an unflattering set of wheels, you can save money with a company like Rent-a-Wreck (❽www.rent-a-wreck.com) that specializes in well-used vehicles. In well-populated areas, this should be fine, but it may not be great for the long desert crossings.

Another option to rental is a "drive-away". Car owners who want to transport their vehicles long distances (typically from coast to coast) but don't want to do the driving themselves, leave their cars with a driveaway agency (⊛www.autodriveaway.com). For a fee, the agency guarantees delivery of the vehicle and finds drivers – drivers like you. You're expected to cover about 600 kilometres per day in the direction of your destination, but that does leave some room for small side-trips and adventures. Some agencies help out with pocket money, others don't. You'll probably be expected to cover the petrol charges, which add up to about $150/£96 for a fuel-efficient car and $300/£193 for a gas-guzzler on a cross-country trip. Check the phone book under Automobile Transporter for local agents and sign up a week to a month in advance.

Buying a car

Buying a car in the US is relatively easy; check out ⊛www.autotrader.com and ⊛www.newspapers.com. You'll need cash, but you can pick up a rust-bucket for as little as $200/£130. A low-mileage, zippy car with air-con that you can sell for a good price will set you back $8000–$10,000/£5145–£6430. Whatever the state it's in, take the car to a mechanic to see which things need replacing to make it roadworthy, and pick up a $70/£45 AAA membership (⊛www.aaa.com) to assist with breakdowns – consider AAAplus ($100/£64) if you're taking an old car through remote areas, and you might want to buy a cheap cell phone so you can take advantage of your insurance. Watch out for cars that have been scrapped then salvaged from a junkyard and touched up to sell to an unsuspecting buyer. Ask for the Vehicle Identification Number and check online at ⊛www .vehicleidentificationnumber.com

Don't forget about the fuel efficiency. Sure, it would be fun to drive down the road in a classic American houseboat-sized car with a set of old bull horns strapped to the front, but most of these drink preposterous amounts of fuel, and you'll be kicking yourself each time you head to the pump. Despite the continent's fascination with sport utility vehicles, you do not need four-wheel drive. But, if you're driving in the south or southwest in the summer, you will want air-con strong enough to deep-freeze a large steak.

Think in terms of resale when you buy. Study the online newspaper classified ads where you're selling and compare them to the prices where you're buying: ⊛www.kbb.com will give you the official value of a car, but that's just a starting point for negotiations. You can also use the site to calculate the depreciation of the mileage you'll be adding. Stay away from off-beat colours: silver metallic is always a safe bet. And consider buying a car somewhere like California or Florida, where the climate is gentle, and selling it someplace with tough winters, such as Minnesota or Boston, where they'll be impressed that the car is still in such good condition. Just keep in mind that northern buyers may not be as interested in peppy sports cars that can't handle snow.

Car camping

Sleeping in your car at rest stops is a dodgy plan. One idea, provided you arrive well after dark, is to look for nice residential areas and park among expensive cars. If the owners are willing to leave them on the street overnight, it's logical to assume it must be quite safe. Only problem here is that if police are patrolling the area, they may not like you camping there, so be discreet – arrive late, leave early and buy some little screens for the windows.

Bikes

North America is a reasonably good place to bike. The distances are long, often with very little of interest in between the towns, and the bigger cities are rarely bike-friendly. There are, however, excellent places to mountain-bike and some exceptional stretches of road. Think ski towns and areas in or near national parks. In many of the biking hubs, it's possible to rent a top-end set of wheels ($30/£19–$40/£26 per day). Cycling in June to August in the south will be extremely warm, and, conversely, if you're going to the north in November to March, take your thermals.

Hitching

Beyond the standard warning against hitching in general, here's an added one for the US: Forgetaboutit! It's considered especially unwise, probably due to the amount of well-armed people out there who never quite made it on the Jerry Springer show. Canada is safer. In both cases, hitchers not dissuaded by this warning should take heed of the safety information on p.136.

Reading list

- Margaret Atwood *Surfacing*
- John Berendt *Midnight in the Garden of Good and Evil*
- Truman Capote *Breakfast at Tiffany's*
- Jack Kerouac *On the Road*
- Armistead Maupin *Tales of the City*
- Toni Morrison *Beloved*
- J.D. Salinger *Catcher in the Rye*
- Alexis de Tocqueville *Democracy in America*
- Mark Twain *The Adventures of Tom Sawyer*
- Tom Wolfe *The Bonfire of the Vanities*

Visas

With an onward ticket, no visa is required (for a stay of up to 90 days) for citizens of Australia, Austria, Belgium, Denmark, Finland, France, Germany, Italy, Japan, the Netherlands, New Zealand, Portugal, Slovenia, Spain, Sweden, Switzerland and UK.

South America

Botanists love South America, possibly the most geographically dynamic continent on the planet, with the world's largest rainforest and the world's driest desert (Chile's Atacama) a bus ride or two away from each other. Anthropologists and sociologists are still combing the rainforest, studying indigenous, isolated tribes. Climbers have a selection of scaleable peaks that stretch from Colombia to Patagonia. Amateur adventurers are lured by the challenges of overland travel as well as the stunning Inca ruins. For urbanites, the cities offer a combination of congestion, coastal vistas and fantastic salsa and samba clubs. And soccer-lovers are in for a real treat: some of the world's most acrobatic stylists come from these parts.

The most common language is Spanish (many people elect to begin their trips with a short language course, which is a huge help), but from country to country the dialect can be as different as Australian and American, complete with unique words and expressions. On average, travellers here tend to be a little older and more experienced than the ones who visit Europe or Australia. They seem less in search of spiritual enlightenment than the ones in India and less tan-hungry than the ones in Thailand. Couple the scary diseases with even scarier political regimes and rebel groups, and it's easy to understand why the travel routes haven't turned into tourist superhighways.

Main attractions

● **Machu Picchu/Cuzco** Peru. Once the head of the Inca Empire, the town of Cuzco now serves as the springboard for trips to Machu Picchu, the mountainous "Lost City" (discovered by American historian Hiram Bingham in 1911). Most budget travellers prefer to arrive on foot by way of the Inca Trail, a sometimes-crowded four-day trek that takes in high-altitude passes, countless scenic overlooks and lush cloud forests.

● **Angel Falls** Venezuela. It can't be seen in one glance. You need to start at the bottom and slowly tilt your head back to take in all 979 metres of the freefalling water. The world's highest waterfall isn't that easy (or cheap) to get to. This southern Venezuelan wonder is most commonly seen out the window of a plane, but it's possible to take a multi-day trip in a motorized dugout canoe.

● **Rio de Janeiro** Brazil. This city is easily one of the most breathtaking on the planet. A 27-metre-tall statue of Christ looms over the nine million caipirinha-drinking, samba-dancing, beach-football-playing Cariocas (inhabitants of Rio). Rio kicks into high gear during Carnaval, as everyone tries to rack up forty days' worth of eating, drinking and sinning before Lent arrives.

● **Galapagos Islands** Ecuador. This barren, volcanic thirteen-island archipel-

SOUTH AMERICA

NORTH
ATLANTIC
OCEAN

Caracas
VENEZUELA
Georgetown
GUYANA
Paramaribo
Cayenne
Bogotá
SURINAM
FRENCH
GUIANA
COLOMBIA

Quito
ECUADOR

PERU
Lima

BRAZIL

La Paz
BOLIVIA
Brasília

PACIFIC
OCEAN

PARAGUAY
Asunción

CHILE

Santiago
URUGUAY
Buenos Aires
Montevideo
ARGENTINA

SOUTH
ATLANTIC
OCEAN

Falkland
Islands

0   1000 km

South
Georgia

ago located 1000km off Ecuador's coast is best known for its unique wildlife, and the man who pointed out the process of natural selection that got them that way: Charles Darwin. The absence of natural predators affords humans an intimacy with the animals unheard of elsewhere. You can swim with sea lions, float alongside penguins, step over blue-footed boobies and pose for pictures next to marine iguanas.

● **Amazon rainforest** Often called the

"lungs of the world", the Amazon rain-forest, an impenetrable snarl of vegetation bigger than Western Europe, produces twenty percent of the planet's oxygen. It accommodates the world's second-longest river (over 6300km), which carries twelve times more water than the Mississippi and discharges it upwards of 250km out into the Atlantic. Despite its ongoing destruction, it's the most bio-diverse natural phenomenon going and can be best explored in Brazil, Bolivia, Peru and Ecuador.

When to go

The weather in South America is welcoming year-round, especially if you're flexible. Often, that doesn't mean fleeing far. If it gets too steamy in the coastal lowlands, just head for the cooler surrounding hills. A few things to watch for: in the south of Patagonia, winter can get awfully cold, things close and the remote dirt roads near the Amazon basin get muddy and impassable during rainy season (Jan–April). That's also when the Inca Trail becomes wet and slippery and the Galapagos Islands are hot and drizzly. There are two peak seasons: South Americans tend to go on holiday from mid-December until Carnival in February; and most foreigners arrive in July and August.

Costs

Argentina, Chile, Brazil, Venezuela and Uruguay are slightly more expensive than the rest of Latin America, but you may be more likely to find larger price differences between cities and rural areas than between the countries themselves. Because South America has fewer hostels and more guesthouses (ie fewer dormitories), it's possible to make

Lowest daily budget
Expensive ($40+/£26): French Guiana, Falkland Islands
Mid-range ($25–$40/£16–£26): Chile, Argentina, Brazil, Venezuela, Uruguay
Budget ($8–$25/£5–£16): Bolivia, Peru, Ecuador, Colombia, Paraguay

significant savings by travelling with another person.

Getting around by air

One look at the point-to-point air travel prices, and it's easy to understand why overland travel is so popular among budget travellers. As usual, domestic flights are often significantly cheaper, even over longer distances, so if it's just a matter of taking a little pressure off your kidneys, that's a decent alternative.

Air passes
There are a variety of air passes you can turn to, but unfortunately, most are single-country passes and have to be purchased before you arrive. If you fly to the continent with a South American

Sample fares
Caracas to: Bogotá $250/£161 Lima $360/£231 Quito $300/£193 Santiago $420/£270
Rio de Janeiro to: Buenos Aires: $400/£257 La Paz $430/£276 Quito $900/£579 Santiago $570/£367

carrier, you can often get significant savings (up to $100/£64) on their air pass.

● **Latin AirFlex Pass** (🌐www.exitotravel .com). You buy a minimum of four coupons ($200/£129 each) and maximum of 16 and can fly between Peru, Brazil, Chile, Argentina and Bolivia for up to 60 days.

● **Merco Sur Airpass** (🌐www.exitotravel .com). The minimum purchase is one coupon for an international flight and the maximum is five coupons (coupons are based on length of flight and range from $225/£145 to $870/£559). Flights must be used within 30 days. Participating countries include Argentina, Brazil, Chile, Paraguay and Uruguay.

● **Argentina** Visit Argentina Pass: $500/£320 for 4 flights within 30 days. 🌐www.turismo.gov.ar/eng/Information/ mvisit.htm

● **Bolivia** LAB (Lloyd Aereo Boliviano) pass: $173/£111 for 5 flights within 30 days. The pass can be purchased within Bolivia. 🌐www.labairlines.com/Bolivia.

● **Brazil** Brazil Airpass: $490/£315 (low season) $540/£350 (high season) for 4 flights within 21 days. 🌐www.brol.com/brazilairpass.asp

● **Chile** Visit Chile Pass: $350/£225 for 3–6 flights not including Easter Island. Additional flights are $80/£50.

● **Colombia** Descubra Colombia: $180/£115 (low season) $200/£130 (high season) for 5 flights in 21 days. Three extra flights for $40/£26 each.

● **Peru** Inka Air Pass: up to 5 flights for $90/£60 each.

Overland routes

The classic South American overland route brought travellers down from Central America to Tierra del Fuego via the Panamerican Highway. Even Butch

Cassidy and the Sundance Kid reportedly got as far as central Patagonia. Roads around the Amazon rainforest and the mountain highlands (Peru, Bolivia, Ecuador) are the among the slowest going. The main routes in Argentina, Brazil, Chile, Colombia and Venezuela are relatively well surfaced and allow traffic to move perhaps a little too fast for your own comfort level.

Buses

For short and mid-range distances, buses are the most common, convenient and usually the cheapest way to get around South America. Here's a general rule of thumb: the cheaper the bus ride is per hour, the slower you're going, the rougher the ride, and the greater the chance that something can further delay your journey. In addition to the terrain, politics can slow things down. Major political disagreements usually find their way to the surface in the form of road blocks. Locals may drag a few trees across the road or go on strike, but generally if you wait for a few days the path clears.

Trains

There's no extensive rail network, but a number of classic train journeys are well worth the ride, such as the line from Salta to San Antonio de los Cobres (train to the clouds), which runs through the foothills of the Argentinian Andes. There's the Bolivian eye-popper from Oruro to Villazon via a bottomless gorge and a Peruvian gem from Arequipa to Puno by way of a 4600-metre pass.

Cars

Renting

Rental isn't such a great deal, but with a few travellers sharing the cost it can be. All you need to rent a car is a valid driving licence, major credit card or cash

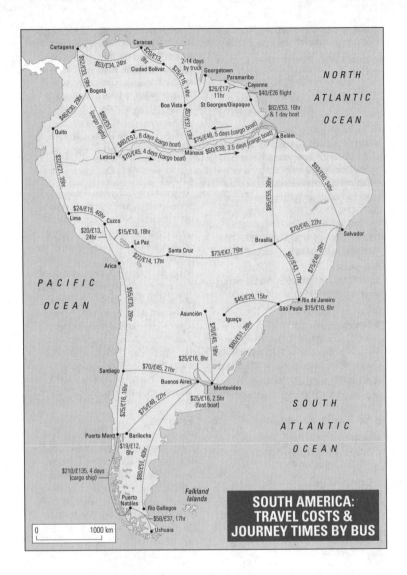

Cartagena
$52/£33, 19hr
$53/£34, 24hr

Caracas
$20/£13, 9hr
Ciudad Bolívar
$25/£16, 14hr

2-14 days by truck
Georgetown
Paramaribo
$26/£17, 11hr
Cayenne
$40/£26 flight

$46/£30, 29hr
Bogotá
$90/£51 (cargo flight)

Boa Vista
$57/£37, 13hr

St Georges/Oiapoque
$82/£53, 16hr & 1 day boat

NORTH
ATLANTIC
OCEAN

Quito
$32/£21, 35hr

$80/£51, 8 days (cargo boat)
$75/£48, 5 days (cargo boat)
$60/£39, 3.5 days (cargo boat)
Belém

Leticia
$10/£45, 4 days (cargo boat)
Manaus

$53/£80, 34hr

$85/£55, 36hr

Lima
$24/£15, 40hr
Cuzco
$15/£10, 18hr
La Paz
$22/£14, 17hr
Arica

$20/£13, 24hr

Santa Cruz
$73/£47, 75hr

Brasília
$70/£45, 22hr
$67/£43, 17hr
$75/£48, 28hr

Salvador

PACIFIC
OCEAN

$55/£35, 26hr

Asunción
$70/£45, 18hr
Iguaçu
$45/£29, 15hr
Rio de Janeiro
São Paulo $15/£10, 6hr
$60/£51, 20hr

$25/£16, 8hr

Santiago
$70/£45, 21hr
Buenos Aires
Montevideo
$25/£16, 2.5hr (fast boat)

$25/£16, 16hr
$75/£48, 22hr

SOUTH
ATLANTIC
OCEAN

Puerto Montt
Bariloche
$19/£12, 6hr

$80/£51, 40hr

$210/£135, 4 days (cargo ship)

Puerto Natáles
Río Gallegos
$58/£37, 17hr
Ushuaia

Falkland
Islands

0   1000 km

SOUTH AMERICA:
TRAVEL COSTS &
JOURNEY TIMES BY BUS

deposit, and in some countries (Bolivia, Argentina, Colombia, and Surinam) an international driving permit (ⓦwww.theaa.co.uk). Driving is on the right-hand side, except for the daredevil passing that takes place on some roads.

For longer-term rentals, look around for deals once you're in the city centre. Make sure insurance is included with the quoted price of the vehicle, as it's usually mandatory. Also, watch out for sneaky offers, such as not having to

Avoiding the Darién Gap

To get from Central to South America (Panama to Colombia), there are a few options. There's the **Darién Gap**, a rough and lawless jungle between Colombia and Panama considered by many to be the most notorious overland stretch in the world. If you get robbed only once you're considered to have had excellent luck – some people get kidnapped for months, some never come out. This route should not be attempted.

Instead, take a $45/£29 flight to Puerto Obaldia, then a walk or boat to Capurgana, then a boat to Turbo, and from there a cargo boat (2 days; $35/£23) to Cartagena. Option two is a $27/£17 flight from Panama City to Porvenir, then a sailing boat service (4–5 days; $185/£119) to Cartagena via the San Blas Islands. From a budget perspective, however, neither of these is cheaper than flying: $190/£122 from Panama City to Cartagena.

pay for damage in the event of an accident. The catch? You have to pay seventy percent or so of the daily rate for as long as it takes to fix the vehicle. And you can guess how long it'll take to complete the repairs.

Buying a car

One of the best places to buy a car is Chile, specifically Iqueque, a duty-free port town well north of Santiago: customs officers there are reportedly accustomed to handling the international paperwork. Santiago also has a good reputation for car purchasing. With some luck you can even sell the vehicle for a profit in Peru, Bolivia, or elsewhere. Asuncion in Paraguay may be the best place to sell if you can get there. The paperwork necessary for heading over borders can be gathered at embassies and consulates along the way, but it can be a hassle.

You'll need a Carnet de Passage (p.42) or Libreta de Pasos por Aduana. When it comes to choosing a car, you'd do well to pick up a Toyota Land Cruiser, especially if you've got some off-roading in mind. It's popular, attractive even with a few scratches, and easy to sell. More important, it rarely breaks down. Tagging along behind buses after dusk is a good option, as there are scores of roads that become dangerous by night. But don't get too close on gravel roads as windscreens crack easily from stray flying pebbles. Petrol isn't that cheap, especially in the southern half of the continent and difficult-to-reach areas, where it can rival European prices.

Bikes

Cyclists can find nicer, less chaotic roads, such as those in Southern Argentina and Chile. The cyclist community is small, but it exists all over South America. For more on travelling by bike, see p.43.

Hitching

The plausibility of hitching varies from region to region, but is sometimes the only means to reach out-of-the-way spots. In Chile, hitching is particularly popular, even among young Chilean travellers. Because traffic can be sparse along many routes, adequate food and water is a must. See p.136 for hitching tips and safety issues.

Reading list

● Isabel Allende *Eva Luna*
● Jorge Amado *Doña Flor and Her Two Husbands*

Visa requirements for South America

	EU	US/Can	Aus/NZ
Argentina	By air, visa issued upon arrival for free: 90-day. Prior visa required with land entry only.	By air, visa issued upon arrival for free: 90-day. Prior visa required with land entry only.	By air, visa issued upon arrival for free: 90-day (NZ must pay $24/£15). Prior visa required with land entry only.
Bolivia	Visa issued upon arrival for free: 90-day, but each crossing may have its own requirements.	Visa issued upon arrival for free: 30-day, but each crossing may have its own requirements. For a 90-day visa, apply before or request one at the border.	Visa issued upon arrival for free: 30-day, but each crossing may have its own requirements. For a 90-day visa, apply before or request at the border.
Brazil	Only British do not require a visa. EU citizens must get a visa (90-day) and must use it within 90 days of issue. $20/£13	Visa required (90-day) and must use it within 90 days of issue. Americans pay $65/£42, Canadians pay $40/£26	Visa required (90-day) and must use it within 90 days of issue. Australians pay $35/£23, NZ pay $20/£13
Chile	Issued upon arrival for free: 90-day stay.	Issued upon arrival for free: 90-day stay.	NZ citizens require visa prior to arrival.
Colombia	Issued upon arrival for free: 30-, 60- and 90-day stays (at the whim of the immigration official). Extensions are allowed up to 90 days. Czech Republic and Slovakia require prior visa.	Issued upon arrival for free: 30-, 60- and 90-day stays (at the whim of the immigration official). Extensions are allowed up to 90 days.	Issued upon arrival for free: 30-, 60- and 90-day stays (at the whim of the immigration official). Extensions are allowed up to 90 days.
Ecuador	Issued upon arrival for free: up to 90-day tourist visa in any 12-month period. UK citizens may stay longer.	Issued upon arrival for free: up to 90-day tourist visa in any 12-month period.	Issued upon arrival for free: up to 90-day tourist visa in any 12-month period.

	EU	US/Can	Aus/NZ
Guyana	Issued upon arrival for free: 30-day stay	Issued upon arrival for free: 30-day stay	Issued upon arrival for free: 30-day stay
French Guiana	No visa required	No visa required for US. Canadians should apply at French embassy; $25/£16	Visa required: apply at French embassy; $25/£16
Paraguay	No visa required	No visa required for US. Canadians require visa prior to arrival	Visa required prior to arrival
Peru	Issued upon arrival for free: 30–90-day visa	Issued upon arrival for free: 30–90-day visa	Issued upon arrival for free: 30–90-day visa
Surinam	Issued in a few days for $30/£19 in consulates in Guyana or French Guiana (longer from overseas). UK, Denmark, Finland, Norway, Sweden and Switzerland citizens do not require visa.	Issued in a few days for $30/£19 in consulates in Guyana or French Guiana (longer from overseas)	Issued in a few days for $30/£19 in consulates in Guyana or French Guiana (longer from overseas)
Uruguay	Issued upon arrival: 90-day tourist card	For US, issued upon arrival: 90-day tourist card. Canadians require visa prior to arrival ($30/£19).	Visa required prior to arrival
Venezuela	By air: issued upon arrival for free: 90-day tourist card. By land: depends on consulate. Anything from free 90-day tourist card to one with $40/£26 fee, to 72hr transit pass	By air: issued upon arrival for free: 90-day tourist card. By land: depends on consulate. Anything from free 90-day tourist card to one with $40/£26 fee, to 72hr transit pass	By air: issued upon arrival for free: 90-day tourist card. By land: depends on consulate. Anything from free 90-day tourist card to one with $40/£26 fee, to 72hr transit pass

- Bruce Chatwin *In Patagonia*
- Charles Darwin *On the Origin of Species by Means of Natural Selection*
- Peter Fleming *Brazilian Adventure*
- Ernesto "Che" Guevara *The Motorcycle Diaries: a Journey Around South America*
- Machado de Assis *Quinincas Borba*
- Gabriel García Márquez *One Hundred Years of Solitude*
- Pablo Neruda *Selected Poems*
- Mario Vargas Llosa *The Notebooks of Don Rigoberto*

Visas

Most travellers landing in South American countries will find visas are generally handed out upon arrival (or can be purchased at that time). Brazil is the typical exception, but watch out for overland entry requirements, which are often different from plane arrivals. See pp.290–291 for more.

First-Time
Around the World

Basics

Transport

RTW flight specialists

ⓦ**www.airbrokers.com** A US-based quick and simple RTW planner

ⓦ**www.airtreks.com** A do-it-your-self RTW web planner

ⓦ**www.roundtheworldflights.com** A UK-based planner

ⓦ**www.statravel.com** Student and budget travel experts with world-wide shops

ⓦ**www.trailfinders.co.uk** Well-informed UK-based agents

ⓦ**www.westernair.co.uk** RTW and budget trip specialists

RTW alliance sites

ⓦ**www.oneworld.com** Eight-member alliance

ⓦ**www.star-alliance.com** Background information on Star-Alliance airline consortium

ⓦ**www.thegreatescapade.com** An alliance with a good online RTW planner

Flight booking engines

ⓦ**www.expedia.com** Microsoft's online travel agency

ⓦ**www.orbitz.com** The airlines' Web project – a group booking engine with fares from 450 airlines

ⓦ**www.travelocity.com** A leading booking site powered by the Sabre reservation system.

Airlines and airports

ⓦ**http://flightview.com** Allows you to check the status of any flight

ⓦ**www.airlineandairportlinks.com** Links to all airports

ⓦ**www.sleepinginairports.net** A guide to sleeping in airports

ⓦ**www.travel-watch.com/airlink.htm** Links to every airline worldwide

International air passes

ⓦ**www.bestfares.com/travel/desks/story.asp?id=1813** Listings of airpasses with links

Budget airlines in Europe

ⓦ**www.BuzzAway.com** Flights from the UK mainly to France, plus Spain, Germany and a few others

ⓦ**www.EasyJet.com** Flights from the UK to the Mediterranean and around the UK

ⓦ**www.RyanAir.com** Flights all over Europe can actually be so low as to be free – you just pay taxes and charges

ⓦ**www.Virgin-Express.com** Bargain flights to Scandinavia, Italy, France, Spain and Belgium

Trains

ⓦ**www.raileurope.com** Europe Rail Passes

ⓦ**www.railserve.com** Links to rail services around the world

Cars and motorbikes

ⓦ**www.viamichelin.com** The Michelin Route Planner gives driving directions throughout Europe

ⓦ**www.aaa.com** American Automobile Association – your best friend after you buy the world's cheapest car in the US

ⓦ**www.caa.ca** Canadian Automobile Association – offers Carnet information for Americans as well

www.rac.co.uk The Royal Automobile Club, which offers similar services to the AA

www.theaa.com The UK's Automobile Association for all things automotive

www.Unlimitedhorizons.com Tips and tales on motorcycling around the world

Ferries and freighters

http://members.aol.com /CruiseAZ/freighters.htm UK-based freighter bookers

http://routesinternational.com/ ships.htm Links to ferry services around the world

www.freightertravel.hb.co.nz/ NZ-based freighter bookers

www.freighterworld.com Helps book passage on freighters worldwide

www.tcpltd.com/tcpltd1.htm Canada-based freighter bookers

www.travltips.com /freighterdirectory.html Directory provides a sample of the freighters on the move and will help with booking

Money

Currency exchange rates

www.orlanda.com Quick conversions with 164 currencies

ATMs worldwide

www.mastercard.com/ cardholderservices/atm/ For Mastercard users

www.visa.com/pd/atm/main.html For Visa card owners

Money transfer

www.moneygram.com Urgent money-sending and bill-paying, affiliated with Thomas Cook, American Express and various banks and post offices

www.westernunion.com For sending money urgently overseas between Western Union offices

AmEx travel offices

http://travel.americanexpress .com/travel/personal/resources/tso/ A list of AmEx offices worldwide

Discount cards

www.isecard.com International Exchange Student Cards

www.istc.org International Student Identity Cards, Teacher Cards and Youth Cards

Working abroad

www.anyworkanywhere.com Find work in 41 countries and get help with visa information

www.jobmonkey.com Search by job type, from skiing to teaching

www.jobsabroad.com This site allows searching by country or job type, and has links to study and

volunteer programmes
Ⓦ **www.liveworkplay.com.au** A down-under guide with useful working-holiday information, complete with the lowdown on visas
Ⓦ **www.michaelpage.com**

Professional work placement agency
Ⓦ **www.monster.com** This site helps place skilled workers
Ⓦ **www.wwoof.org** Directory of World Wide Opportunities on Organic Farms

Travel tools

Online maps

Ⓦ **www.mapblast.com** Good graphics, and places items such as hotels or petrol stations on map as well
Ⓦ **www.maporama.com** Another dependable online map site that allows you to zoom in to nearly any spot on the globe

Conversions

Ⓦ **http://convert.french-property .co.uk** This site converts weights, measurements, distances and so on

Global adaptors

Ⓦ **www.kropla.com/electric.htm** The lowdown on how to plug in any electrical appliances you may be lugging with you
Ⓦ **www.kropla.com/phones.htm** For phone adaptors and line checkers – all the tools you'll need, and some you won't

Times and dates

Ⓦ **www.festivals.com** or
Ⓦ **www.world-party.com** Find out when and where the party is on, no matter where you go
Ⓦ **www.worldtimeserver.com** A quick guide to the time worldwide
Ⓦ **www.holidayfestival.com** Calendar of global holidays

World facts

Ⓦ **www.countryreports.org** From flags to maps to national anthems, here's a good starting point for learning a little about the countries you're heading to
Ⓦ **www.nationalgeographic.com** The National Geographic Society offers a top-end presentation of our fascinating planet
Ⓦ **www.odci.gov/cia/publications /factbook/** It's no secret that the CIA World Facts Guide is one of the best sources of information around

Weather

Ⓦ **www.intellicast.com/Travel /World/** Global five-day forecasts
Ⓦ **www.worldclimate.com** Get the scoop on world climates – lists average temperature or rainfall for a huge number of destinations

Language

Ⓦ **www.babblefish.com** Free online translations for several European languages
Ⓦ **www.travlang.com** The Rosetta Stone of websites, translating most languages to most other languages
Ⓦ **www.word2word.com** Provides access to foreign dictionaries

Travel gear

Ⓦ **www.altrec.com** An online-only retailer with gear from all brands
Ⓦ **www.ems.com** Loads of gear with many Web deals
Ⓦ **www.gear-zone.co.uk** A UK-based gear bonanza with easy-to-use layout

Ⓦ **www.menda.com.au** A site for getting gear down under – they even have all the cheap stuff (ear plugs, sink plug etc) for one-stop shopping
Ⓦ **www.rei.com** The megastore US retailer has regular online specials

Communication

Ⓦ **www.ekit.com** Also known as ISIconnect and eKno, this full-service budget communication package offers an excellent service
Ⓦ **http://e-worldphone.com** If you just want the prepaid budget phone service, this is one option
Ⓦ **http://phonecallworld.com /1callback.html** For those who'd rather be billed monthly than have to load up a budget phone account beforehand

Callback services

Ⓦ **www.newworldtele.com**,
Ⓦ **www.owcusa.com** and
Ⓦ **www.world-link.com/services .html** all offer callback services, which work well if you're calling from abroad, but not on the move
Ⓦ **www.escapeartist.com/ internet/callback.htm** Offers a more complete list of callback companies

International phone cards

Ⓦ **www.besttelephonerates.com** If you want some phone cards before arriving in a country, here's a place to find them

Cybercafés

Ⓦ **www.cybercafes.com** A search engine for thousands of cybercafés in nearly every country

Webphones

Ⓦ **www.net2phone.com** and
Ⓦ **www.iconnecthere.com** Both have fantastically low prices, but the quality of the connection can be low as well: stay tuned for improvements

Country calling codes

Ⓦ **www.countrycallingcodes.com** Get the dialling numbers to every country, plus the ones you need to dial out of the country you're in

Health and safety

Ⓦ **www.cdc.gov** The US Center for Disease Control has the latest updated information on vaccinations and outbreaks

Ⓦ **www.who.org** Features a country-by-country health profile

Travel advisory

Ⓦ**http://travel.state.gov/travel _warnings.html** The US State Department warnings can be a little imprecise – if one spot is potentially dangerous, they put the whole country on the list

Ⓦ**www.dfat.gov.au/consular /advice/advices_mnu.html** Australia's consular advice

Ⓦ**www.fco.gov.uk** The UK's Foreign Office is a good starting point

Ⓦ**www.voyage.gc.ca/destinations /menu_e.htm** Canada's warning page

Ⓦ**www.lonelyplanet.com/travel _ticker/** Lonely Planet's monthly update of travel advisories

Embassies

Ⓦ**www.embassyworld.com** Find an embassy anywhere in the world and get updated visa information

Customs

Ⓦ**www.travel.com.hk/customs.htm** How to figure out what you can bring in and take out of countries

Ⓦ**www.tiglion.net/scripts/travdb /currency/exe/index.asp** Country-by-country regulations on how much money you can bring in and take out

Your stay

Tourist information

Ⓦ**www.towd.com** Find a tourist bureau worldwide

World heritage sites

Ⓦ**http://whc.unesco.org/heritage .htm** World Heritage Sites around the globe

Accommodation

Ⓦ**http://servas.org** SERVAS is a global homestay service with a large database – travellers allowed to stay two nights

Ⓦ**www.bandb.com** An international bed & breakfast directory

Ⓦ**www.elderhostel.org** Elderhostel information and hostel locator for the over-55s

Ⓦ**www.homexchange.com** HomeExchange is a membership-based ($30) home-swapping service with 5000 listings in 50 countries

Ⓦ**www.hostels.com** Global hostel finder

Ⓦ**www.iyhf.org** Hostelling International's main site

Museums

Ⓦ**http://wwar.com** World Wide Art Resources has links to 10,000 museums – buy your ticket online and avoid the queues

Ⓦ**www.hermitagemuseum.org** Russia's largest art museum

Ⓦ**www.louvre.fr** Check out the Louvre

Responsible tourism

ⓦ**www.tourismconcern.org.uk**
Organization campaigning for smart,
responsible tourism

ⓦ**www.pirt.org**
Tourism operators concerned about
the impact of tourism, particularly
on indigenous peoples

Reading resources

Guidebook sites

ⓦ**www.fodors.com** A very user-
friendly site aimed at travellers with
more pocket change than the average

ⓦ**www.letsgo.com** Let's Go is an
American classic for the college
stomp in Europe, but its core audi-
ence are now expanding their hori-
zons

ⓦ**www.lonelyplanet.com** This site
covers every country on the planet
and has a much-subscribed travel-
discussion site called the Thorn
Tree

ⓦ**www.roughguides.com** Set up
for independent travellers of all
budgets, with online chat boards,
travel tips and in-depth country
information

ⓦ**www.travelerstales.com**
Pushing the experiential side of
guiding, *Travelers Tales* offers a
sampling of literature to enrich your
trip

Budget travel magazines

ⓦ**www.bigworld.com** Down-to-
earth world travel on a budget.

ⓦ**www.msnbc.com/news/bt-
front_front.asp** Arthur Frommer's
Budget Travel Magazine is mostly
focused on cheap holidays, but has
good information for longer trips as
well

ⓦ**www.outpostmagazine.com**
Shoestring globetrotting with a
pleasing layout

ⓦ**www.tntmagazine.com/uk/** *TNT*
magazine, with UK and Aus/NZ editions for work and flat finding

ⓦ**www.transitionsabroad.com**
Great information on working,
studying and living overseas

Adventure travel magazines

ⓦ**www.bluemagazine.com** A budget adventure magazine with an
edgy layout

ⓦ**www.getaway.co.za** *Getaway* is
a South African publication with an
African emphasis

ⓦ**www.nationalgeographic.com
/adventure/** *National Geographic's*
award-winning adventure magazine:
tight writing with an outdoor activity
slant

ⓦ**www.outsidemag.com** Excellent
writing with an extreme sport and
activity bias as well as eco and
travel pieces

ⓦ**www.wanderlust.co.uk**
Wanderlust Magazine covers the
classic travel destinations, plus
reviews and interviews

Upmarket travel magazines

ⓦ**www.islands.com** More cultural depth than you might expect, although you can practically get a tan flipping through the pages

ⓦ**www.nationalgeographic.com /traveller/** An upmarket, well-crafted travel magazine that's not afraid to show the effects of tourism – or the benefits of a comfortable room

ⓦ**www.travelandleisure.com** Ranks everything from hotels to airlines and finds some room for interesting (albeit comfortable) travel in between

Newspaper travel sections

ⓦ**www.newspapers.com** Has links to newspapers all over the world. The pick of the international bunch are:

ⓦ**http://travel.independent.co.uk**

ⓦ**http://travel.guardian.co.uk/**

ⓦ**www.nytimes.com/travel/**

ⓦ**www.latimes.com/travel/**

ⓦ**www.smh.com.au/travel/**

ⓦ**www.nzherald.co.nz/travel/**

ⓦ**www.thestar.ca/travel**

ⓦ**www.canada.com/travel/**

ⓦ**www.observer.co.uk/travel/**

ⓦ**www.timesonline.co.uk/travel**

ⓦ**www.theglobeandmail.com/ travel/**

Travel radio

ⓦ**www.bbc.co.uk/radio1/onelife /travel/** BBC Onelife travel has an impressive and complete travel resource section

ⓦ**www.savvytraveler.com** An American public radio programme devoted to travel in all its various acoustic forms; hear it online

Online-only travel publications

ⓦ**www.bootsnall.com** A great travel resource with anecdotes that explain how to avoid some of the potholes on the road less travelled

ⓦ**www.connectedtraveler.com** Offers a refreshing perspective on cultural travel

ⓦ**www.igougo.com** Swaps photos and travel writing with mileage-type points accrued for your contributions

ⓦ**www.journeywoman.com** This site highlights the female perspective and offers tips and tales

ⓦ**www.kinetictravel.net** Tales of adventure combining mayhem and meditation

ⓦ**www.literarytraveler.com** Tracing the steps of famous authors and learning about their inspirations is just part of the literary journey

ⓦ**www.worldhum.com** A travel version of *Arts and Letters Daily* with original articles, interviews and reviews

Map specialists

ⓦ**www.mapshop.net.au** Australia

ⓦ**www.worldofmaps.com** Canada

ⓦ**www.mapworld.co.nz** NZ

ⓦ**www.stanfords.co.uk** UK

ⓦ**www.randmcnally.com** US

First-Time Around the World

Index
and small print

Index

A

J

K

L

M

N

O

P

R

S

T

Twenty Years of Rough Guides

In the summer of 1981, Mark Ellingham, Rough Guides' founder, knocked out the first guide on a typewriter, with a group of friends. Mark had been travelling in Greece after university, and couldn't find a guidebook that really answered his needs.There were heavyweight cultural guides on the one hand – good on museums and classical sites but not on beaches and tavernas – and on the other hand student manuals that were so caught up with how to save money that they lost sight of the country's significance beyond its role as a place for a cool vacation. None of the guides began to address Greece as a country, with its natural and human environment, its politics and its contemporary life.

Having no urgent reason to return home, Mark decided to write his own guide. It was a guide to Greece that tried to combine some erudition and insight with a thoroughly practical approach to travellers' needs. Scrupulously researched listings of places to stay, eat and drink were matched by careful attention to detail on everything from Homer to Greek music, from classical sites to national parks and from nude beaches to monasteries. Back in London, Mark and his friends got their Rough Guide accepted by a farsighted commissioning editor at the publisher Routledge and it came out in 1982.

The Rough Guide to Greece was a student scheme that became a publishing phenomenon. The immediate success of the book – shortlisted for the Thomas Cook award – spawned a series that rapidly covered dozens of countries. The Rough Guides found a ready market among backpackers and budget travellers, but soon acquired a much broader readership that included older and less impecunious visitors. Readers relished the guides' wit and inquisitiveness as much as the enthusiastic, critical approach that acknowledges everyone wants value for money – but not at any price.

Rough Guides soon began supplementing the "rougher" information – the hostel and low-budget listings – with the kind of detail that independent-minded travellers on any budget might expect. These days, the guides – distributed worldwide by the Penguin Group – include recommendations spanning the range from shoestring to luxury, and cover more than 200 destinations around the globe. Our growing team of authors, many of whom come to Rough Guides initially as outstandingly good letter-writers telling us about their travels, are spread all over the world, particularly in Europe, the USA and Australia. As well as the travel guides, Rough Guides publishes a series of dictionary phrasebooks covering two dozen major languages, an acclaimed series of music guides running the gamut from Classical to World Music, a series of music CDs in association with World Music Network, and a range of reference books on topics as diverse as the Internet, Pregnancy and Unexplained Phenomena. Visit **www.roughguides.com** to see what's cooking.

Rough Guide credits

Text editor: Helena Smith
Series editor: Mark Ellingham
Editorial: Martin Dunford, Jonathan Buckley, Kate Berens, Ann-Marie Shaw, Helena Smith, Olivia Swift, Ruth Blackmore, Geoff Howard, Claire Saunders, Gavin Thomas, Alexander Mark Rogers, Polly Thomas, Joe Staines, Richard Lim, Duncan Clark, Peter Buckley, Lucy Ratcliffe, Clifton Wilkinson, Alison Murchie, Matthew Teller, Andrew Dickson, Fran Sandham, Sally Schafer (UK); Andrew Rosenberg, Yuki Takagaki, Richard Koss, Hunter Slaton (US)
Production: Link Hall, Helen Prior, Julia Bovis, Michelle Draycott, Katie Pringle, Zoë Nobes, Rachel Holmes, Andy Turner, Dan May

Cartography: Maxine Repath, Melissa Baker, Ed Wright, Katie Lloyd-Jones
Cover art direction: Louise Boulton
Picture research: Sharon Martins, Mark Thomas
Online: Kelly Martinez, Anja Mutic-Blessing, Jennifer Gold, Audra Epstein, Suzanne Welles, Cree Lawson (US)
Finance: John Fisher, Gary Singh, Edward Downey, Mark Hall, Tim Bill
Marketing & Publicity: Richard Trillo, Niki Smith, David Wearn, Chloë Roberts, Demelza Dallow, Claire Southern (UK); Simon Carloss, David Wechsler, Megan Kennedy (US)
Administration: Julie Sanderson, Karoline Densley

Publishing information

This first edition published March 2003 by **Rough Guides Ltd**, 80 Strand, London WC2R 0RL
345 Hudson St, 4th Floor, New York, NY 10014, USA
Distributed by the Penguin Group
Penguin Books Ltd, 80 Strand, London WC2R 0RL
Penguin Putnam, Inc. 375 Hudson Street, NY 10014, USA
Penguin Books Australia Ltd, 487 Maroondah Highway, PO Box 257, Ringwood, Victoria 3134, Australia
Penguin Books Canada Ltd, 10 Alcorn Avenue, Toronto, Ontario, Canada M4V 1E4
Penguin Books (NZ) Ltd, 182–190 Wairau Road, Auckland 10, New Zealand
Typeset in Bembo and Helvetica to an original design by Henry Iles.
Printed in Italy by LegoPrint S.p.A

336pp includes index
A catalogue record for this book is available from the British Library

ISBN 1-843-53057-0

The publishers and authors have done their best to ensure the accuracy and currency of all the information in **The Rough Guide to First-Time Around the World**; however, they can accept no responsibility for any loss, injury, or inconvenience sustained by any traveller as a result of information or advice contained in the guide.

Help us update

We've gone to a lot of effort to ensure that the first edition of **The Rough Guide to First-Time Around the World** is accurate and up to date. However, things change and if you feel we've got it wrong or left something out, we'd like to know, and if you can remember the address, the price, the time, the phone number, so much the better.

We'll credit all contributions, and send a copy of the next edition (or any other Rough Guide if you prefer) for the best letters. Everyone who writes to us and isn't already a subscriber will receive a copy of our full-colour thrice-yearly newsletter. Please mark letters: **"Rough Guide First-Time Around the World Update"** and send to: Rough

Guides, 80 Strand, London WC2R 0RL, or Rough Guides, 4th Floor, 345 Hudson St, New York, NY 10014. Or send an email to **mail@roughguides.com**

Have your questions answered and tell others about your trip at **www.roughguides.atinfopop.com**

Acknowledgements

This book is dedicated to Signe,* my recurrent travel companion, soul mate, literary critic, copy editor, personal physician, and – by sheer coincidence – wife. And also my two-year-old daughter, Sienna, who frequently hopped onto my computer while I was briefly out of the room and inserted several hundred pages of the letter "R". For your reading pleasure, most of them have been removed.

I'd like to thank Jonathon Werve, a friend, ultimate Frisbee player and champion of noble causes, who flew all the way to Sweden just to lend me some of his invaluable research expertise.

I'm particularly thankful to the travellers who shared their adventures and misadventures in the interview sidebars throughout the book: P.J. O'Rourke, Tim Cahill, Rudy Maxa, Michael Finkel, Jason Wilson, Chris Anderson, John Flinn, Jonas Persson, John Hoult, Peter Laurin, Beth Wooldridge, Per Andersson, Amy Schrier, Craig Ayre, Sara Hare, Claire Southern, Sally Schafer, Ron Gluckman and Jim Benning, so that we all might avoid the same pitfalls. Many of them, you will notice, have written books (hint, hint).

Finally, I'd like to thank all the people at Rough Guides I've had the pleasure of working with, starting with the publisher, Martin Dunford, who casually mentioned when we first met that he'd like to publish a

book like this, then actually went ahead and did it. Marketing guru Simon Carloss has been especially supportive and deserves his own sentence. As does editorial whiz Kate Berens. Saving the most overworked for last, a cheer for Helena Smith. Without her, this book would have been a single 350-page run-on sentence with improperly placed commas. It would also be riddled with ghastly American spellings, expressions, and references.

Brief Literary Notes on this Book: For purposes of greater cross-cultural understanding, "Joan Rivers" was changed to "Elizabeth Taylor" in the introduction. In Chapter 7, there was a short paragraph removed about why travelers with multiple passports love to tell everyone they have more than one passport. Also, in Chapter 7, there was another paragraph removed in which the author admitted, quite frankly, that most embassies and consulates could certainly provide more traveller services than they currently do. I do not personally endorse, nor was influenced by, the advertisements that appear in this book.

*pronounced: "SING-neh"

The **editor** would like to thank Kate Berens for editorial support, Ed Wright for great work on the maps, Mark Thomas for hunting down the photos, Rachel Holmes for typesetting and picture layout and Karoline Densley for the index.

Photo credits

The Pan-American Highway © H.R. Dörig/
Hutchison
Samburu warrior © David Keith
Jones/Images of Africa
Santiago de Cuba © Rolando Pujol/South
American Pictures
Petra Treasury © Jane Taylor

Things to enrich your journey
01 Playa Cocles beach © Diego Ferrari
02 Chandelier, Ice Hotel © Michael
Freeman/ Corbis
03 Grape harvest © Robert Harding
04 Elephant ride © David Reed
05 Felucca © Doug Lansky
06 Street food, Beijing © Brent Madison
07 Lisa Ball at the Rainbow Gathering,
Australia
08 Roman theatre, Orange, France © Gail
Money/Corbis
09 Diver above reef off Saparua Island,
Moluccas © Louise Murray/Robert
Harding
10 Carsbad Caverns, New Mexico © Adam
Woolfitt/Robert Harding
11 Mongolian wrestlers © Keren Su/Corbis
12 Riding a bicycle © Doug Lansky
13 Kangaroo © Lisa Nellis
14 Street sign © Doug Lansky
15 Delhi street vendor © Brent Madison

16 Relaxing in a Turkish Bath © Adam
Woolfitt/Robert Harding
17 Bhote Koshi rafting © David Reed
18 Red Square © Doug Lansky
19 Barber © Everton Macduff/Corbis
20 Pub, Prague © Trip
21 Tomato Festival, Valencia © Roberto
Arakaki/Robert Harding
22 Tikal, Guatemala © Ian Osborne/
Footprints
23 Back streets of Paris © Mark Thomas
24 Sand surfing © Jamie Budge/Corbis
25 Mt Kilimanjaro © Doug Lansky

Black and whites
Cargo trucks on mountain road, India
© Chloë Roberts p.37
Money-changing © Tony West p.62
Empty hammock © Michael Pole/Corbis p.86
Bull-running © Robert Frerck/Robert Harding
p.98
Man carrying sofa, Simla © Chloë Roberts
p.108
Basic toilet, Agra © Chloë Roberts p.150
Japanese toilet control © Doug Lansky
p.152
Toucan phone © Tony Morrison/South
American Pictures p.163
Dentist sign © Jamie Marshall p.180
On safari © Corbis p.211

TRAVEL • MUSIC • REFERENCE • PHRASEBOOKS

Rough Guides publishes new books every month

Music

Acoustic Guitar
Blues: 100 Essential CDs
Cello
Clarinet
Classical Music
Classical Music: 100 Essential CDs
Country Music
Country: 100 Essential CDs
Cuban Music
Drum'n'bass
Drums
Electric Guitar & Bass Guitar
Flute
Hip-Hop
House
Irish Music
Jazz
Jazz: 100 Essential CDs
Keyboards & Digital Piano
Latin: 100 Essential CDs
Music USA: a Coast-To-Coast Tour
Opera
Opera: 100 Essential CDs
Piano
Reading Music
Reggae
Reggae: 100 Essential CDs
Rock
Rock: 100 Essential CDs
Saxophone
Soul: 100 Essential CDs
Techno
Trumpet & Trombone
Violin & Viola
World Music: 100 Essential CDs

World Music Vol1
World Music Vol2

Reference

Children's Books, 0–5
Children's Books, 5–11
China Chronicle
Cult Movies
Cult TV
Elvis
England Chronicle
France Chronicle
India Chronicle
The Internet
Internet Radio
James Bond
Liverpool FC
Man Utd
Money Online
Personal Computers
Pregnancy & Birth
Shopping Online
Travel Health
Travel Online
Unexplained Phenomena
Videogaming
Weather
Website Directory
Women Travel

Music CDs

Africa
Afrocuba
Afro-Peru
Ali Hussan Kuban
The Alps
Americana
The Andes
The Appalachians
Arabesque
Asian Underground
Australian Aboriginal Music
Bellydance
Bhangra
Bluegrass

Bollywood
Boogaloo
Brazil
Cajun
Cajun and Zydeco
Calypso and Soca
Cape Verde
Central America
Classic Jazz
Congolese Soukous
Cuba
Cuban Music Story
Cuban Son
Cumbia
Delta Blues
Eastern Europe
English Roots Music
Flamenco
Franco
Gospel
Global Dance
Greece
The Gypsies
Haiti
Hawaii
The Himalayas
Hip Hop
Hungary
India
India and Pakistan
Indian Ocean
Indonesia
Irish Folk
Irish Music
Italy
Jamaica
Japan
Kenya and Tanzania
Klezmer
Louisiana
Lucky Dube
Mali and Guinea
Marrabenta Mozambique
Merengue & Bachata
Mexico
Native American Music
Nigeria and Ghana
North Africa

Nusrat Fateh Ali Khan
Okinawa
Paris Café Music
Portugal
Rai
Reggae
Salsa
Salsa Dance
Samba
Scandinavia
Scottish Folk
Scottish Music
Senegal & The Gambia
Ska
Soul Brothers
South Africa
South African Gospel
South African Jazz
Spain
Sufi Music
Tango
Thailand
Tex-Mex
Wales
West African Music
World Music Vol 1: Africa, Europe and the Middle East
World Music Vol 2: Latin & North America, Caribbean, India, Asia and Pacific
World Roots
Youssou N'Dour & Etoile de Dakar
Zimbabwe

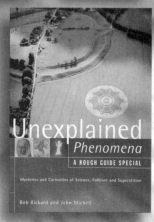

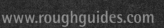

Going abroad?

When you are about to travel abroad you want to be able to feel relaxed and confident that you are prepared. Boots Travel Clinics offer you advice, vaccinations and medication which will help you make the most of your trip.

Your consultation will be carried out with a qualified Nurse acting under the direction of a doctor from MASTA (Medical Advisory Service for Travellers Abroad) a leading supplier of travel health medicine services. Your nurse will advise you on local conditions, from disease outbreaks to political situations, carry out any required vaccinations and supply any necessary anti-malarial medication.

Your details will be entered onto the MASTA e-clinic system, which means that for subsequent trips you can access your records by visiting any MASTA or Boots Travel Clinic in the UK.

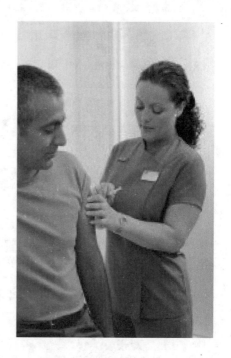

Travel Clinic
in association with **MASTA**

The ideas expressed in this code were developed by and for independent travellers.

Learn About The Country You're Visiting

Start enjoying your travels before you leave by tapping into as many sources of information as you can.

The Cost Of Your Holiday

Think about where your money goes - be fair and realistic about how cheaply you travel. Try and put money into local peoples' hands; drink local beer or fruit juice rather than imported brands and stay in locally owned accommodation. Haggle with humour and not aggressively. Pay what something is worth to you and remember how wealthy you are compared to local people.

Embrace The Local Culture

Open your mind to new cultures and traditions - it will transform your experience. Think carefully about what's appropriate in terms of your clothes and the way you behave. You'll earn respect and be more readily welcomed by local people. Respect local laws and attitudes towards drugs and alcohol that vary in different countries and communities. Think about the impact you could have on them.

Exploring The World – The Travellers' Code

Being sensitive to these ideas means getting more out of your travels - and giving more back to the people you meet and the places you visit.

Minimise Your Environmental Impact

Think about what happens to your rubbish - take biodegradable products and a water filter bottle. Be sensitive to limited resources like water, fuel and electricity. Help preserve local wildlife and habitats by respecting local rules and regulations, such as sticking to footpaths and not standing on coral.

Don't Rely On Guidebooks

Use your guidebook as a starting point, not the only source of information. Talk to local people, then discover your own adventure!

Be Discreet With Photography

Don't treat people as part of the landscape, they may not want their picture taken. Ask first and respect their wishes.

We work with people the world over to promote tourism that benefits their communities, but we can only carry on our work with the support of people like you. For membership details or to find out how to make your travels work for local people and the environment, visit our website.

www.tourismconcern.org.uk

TourismConcern
Campaigning for Ethical and Fairly Traded Tourism

WITH OUR INTERNATIONAL TRANSFER SERVICE YOUR MONEY WILL FLY AROUND THE WORLD

Whether you're sending cash to relatives overseas or buying a home in the sun, we can get your money to wherever it has to go, quickly and reliably. What's more, the funds can be sent in a wide range of local currencies, as well as in sterling. So, if you're after a full range of international payment services that are quick and easy to use, we'd suggest you fly along to your nearest branch of Halifax

HALIFAX Always giving you extra